Aid to Africa

So Much to Do,

...

Aid to AFRICA

So Little Done

Carol Lancaster

A Century Foundation Book

The University of Chicago Press

Chicago & London

The University of Chicago Press, Chicago 60637
The University of Chicago Press, Ltd., London
© 1999 by The Century Foundation
All rights reserved. Published 1999
08 07   5 4 3

ISBN (cloth): 0-226-46838-0

Library of Congress Cataloging-in-Publication Data

Lancaster, Carol.
     Aid to Africa : so much to do, so little done / Carol
Lancaster.
        p. cm.
     "A Century Foundation book."
     Includes bibliographical references and index.
     ISBN 0-226-46838-0 (alk. paper)
     1. International relief—Africa—Evaluation.   2. Economic
assistance—Africa—Evaluation.   3. Africa—Economic
conditions—1960–   4. Africa—Economic policy.   I. Title.
HV640.4.A35 L36   1999
361.2'6'096—dc21
                                            98-33667
                                            CIP

For Curt
and
Douglas

Contents

Foreword

Although the subject of decades of serious academic research and extensive real-world policy debates, the transformation of any nation's economy from underdeveloped status to substantial modernization remains an uncertain and unpredictable process. Indeed, the recent turmoil among the Asian "tigers" and the continuing crisis in Russia serve as sobering reminders that economic policy is neither a science nor an engineering blueprint. Still, during the past fifty years, many countries, especially in Latin America and East Asia, have broken past cycles of poverty and achieved higher levels of prosperity and growth. The optimistic view holds that this progress is based on important new understandings about how to jump-start economies. If so, the lessons are not reflected everywhere. The story in Sub-Saharan Africa, especially, is sobering. Despite decades of foreign aid, international engagement, and numerous "grand plans," average incomes in most of Africa are little improved from what they were at the beginning of the 1960s.

Why is this the case? Given all of the attention and resources devoted to development programs in Africa, why have they generally had little lasting effect?

In the pages that follow, Carol Lancaster provides several possible answers to these questions. Currently on the faculty at the School of Foreign Service at Georgetown University and director of the Master of Science in Foreign Service program, she is a widely published scholar on foreign aid and African development, and has served as deputy administrator of USAID, deputy assistant secretary of state for Africa, and in a number of other government positions. While strongly supportive of the goals of aid programs for Africa, she has a written book that offers both balance and, where appropriate, sharp criticism of the way these programs have been designed and implemented. She provides an expert examination of the performance of the eight major aid agencies operating in Africa, including an inside look at the way bureaucratic politics, special interests, and public opinion interact to shape aid policies.

Lancaster examines both sides of the donor-recipient relationship. On the one hand, there are problems inherent in trying to promote development in countries with limited natural resources, chronic political instability, or inept or corrupt governments. But even more important, she argues, are the problems with the donor governments and aid agencies themselves. Aid programs have had a tendency to be donor driven, both in the sense of being tied to the donor government's diplomatic and geopolitical objectives in Africa, and in the sense of having program design and implementation tightly controlled by the donor. Problems of capacity in the aid agencies also have a negative effect on program outcomes, with many lacking in technical experience and knowledge of the local environment in the recipient countries.

In a series of case studies, Lancaster analyzes the performance of aid programs funded by the United States, Japan, the major donor countries in Europe, and multilateral agencies such as the World Bank. The differences in program management structures and differences in the level of autonomy these agencies have from the political goals of their governments have important implications for the level of success or failure of their programs.

Perhaps most important, Lancaster offers suggestions in her conclusion for a fundamental reorientation in the way aid agencies do business in Africa, with an emphasis on increased reliance on and empowerment of Africans themselves. Most aid agencies still rely overwhelmingly on expatriate staff to implement programs in the field, even though they could benefit significantly from greater engagement of Africans in program design decisions. She also suggests greater coordination among donor governments, who now operate independently without an overall plan for each recipient country.

While the assessment of the efficacy of aid programs in Africa Lancaster presents is quite negative, this book doesn't suggest, as some have, that we throw up our hands and walk away. By taking to heart the lessons we learned from past failures, we can fund aid programs in Africa that will make a real difference.

The Century Foundation has long been concerned about the economic problems and political issues that affect U.S. relations with developing countries. As the Twentieth Century Fund, we supported a series of studies of the crises in Latin America in the 1980s, examined the problems of debt in Africa in *The African Burden,* supported Naomi Caiden and Aaron Wildavsky's study *Planning and Budgeting in Poor Countries,* and over the years have focused on the problems facing individual developing nations such as Haiti and India. Our interest is these issues is ongoing, and we are currently supporting research on Turkey, Korea, and China, as well as another study on the problems facing Africa.

On behalf of the Trustees of The Century Foundation, I thank Carol Lancaster for this important contribution to understanding what works and does not work in this critical area.

Richard C. Leone, President
The Century Foundation
September 1998

Acknowledgments

I would like to thank a number of institutions and individuals for their help and patience as I wrote this book. Most importantly, I wish to express my gratitude to the Century Foundation and its exceptional staff for their invaluable support, patience, and advice. I am also grateful to the Institute for International Economics and its Director, Fred Bergsten, for providing me a venue for much of the research and preparation of the manuscript. I am thankful as well to the Dean and to my colleagues at Georgetown University's School of Foreign Service for their encouragement and forbearance.

I owe a special thanks to several individuals who read the entire manuscript and provided me with useful criticisms and advice: Michael Feldstein, David Gordon, Richard Grant, Catherine Gwin, Mort Halperin, Ray Hopkins, Tony Lake, Vernon Ruttan, Nicolas van de Walle, Jennifer Whitaker, Jennifer Windsor, and several anonymous reviewers. Others were kind enough to read and comment on individual chapters: Hans Abrahamsson, Devesh Kapur, Walter Kennes, Serge Michailof, Bertil Oden, Rosina Salerno, Sergei Shatalov, David Stanton, Noriyuki Wakisaka, Paul White, and Jerry Wolgin. Among those whom I consulted for various chapters were Baroness Lynda Chalker, Barry Eisen, John Howell, Kelly Kammerer, Carolyn Long, Harris Mule, the late Philip Ndegwa, David Newsom, Larry Nowels, Rick Nygard, Carol Peasley, Jean Michel Severino, and Julia Taft. Jean Louis Grolleau of the OECD was helpful with data. Many others, too numerous to list, were helpful with information and advice. Jennifer Harhigh and Sarah Nugent provided assistance on quantitative data and the bibliography.

Mistakes, should any remain after all these efforts, are my own.

Finally, I am especially grateful to my husband for ideas and advice on the manuscript, and to him and to my son for their support and tolerance during the many, many days when I was shut away writing. It is to them that the book is dedicated.

Chapter One

Introduction

"Why," the senator asked, "with so much aid has there been so little development in sub-Saharan Africa?" I was an expert witness at a hearing on foreign aid in Africa.[1] As I groped for a good answer to such a broad and fundamental question, I recalled the lines of the poet Tennyson that Kwame Nkrumah, Ghana's first president, cited at the beginning of his autobiography:[2]

So many worlds, so much to do,
So little done, such things to be.

In 1957, at the time Nkrumah wrote, there had indeed been so much to do to promote development in Africa. But after more than three decades and billions of dollars of foreign aid, there was still so little done. The question was why.

Now, a decade later, many more people—in the United States as well as in Africa—are asking the same question. This book is a effort to provide an answer.

Foreign aid—the transfer of concessional resources from one government to another—is a tool of statecraft. It is often used by the government providing it to encourage or reward politically desirable behavior on the part of the government receiving it. It is also used to spur economic development (defined here as equitable growth) in poor countries through financing investment projects, funding research and technical assistance, and supporting economic and political reforms. This study is concerned primarily with the effectiveness of foreign aid in promoting development in Africa.

1

The issue of aid's effectiveness in Africa is an important one. The amounts of foreign aid to most countries of sub-Saharan Africa have been among the largest in the world relative to the size of their economies. In 1994–95, foreign aid averaged nearly 8 percent of the gross national product (GNP) of African countries, and for many, it was well above that ratio. (Aid as a percentage of GNP averaged only 0.7 percent for Asia, 1.3 percent for the Middle East and North Africa, and 0.4 percent for Latin America.)[3] For most African countries, the relatively high levels of aid had extended over several decades.

Nevertheless, economic development has been disappointing in most of Africa. Average per capita income in the region is nearly the same in the 1990s as it was in the 1960s. Nearly half of Africa's 570 million people live on only one dollar per day. This percentage has not changed over the past decade or so. As a consequence, population growth has added 30 million people per year to the ranks of the impoverished. Moreover, the degree of impoverishment is greater in Africa than in any other part of the world. Social indicators—levels of literacy, life expectancy, health—remain among the lowest in the world and may be deteriorating. The region has seen its share of world trade shrink and has been all but bypassed by the surge in international capital flows beginning in the 1990s. It remains the least industrialized of regions and the most heavily indebted.[4]

Foreign aid is supposed to promote development. It has apparently failed to do so in Africa.

A Preview of the Study

Four main findings of this study explain the puzzle of large flows of aid over an extended period combined with disappointing development. First, the aid itself has been relatively ineffective in Africa. While there have been some remarkable and important successes, on the whole, aid-funded projects and programs have been disappointing. Aid to Africa has typically had the poorest success record of any worldwide (often half or fewer aid-financed activities achieve their goals), and projects and programs there have proven to be the least sustainable. In some cases, only one out of five projects and programs endures after aid funding is terminated. Particularly problematical have been "complex interventions" that have included multiple activities or required behavioral, institutional, or political changes on the part of Africans. There is also evidence that the large and continuous aid flows have in some cases had negative side effects on development in the region.

Second, it is primarily to the donors of aid that we must look for an explanation of its failure. Of course, the effectiveness equation has two sides: conditions in the country receiving the aid and the capacities and policies of the governments to which it is provided; and the policies and capacities of the governments and organizations donating the aid. On one level, the often limited natural-resource base, harsh physical environment, faulty policies, and weak institutions in many African countries go far in explaining the relative ineffectiveness of foreign aid in the region. It is difficult for foreign aid to bring about beneficial and sustainable changes where economic growth itself is stymied by government policies that discourage investment, by ineffective or corrupt public institutions, or by political repression and instabilities—all problems evident in much of the region.

But at a deeper level, this explanation for the ineffectiveness of aid in Africa is unsatisfying. Those deciding whether to aid African countries or not have been the donors of that aid, both governments and international organizations. They could always have decided to terminate aid where it was clearly ineffective. Moreover, in Africa more than in any other region of the world, the donors have had the major say over how the aid has been used. African governments have typically been exceptionally eager to obtain as much foreign aid as possible and have rarely rejected donor-proposed aid programs. As a result, Africans have frequently ceded much of the responsibility for identifying, designing, and implementing aid-funded activities to the donors, which have for the most part gladly seized the initiative. Both aid agencies and African officials have acknowledged the phenomenon of "donor-driven" aid. General Obasanjo, former president of Nigeria, once lamented, "In education and in industrialization, we have used borrowed ideas, utilized borrowed experiences and funds and engaged borrowed hands. In our development programmes and strategies, not much, if anything, is ours."[5]

Third, on the basis of the case studies of eight major donors operating in Africa (the United States, United Kingdom, France, Sweden, Italy, Japan, the World Bank, and the European Union), it is clear that the principal causes of the developmental ineffectiveness of aid have been two. One is the allocation of that aid for nondevelopmental purposes—primarily diplomatic and commercial. But contrary to widely held views (especially among development practitioners), this is not the main problem. The primary problem is the lack of capacity on the part of aid agencies to undertake the kind of interventions they have attempted with the amount of aid they have tried to disperse. Most donors have attempted to commit large and (until recently) rising amounts of aid to African countries, an increasing quantity of which has funded the complex interventions mentioned above. While the problems donors have attempted to address with this aid are key ones in African development, the aid agencies themselves have often lacked the technical experience, local knowledge, staff, and appropriate processes to manage such projects and programs effectively. And they have usually been driven by bureaucratic and political imperatives to spend the monies available to them, often regardless of the economic and political conditions in recipient countries or their own capacity to design and manage effective projects and programs. A major study of the World Bank observed that "the Bank committed the very error that it saw as the root of the region's problems: like the SSA [sub-Saharan African] state, it manifested a marked inability to judge institutional limitations. Though it correctly saw institutional weakness as the heart of the region's predicament, it overestimated its own ability to help in such matters."[6] What is true of the World Bank—among the more capable aid agencies—is true of the others. Aid agencies have overreached in Africa. And their individual weaknesses have been multiplied by the large number of agencies (usually numbering forty to fifty per country) operating without strong coordination among them.

Fourth, the performance of aid agencies in Africa is not uniform. While they share common patterns of performance, there are also important differences. These differences, described in detail in the case studies, are the result of the autonomy (that is, ability to make policy and allocative decisions based on developmental criteria) and the capacity of individual aid agencies. Each of these characteristics is determined by a number of specific factors. Among those factors, geopolitical posture and domestic political institutions and players (including other government agencies, legislatures, political parties, nongovernmental organizations, and other organized and informal groups) claim the major roles. Nongovernmental organizations (NGOs) have gained increasing influence over the aid programs of a number of the countries examined here. Foreign aid may be a tool of development, but its use is greatly affected by domestic factors peculiar to the aid-giving countries.

The study concludes with a number of recommendations intended to enhance the effectiveness of aid in Africa, involving a significant reorientation in the way aid agencies do business in the region.

Foreign Aid and Development: The Conceptual Landscape

There is a large and diverse literature on the impact of foreign aid on development, of which only the most summary description will be offered here to indicate the location of this study in the broader discourse and to identify some of its intellectual precursors. This discourse on aid and development has taken place at both the theoretical and practical (or empirical) levels and in a number of disciplines.

At the risk of some oversimplification, we can identify two main approaches to analyzing the impact of aid on development. There is the "contextual" approach, which tends to be more theoretical and considers that the impact of aid on development is primarily a function of the broader economic and political context in which it is provided. And there is the "instrumental" approach, which is more empirically oriented and evaluates the impact of aid largely in terms of the success or failure of the programs and projects it finances.

Within the contextual approach, there are several different theories of the impact of aid on development. One emphasizes the relations of power between rich and poor countries. An example of this is the "dependency" school, which views underdevelopment and poverty as a consequence of the exploitation by powerful capitalist countries (the "center") of weak developing countries (the "periphery").[7] "Dependendistas" have viewed aid as a tool of capitalism to reinforce exploitative behavior and, therefore, deepen underdevelopment and poverty.[8] The polemical nature of many of these works, their weak empirical bases, and the very real economic progress evident in much of the developing world have discredited this approach in scholarly circles. (Not surprisingly, it never had much currency among Western development practitioners.)

During the 1990s, another, related view of aid and development appeared. "Deconstructionism" was inspired in part (like the dependency school) by the great disparity of power between the rich, developed world and the poorer developing regions of Asia, Africa, and Latin America. The deconstructionist approach—reflected primarily in the writings of anthropologists—attacked the validity of the very idea of "development" and the concepts and discourse it has engendered as an invention of Western capitalism, intended to create "an extremely efficient apparatus for producing knowledge about, and the exercise of power over, the Third World,"[9] but with little basis in the realities of that world, which in any case, it was argued, cannot easily be known or articulated accurately by Westerners. Foreign aid is simply a tool for the exercise of power by the donor, with little relevance to (and possibly with negative consequences for) the lives of recipients.

In its extreme form, deconstructionist discourse is highly polemical and poorly grounded empirically. Taken to its logical conclusion, it implies that the scientific method itself is artificial. In effect, one cannot know; one can only imagine. However, its more moderate, empirically oriented adherents have produced insightful studies analyzing the impact of aid on the societies in which it is provided. One such work is by James Ferguson,[10] who examined an aid-financed rural development project in Lesotho and found that it failed to achieve its goals largely because the "development apparatus" providing it, immersed in a discourse of its own creation, misunderstood the social and political environment in which it was working. Additionally, the project had the effect of expanding bureaucratic power and "depoliticizing" poverty by treating it as if it were a technical problem rather than a consequence of the unequal distribution of political power within Lesotho.

Another, very different approach to the contextual analysis of the impact of aid on development revolves around assumptions about states and markets. For much of the second half of the twentieth century, the "mainstream" discourse on aid and development has been conducted by Western-trained economists and, to a lesser extent, political scientists. It is also this discourse (on which more detail is provided in chapters 2 and 3) that has been the main influence on aid policies. Mainstream development specialists during the 1950s and 1960s viewed underdevelopment as a result primarily of the lack of savings and investment in poor countries. It was further assumed that states—even in poor countries—could plan and implement effective development policies and programs and that because of the weakness of markets, they should do so. Where state capacity was weak, technical assistance could overcome that weakness. Deficiencies in resources could be remedied with increased amounts of money and technical assistance from external sources—primarily in the form of concessional loans and grants from foreign governments, since for much of this period, only a very limited amount of private international capital was available to poor countries. Foreign aid would thus help stimulate growth and reduce poverty. Perhaps the best-known articulation of this view was by Hollis Chenery and Alan Strout in "Foreign Assistance and Economic Development," published in the *American Economic Review* in 1966.

While this approach informed much of the early discourse on aid and development, it was not unchallenged by those who were much more skeptical of the ability of states (because of their ineptitude and, often, their capture by greedy elites) to play a positive role in managing development and much more confident of the ability of markets—if left alone by governments—to spur growth. Peter Bauer of the London School of Economics, for example, argued that the main impediments to growth were misguided government policies and that foreign aid would simply strengthen and even expand those impediments.[11]

The 1980s and 1990s saw a blend of these two contrary views of the capacity and roles of states and markets and their implications for foreign aid. The failure of many states in the developing world as well as in the former Socialist bloc countries to promote healthy growth (spotlighted by the debt crisis and the collapse of Communism in the 1980s) led mainstream economists to argue that the influence of states over markets needed to be circumscribed. Foreign aid could be effective in promoting development when provided to states as an incentive to encourage policy and regulatory reforms, which would free markets and stimulate investment and growth. Anne Krueger articulated this role of aid in development in her "Aid in the Development Process" in the World Bank's *Research Observer* in 1986.

Once economic-policy change, or "structural adjustment," became a focus of the discourse on aid and development, it was only a short step to ask why governments of developing countries adopted policies that appeared to defeat their stated goals of promoting economic growth, and how foreign aid might influence policymaking by those governments. A number of political scientists and economists in the 1980s demonstrated that governmental policies reflected the interplay of powerful political interests within countries (and within the governments themselves).[12] In this "political economy" approach, aid and aid agencies, it was argued, could play the role of external constituents for economic-policy change— in effect, substituting for or strengthening domestic constituencies for reform. Two notable contributions to the literature of aid and the politics of economic reform are *The Politics of Economic Adjustment,* edited by Stephan Haggard and Robert Kaufman, and *Economic Crisis and Policy Choice,* edited by Joan Nelson.

By the mid-1990s, a number of aid agencies had extended the logic of leveraging economic-policy change into the political realm, attempting to use their assistance as an inducement for political reform, including improved governance (involving greater transparency, accountability, and predictability) and, often, democratization on the part of recipient governments. While there was little dispute that transparent, accountable governments supporting the rule of law were important to create an environment for investment and development, the assumptions, made by a number of aid agencies, that democracy was key to ensuring both good governance and development and that foreign aid was an effective tool in promoting democracy in developing countries were still controversial.

Another contextual approach to aid and development focused not on states and markets but on the distribution of income within particular states. Proponents of this approach (popular particularly in the 1970s) argued that where there was an inequitable distribution of income (and this included most poor countries), economic growth would benefit the poor little and might even make them poorer. Aid could be effective in bettering their lives only if it were used to fund government programs and projects intended to benefit the poor directly. For example, Dudley Seers of the Institute of Development Studies at the University of Sussex and Mahbub ul Haq of the World Bank argued that the focus of aid should be to address problems of unemployment and poverty.[13] The latter argument had a considerable impact on aid policies during the 1970s, leading to an effort on the part of a number of agencies to target the basic human needs of the poorer elements of the populations of developing countries. Targeting aid directly on the poor remains a core element in the policies advocated by many NGOs and others in the development community today.

Turning to the instrumental approach to assessing the impact of aid on development, we find two clusters of literature. One involves highly polemical exposés of the iniquities of aid donors, usually based on a series of anecdotes presented by the author. One of the numerous examples of this genre is *Lords of Poverty* by Graham Hancock, who asserted that foreign aid as a tool of development is fundamentally flawed by the misguided policies, bureaucratic inefficiency, self-interest, and corruption of official aid agencies—and should be terminated.[14]

More sober and balanced and far more important contributions to the instrumental approach to evaluating aid and development are the efforts by scholars and practitioners to assess the impact of aid, based on available evaluations, studies, and other empirical materials. By the 1980s, with the increasing amount of data on aid and growth and the evaluations undertaken by aid agencies, a number of scholars attempted to determine whether foreign aid had had a positive impact on development. One group took a quantitative approach, examining the statistical relationship between aid flows and economic growth.[15] They found no significant, systematic relationship between aid and growth, suggesting that aid either was too small to have an impact or was not able to deliver the growth benefits it promised. A 1996 quantitative study done by Craig Burnside and David Dollar of the World Bank found that when monetary, fiscal, and trade policies in recipient countries were taken into account, aid had a positive impact on growth in supportive policy environments.[16]

Another group of analysts took a different approach. Robert Cassen and associates in *Does Aid Work?* examined evaluations of a large number of aid-funded projects and programs in various parts of the world and concluded that aid was effective in achieving its goals most of the time.[17] Where aid was ineffective, Cassen pointed to donors' multiple goals (other than development) as a key factor. Another study, by Vernon Ruttan, Anne Krueger, and Constantine Michaelopolous, based on country and sectoral case studies, also found evidence for the effectiveness of aid when the policy environment was supportive.[18]

A few studies of aid, located primarily in the field of public administration and organizational analysis, addressed another influence on the effectiveness of aid: the nature of aid agencies themselves. Two notable examples of this approach are Judith Tendler and Dennis Rondinelli,[19] who have both examined the organizational characteristics of one aid agency—the United States Agency for International Development (USAID)—and how they affected its performance. Their findings have identified the problem of "fit" between the operational processes of aid agencies, often aimed at control, and the realities of managing what are often highly experimental interventions in foreign lands. They have also examined the incentives and constraints on decisions and actions created by aid bureaucracies themselves—for example, the pressures to spend all available monies. This book draws on a number of their insights in explaining the developmental effectiveness of aid in Africa.

Other scholars have examined particular types of aid. On aid for policy reform, Paul Mosley, Jane Harrigan, and John Toye, in *Aid and Power,* found a mixed record of effectiveness in World Bank structural-adjustment lending, with the political conditions in the borrowing countries themselves playing a key role.[20] Uma Lele, in her ambitious and valuable *Aid to African Agriculture,*[21] found evidence of limited effectiveness of smallholder agricultural projects in a number of African countries, with a combination of weak African institutions and poor donor practices at the core of the problems.

Uma Lele's study was the first major examination of the effectiveness of aid focused entirely on Africa. Robert Cassen had found earlier that aid in Africa had been particularly disappointing but did not attempt to explain why in detail. But with the deteriorating economic situation in Africa, others followed Lele's lead. Tony Killick, in a study for the World Bank in 1991,[22] primarily blamed recipient countries' policies for the apparent failure to improve economic performance. Like Cassen, Killick identified the nondevelopmental goals of donors (that is, promoting foreign policy or commercial interests) as important in the poor performance of aid.

Another book focusing on the effectiveness of aid is *Improving Aid to Africa,* by Nicolas van de Walle and Timothy Johnson.[23] This short study accepted that aid had been largely ineffective in promoting development. It pointed to policy, institutional, and financial weaknesses on the part of recipients and, echoing the findings of others, to problems with the multiple goals and bureaucratic politics of donors.

The Locus of This Study

This study builds on the findings of many earlier studies of aid's effectiveness. It shares the "mainstream" assumptions that underdevelopment and poverty are objective, measurable phenomena, and that foreign aid, when designed and implemented appropriately in a supportive policy and institutional environment in recipient countries, can further development. The study examines in some detail the record of aid in Africa, including the size and duration of aid flows, as well as the type of assistance (project, program, technical) and sector to determine what sorts of aid-funded activities have been more or less effective.

The principal focus is on the performance of aid agencies in Africa and the factors affecting that performance. But aid donors differ considerably in their policies, programs, and procedures. To assess the performance of different donors, the study provides a comparative analysis of eight bilateral and multilateral donors, representing 60 percent of the total concessional assistance to Africa. These are the United States; the two major colonial powers, France and the United Kingdom; Japan, the second largest bilateral donor after France; Sweden, the largest of the Nordic donors; and Italy, among the largest donors in the early 1990s (and whose performance in Africa has particularly interesting lessons). Also included are the two principal multilateral donors—the World Bank and the European Union. Finally, this is an "agency centered" study, focusing specifically on the autonomy and capacity of aid agencies and the factors influencing those two key characteristics.

The Plan of the Study

This study attempts to understand a problem—the disappointing impact of foreign aid on development in Africa. As such, it inevitably cuts across several social-science disciplines, including political science, economics, and sociology. However, the focus is primarily on politics because at the core of the problems of development in Africa and the performance of aid agencies are political factors: power, policy choice, the influence of political institutions, and the functioning of public organizations. To examine these political factors, the study applies concepts from a number of areas of political science, described below.

Following this introductory chapter, the second chapter reviews development in Africa and asks why it has proven so disappointing. Building on the extensive literature on African politics and African political economy, the chapter emphasizes the key roles of economic policies, the institutional weaknesses of African governments, and the political and social factors explaining the unsustainable development model adopted in much of the region. A final section examines the African side of the effectiveness equation—the impact of government policies and institutions (including the way Africans sought to manage their aid and their aid relationships with donors) on aid's effectiveness.

The third chapter scrutinizes the phenomenon of foreign aid itself, including its size and impact in Africa. This chapter draws on the literature of aid and development as well as the growing literature on aid's effectiveness, already previewed above. Empirical data is drawn primarily from the studies and evaluations of aid projects and programs generated by the aid agencies, bilateral and multilateral, managing that aid. The fourth chapter introduces the eight case studies of the performance of aid agencies. In describing a framework for analyzing their performance, it borrows insights from works on policy choice, including bureaucratic politics, the "new institutionalism," and collective action, as well as from public administration and the smaller field of policy implementation. The case studies of aid agencies, organized in four chapters, include the eight donors, and these studies draw on articles, books, documents, and interviews. These case studies draw brief conclusions on the factors affecting the effectiveness of their aid in Africa, to be further analyzed and compared in a final chapter. That chapter offers conclusions on effective aid, a comparison of the policies and politics of the different aid agencies, and a discussion of trends in foreign aid, and proposes a set of reforms to improve the effectiveness of aid in Africa.

Sources and Methods

This study is based on extensive empirical research. But it is also informed by my own experience in the U.S. government, most recently as the deputy administrator of USAID, where I had to deal with issues of politics, policy, resource allocation, program implementation, and agency management. My experiences have sharpened my instincts and insights on how the policy process actually works and on how institutions and individuals relate to one another on foreign-assistance issues. I have also had a chance to observe the policy process in other governments and institutions examined here. Further, my experience in the senior management of an aid agency has heightened my appreciation for the roles of organizations and processes in the implementation of policy and program choices. Because of that experience, this book, the writing of which was interrupted by my three-year service in USAID, has a shape quite different from its original plan.

For the materials in the case studies of eight aid agencies, I have relied on studies and evaluations, primarily funded by the aid agencies themselves, supplemented by other studies, both official and scholarly. I have not read all the audits, completion reports, and impact evaluations produced by the agencies discussed in this book—that would be humanly impossible, since they number in the thousands. And in any case, it would not produce robust, finely grained comparisons since the scope and rigor of evaluative materials varies enormously. I have relied therefore on impact studies, summaries of completion reports, particular evaluations where available, studies, and other relevant materials to draw conclusions about the effectiveness of the aid of individual agencies. These materials permit only broad generalizations or comparisons among aid agencies. They nevertheless provide abundant insights into patterns of effective or ineffective aid.

In assessing the autonomy and capacity of aid agencies, I have used published and unpublished documents of governments and international institutions as well as official policy statements and studies by aid agencies themselves. I have also consulted the staffs and drawn on studies of aid agencies undertaken by various research institutes in Europe and the United States, including the Overseas Development Council in Washington, the Overseas Development Institute in London, and the German Development Institute in Berlin. I have consulted scholarly books, articles, and, where relevant, newspaper reports. Supplementing these written materials are interviews with current or former officials of all the aid agencies examined here, officials from other parts of donor governments, officials from the Development Assistance Committee of the Organization for Economic Cooperation and Development (OECD), outside experts, NGO staff, journalists, and African officials and experts on aid. When I can, I cite those I have interviewed. In some cases, I must protect the confidentiality of those still associated with their governments or multilateral aid agencies or others in sensitive positions. I have also drawn on my own extensive experience with officials of the agencies included here (and other experts) and the hundreds of discussions I have had, particularly when I was a government official myself, on the issues examined in this book.

The scope of this study is uncomfortably broad, as it must be to answer the practical and fundamental question it raises. It identifies patterns of policy and performance and draws conclusions on the basis of those patterns. Inevitably, there will be exceptions to generalizations about the effectiveness of foreign aid in Africa and on the behavior of aid agencies. I trust that the weight of evidence and argument is nevertheless compelling. I hope that this book leads to debate and to further research on those many aspects of aid effectiveness and donor performance that are controversial and uncertain.

There is one concluding point to make. While this book focuses on the problems of effective aid in Africa, its intent is not to attack aid but to understand and improve it. This study's findings indicate not that aid should end but that we should examine it dispassionately in order to better its effectiveness. There is plenty of evidence that this is both possible and urgently required. There is still in Africa so little done and so much to do.

Chapter Two

Africa—So Little Development?

This book began with the question, "Why, with so much aid, has there been so little development in Africa?" It is the task of this chapter to examine the second part of that question—whether there has been "so little development." We begin by clarifying what is meant by *development* and how it occurs. We then turn to the history of development in Africa.

The Phenomenon of Development: A Brief Primer

Economic development has been defined in numerous ways. It has been used by some to refer solely to economic growth—the expansion in national production and income. It has been used by others to include the achievement of an array of conditions, such as high levels of per capita income, broad access to social services, political empowerment, human security, and gender equality.[1]

In this study, economic development refers to a process of economic change that includes both growth in national production and income and an improvement in the standard of living of the poor.[2] The latter may encompass increased access to productive assets (e.g., land, jobs, or capital) and to education and health services that not only bring improvements in the quality of life but increase productivity and income-earning potential. We shall use several indicators to assess development, specifically changes in per capita income (to indicate the extent of economic growth) and access to education and health services, as well as average rates of literacy and life expectancy (to indicate advances or decreases in the standard of living of the poor). These two groups of indicators are imperfect measures of development, but they are the best we have available for Africa, given the severe limits on the quantity and quality of statistical data.

Development is a process of change. How does it occur? There is a vast literature and considerable continuing debate on the factors affecting economic development.[3] We shall not review that literature here but simply indicate several elements critical to economic development about which a broad consensus has evolved over the past five decades. These elements include the role and importance of economic growth and strategies for achieving it, the problem of poverty and its reduction, the impact of economic policies, and the importance of institutions.

Economic Growth

There is little doubt that an expansion in national production and income is necessary to raise the standard of living of the poor and that the expansion must be sustained and sustainable—that is, it must continue over a period of time and must not destroy the resource base necessary to future prosperity. One source of economic growth is an increase in one of the factors of production—land, labor, and capital. The amount of land available is often fixed or expandable only slowly (where unused land can be brought into production). The supply of labor typically grows slowly also, through reductions in death rates, increased birth rates, increased labor market participation, or immigration. Capital—fixed capital as well as "human capital" (gained through investments in education and health)—can increase rapidly if savings are available to finance it. Investments in human capital are especially important in poor countries, where they typically bring high rates of return, both private and social.

Another source of growth is technological innovation—changes in the factors of production that increase efficiency and productivity.[4] Technological innovation typically results from basic and applied research and the dissemination of the results to productive enterprises. Innovations may take the form of new machinery, new combinations of inputs, or improvements in the management of resources—in effect, new products as well as new processes. One of the major technological innovations spurring development in poor countries over the past forty years has been in the key sector of agriculture: the "green revolution" that combined new, high-yielding varieties of wheat and rice with fertilizer and water control to produce significantly larger harvests on the same amount of land.

Finally, there are exogenous and often temporary sources of growth—for example, an increase in the value of a country's exports because of changed market conditions. The surge in petroleum prices in the 1970s led to an increase in the gross national products of petroleum exporters. But changes in market conditions can prove temporary and volatile, decreasing the value of a country's exports as well as increasing them, as the petroleum producers discovered in the 1980s.[5]

Growth Strategies

Investments in expanding the factors of production or in research for technological innovation are usually guided by a strategy of development that decides which investments have priority. While recognizing that strategies must fit the economic potential of individual countries, development specialists during the period just after the Second World War tended to give the greatest priority to industry, as the sector that was most capital intensive (and hence had the most potential for rapid growth) and in which market demand was believed to be the strongest. (Many economists believed at that time that highly competitive international markets for primary products doomed the prices of those commodities to a secular decline vis-à-vis those of manufactured goods.) Industrial development was to be stimulated through import-substituting industrialization policies in which high trade barriers would encourage investments and protect domestic producers from foreign competition so that they could establish themselves. This approach was later rejected by most economists as inappropriate and usually unworkable. Over the past several decades, it has become widely accepted that freer markets and greater competition (even from abroad) will in most cases attract the investment and encourage the efficiency that is needed for sustained growth. Investments in agriculture, where the bulk of the world's poor still gain their livelihood, are a priority if slow growth in agricultural output is not to become a drag on overall economic progress and if the standard of living of the poor is to be raised.

Financing Growth and Poverty Reduction

Capital accumulation and investment in technological research (or its acquisition from abroad) must be paid for. Financing must come from domestic savings or from foreign investors or foreign loans and grants. In poor countries, the size and rate of domestic savings are often low.

Thus, raising savings rates and accessing foreign financing are critical factors in influencing a country's rate of growth. And growth is necessary to reduce poverty over the long term.

During the 1970s, many development experts adopted the view that growth does not guarantee decreased poverty—at least not in any reasonable period of time—and in the short term, it can actually increase poverty and income inequality.[6] Thus, they argued, development policies and projects needed to target the poor to help alleviate poverty through providing for their "basic needs." By the 1980s, evidence suggested that the idea that growth failed to benefit the poor was false; in fact, they were unlikely to gain better lives in the absence of growth. Evidence also increasingly suggested that the greater access to assets (e.g., land, social services) that the poor have, the more they contribute to and benefit from economic growth and the more rapid that growth is likely to be.[7]

Economic Policies and the State

One continuing debate in the development field is whether the challenge of economic growth in poor countries is different from that in developed countries—whether, for instance, structural rigidities and market imperfections in poor countries require the intervention of the state to ensure appropriate investments. In the 1950s and 1960s, mainstream economists and practitioners agreed that the state had an important role in the planning and management of economic growth in poor countries. By the 1980s, this view had changed because of the many cases of flawed state intervention in developing countries (and in Socialist bloc countries as well). A consensus developed among economists in the World Bank, International Monetary Fund, and a number of bilateral aid agencies, among officials of many developing countries, and among significant portions of the scholarly community that government policies often impeded development by allocating resources wastefully and discouraging private investment. But (reminiscent of the focus on "absorptive capacity" in the 1960s) these views shifted in the 1990s to an emphasis on effective public organizations.[8] There is considerably less consensus on how to make public agencies more effective.

Institutions

In the 1990s, a number of specialists also began to give increased attention to the role of "institutions" in development, not only the formal organizations of government and private-sector entities but the "humanly devised constraints that shape human interaction."[9] These constraints— often in the form of rules or norms—create incentives that affect human behavior, including investment decisions and other activities affecting economic performance. One of the most important of these rules is property rights. Where those rights are not protected by law and practice, the costs of economic transactions can be high (e.g., in terms of risk or uncertainty), savings and investment can be discouraged, and growth can be diminished.

The focus on policies and institutions has taken development beyond the field of economics and into politics, sociology, and anthropology. Economic policies are the result of political processes that are complex and often particular to individual countries. Institutions are the product of political processes as well as cultural norms, involving even more complex and often poorly understood sets of relationships and particularities, as we shall now see in the case of development in Africa.

To recap briefly, the understanding of what development is and how it occurs has evolved over the past half century, informed by continuing debates and the experience of experts and practitioners in the field. It moved away from an exclusive focus on economic growth and the investments in fixed and human capital and research needed to promote it, to a concern for reducing poverty, and, subsequently, to an emphasis on the need for appropriate policy and institutional environments to encourage both growth and poverty reduction. Earlier concepts of development have not so much been discarded as included in an ever-broadening perspective on the change necessary to achieve economic prosperity. And that perspective, it is now widely recognized, encompasses not only economics but also politics and society.

Development in Africa

The lowering of the British flag and the raising of the flag of the new state of Ghana at midnight on March 6, 1957, is generally regarded as the beginning of the independence period in sub-Saharan Africa. Much of the rest of Africa had gained its independence by 1965. In these early years of freedom, economists were upbeat about the future of the region. Ghana, with its agricultural and mineral resources, was seen as poised to compete with South Korea. Africa as a whole was favorably compared to East Asia as a promising developing region. But by the late 1980s, when real per capita income in Korea had increased by 700 percent since the early 1960s, average real per capita income in Africa was no larger than three decades earlier.[10]

This stunning outcome was a result of two trends in Africa: very low overall economic growth rates combined with high population growth rates. From 1973 to 1980, economic growth rates for African countries (excluding Africa's largest country—oil-rich Nigeria) averaged only 1.7 percent per year. (If Nigeria is included, annual growth rates in the region averaged 2.5 percent during this period.) The 1980s were only slightly better, with average growth rates of 2.3 percent per year. (Including Nigeria reduces the average annual growth rate to 0.5 percent.) At the same time, population growth rates accelerated during these three decades, rising from an average of 2.5 percent in 1960[11] to just over 3 percent per year during the 1980s.[12] Africa's economic growth during the 1970s and 1980s would have been poor with no increase in population. But the rapid increases in population overwhelmed growth in income during these decades.

It is important to note that two African countries are significant exceptions to these generalizations: Botswana and Mauritius, both of which have enjoyed high rates of growth over a long period. Botswana (thanks to exports of diamonds and other minerals combined with good economic management) has grown at around 10 percent per year for several decades, one of the highest rates of growth in the world. Mauritius is one of the few African countries to diversify its exports with a stable polity and a supportive economic-policy environment—both contributing to an influx of foreign investments in textiles and tourism. And for a period during the 1960s and 1970s, Ivory Coast, Cameroon, and Kenya enjoyed respectable rates of growth. It should also be noted that growth rates improved in much of Africa between 1994 and 1996, with twenty-eight African countries experiencing a positive growth in their per capita incomes in 1996.[13] It is too soon to say whether this hopeful improvement indicates the beginning of an economic upturn or is transient, simply reflecting good rains, an improvement in primary-product prices on the world market, and the devaluation of the CFA franc—the overvaluation of which had long depressed exports, investment, and growth in the fourteen African countries that share it as a common currency.[14]

Two important factors in the disappointing rates of growth in Africa are low levels of investment and of savings. Economists suggest that developing countries need to invest roughly a quarter of national resources to gain the rates of growth that will raise them from poverty. In fact, investment as a proportion of gross domestic product (that is, gross national product less the value of imports) in low-income countries world-wide in 1995 averaged 35 percent, in sub-Saharan Africa 18.5 percent.[15] In the latter case, this level of investment is greater than the average proportion of GDP allocated to investment in Africa in the 1980s, but still below the average of just over 20 percent in the first two decades of the independence period. Available data also show a low and declining rate of productivity of investment in Africa.[16]

Savings rates in much of Africa have been low, averaging 19 percent of GDP between 1965 and 1973, 23 percent between 1974 and 1980 (but excluding Nigeria and South Africa, only 17 percent during that period), and 16 percent in 1996.[17] Of those thirty-nine countries for which savings data were available for 1996, only twelve had savings rates above 15 percent, and four of those (Nigeria, Cameroon, Congo, and Gabon) were petroleum exporters.[18] (The difference between savings and investment rates is made up with foreign aid, foreign investment, or domestic or foreign borrowing.) This data on investment and savings suggests that the most basic elements in the growth equation have long been weak in Africa and continue to be so.

When we turn to the performance of African countries over the past three and a half decades in expanding social services and infrastructure—essential to sustain economic expansion—we find a more positive story. Throughout much of Africa, there has been a rapid expansion in education and health services and in physical infrastructure. The percentage of the eligible age group in primary school has jumped from just over 40 percent in 1965 to nearly 70 percent two and a half decades later.[19] The ratio of nurses to total population has doubled, and child immunization rates have risen significantly. These advances are reflected in dramatic improvements in indicators of the quality of life. While life expectancy at birth in 1960 was only thirty-nine, by 1995, it had reached fifty-two years. Childhood mortality declined from 165 per 1,000 in 1965 to 92 per 1,000 in 1995. Literacy rates rose from 16 percent in 1960 to 50 percent in 1990. Ports, airports, roads, and communications facilities throughout most of Africa have also expanded significantly since the 1960s, facilitating internal and external trade and transport.

The quality-of-life indicators are all lower for Africa than any other region of the world. But their improvement nevertheless indicates progress in putting into place the basic building blocks of development, especially education and infrastructure. That being said, it is also important to note that low rates of overall growth over the past several decades, with associated government budgetary stringencies and foreign-exchange shortages, have resulted in a slowing in the expansion in education and health services. This has occurred in the face of increasing population and a rising demand for these services. Some of the past gains, in short, are being eroded.

How can we explain this picture of social development without economic growth in Africa? And how sustainable has it proven to be?

Why Africa's Disappointing Economic Performance?

The problems of African poverty and growth have been the subject of lively debate over the past four decades. The physical characteristics of much of the region—a harsh and unpredictable climate, weathered and often fragile soils, the incidence of a variety of debilitating diseases affecting both humans and animals—make development there a challenge. Furthermore, most African countries gained independence at a very early stage of development, with a limited infrastructure, often few educated nationals, a largely subsistence agriculture, and almost no industry. But these problems do not present insuperable obstacles to economic progress in Africa any more than they have done in other parts of the world. South Korea, after all, faced the 1950s with few natural resources, little industry, and a devastated infrastructure.

The experience of colonialism and the relationship of independent African countries to the world economy have been proposed as explanations for African underdevelopment by a number of commentators.[20] The "dependency" school of analysis, prominent during the 1960s and 1970s and described briefly in chapter 1, attributed African underdevelopment (and indeed, underdevelopment throughout the world) to the peripheral and economically weak position of the region in the world economy, forcing it to export its primary products at relatively low prices and import manufactured goods from developed, capitalist countries at relatively high prices. As a result of this exploitative relationship, it was argued, capital was in effect withdrawn from peripheral countries (including those in Africa), dooming them to perpetual poverty. By the mid-1990s—nearly a half century since the beginning of African independence—theories attributing African development failures to colonialism retained little credibility among scholars. And the obviously successful development of formerly poor countries in Asia and Latin America undercut the arguments of dependency theory generally.

A view long held by development practitioners and Africans is that a lack of investable funds has constrained development in the region. Some have pointed to the decline in the terms of trade of Africa's many primary-product exporters as having reduced export earnings and investable capital. It is true that the collapse in primary-product prices deepened Africa's economic woes during the late 1970s and 1980s. But those woes, as we shall see below, were already serious before the international economy went sour. Others have complained of too little foreign aid. But as we shall also see, foreign aid was large relative to the size of most African economies. Further, it is difficult to put the lack of investable resources at the center of Africa's development problem when one considers the low and declining efficiency of capital in much of the region[21] and the evidence of large-scale financial waste and corruption. Economic policies and institutions affect the efficiency of capital as well as the general performance of a country's economy. It is here we must look for an explanation of the disappointing development record of so much of Africa.

In fact, there is little debate today that weak public institutions and faulty economic policies pursued by African governments have been key sources of the region's development problems. Those faulty policies have included overvalued exchange rates, excessive regulation of economic activity, high taxes on agricultural producers and price controls, high tariffs and nontariff barriers to trade, bloated and inefficient state sectors—all contributing to a waste of resources and discouraging investment, savings, and growth. These policies were not accidental. They were typically part of a development "model" followed to varying degrees throughout the region.[22]

Toward a Model of Unsustainable Development

The economic policies common to much of Africa had their origins in the state-led development strategies adopted by leaders in the early post-independence period. Many leaders, like Kwame Nkrumah of Ghana and Julius Nyerere of Tanzania, couched their approaches to development in the language of "African socialism." A few others, like Houphouët-Boigny of the Ivory Coast, spoke more of free markets and open economies. However, these leaders differed not over whether the state should play a prominent role, but the extent of that role.[23]

State-led development had three interrelated components. First was a rapid expansion in social services (especially education and health) and in physical infrastructure, undertaken and financed by the state (and by foreign aid). Second was the priority placed on the development of industry, usually through the erection of protective trade barriers, the imposition of pricing policies favorable to industry (e.g., low domestic food prices), and the allocation of budgetary resources and the channeling of credit to industrial enterprises (often state-owned). Some governments went further and nationalized existing private enterprises and discouraged private investment, believing that state ownership of the means of production would ensure more rapid and equitable growth (and would prevent a concentration of economic power in the hands of ethnic minorities or foreigners).

The third component of this approach involved the financing of government expenditures. One of the principal sources of government finance was the taxation of primary commodities for export—mainly agricultural commodities but, where possible, minerals as well.[24] The vehicles for the taxation of agriculture had been left in place by the colonial powers who had created government marketing boards to buy export products from farmers and resell them—often at prices far higher than the farmers received—on the world market. The original intent was to encourage expanded production by using the revenues from export sales to stabilize the prices received by farmers. This purpose was soon discarded by the newly independent governments and the proceeds turned to the general use of government or to political parties. State-led development had the predictable consequence of expanding rapidly the size and cost of government. The public sector in Africa rose from an average of 18 percent of GDP in 1966 to almost 30 percent of GDP by the early 1980s.[25] And during the 1960s, state employment grew by an average of 7 percent per year, reaching 60 percent of wage earners in the modern sector by 1970.[26]

The strategy of state-led, industrially based growth was consistent with mainstream economic thinking (as well as the approach to development by many aid donors) during the 1960s, when most African countries first formulated their development strategies. Tony Killick, in his study of Ghana's economic policies during this period, observed,

> Until the fall of Nkrumah early in 1966, economic strategy in Ghana was inspired by a vision of economic modernization similar to, and influenced by, that of many professional economists who were concerning themselves with the problems of underdeveloped countries: a "big push" primarily involving a major investment effort, a strategy centered around an industrialization drive, emphasizing import-substitution, structural change and a less open economy, to be achieved largely through the instrumentalities of the state.[27]

State-led development reflected a key source of influence over most African countries. Agricultural interests—mostly made up of small, subsistence farmers—were typically unorganized, poorly educated, and ill informed. They were not able to play an influential role in postindependence politics or in the economic-policy choices of their governments. (There were exceptions: farmers in Ivory Coast and Kenya, for example, were organized and did influence economic policies in their favor.)[28] Politically influential groups in the new states tended to be urban based and associated with government. The choice of economic policies reflected and reinforced this essentially urban, state bias in politics in the new Africa. State-led development also coincided with the inclination of Africa's new leaders to consolidate their rule by concentrating power—including economic power—in their hands. There were few "agencies of restraint"[29] within their governments—like independent central banks or judiciaries—and there were rarely groups within their societies able or willing to resist the monopolization of power by increasingly autocratic and often repressive rulers.

The economic roller coaster of the 1970s gave another boost to the impulse toward economic control by Africa's leaders. That decade was characterized by a surge and then collapse in the prices of most of the commodities produced and exported by African countries. First came a quadrupling in petroleum prices in 1973, creating an enormous economic windfall for Africa's oil producers: Angola, Nigeria, Cameroon, Gabon, and Congo. The surge in oil prices created fears of shortages in other minerals markets, and soon speculation drove those prices up too, producing a sudden ballooning in export revenues for Africa's copper producers—Zambia and the Democratic Republic of the Congo (formerly Zaire). The increase in petroleum prices spurred a search for alternative energy sources (including nuclear energy) in developed, oil-importing countries. This in turn led to an increase in uranium prices, benefiting Niger, which exports the mineral.

It was also in 1972 that the prices for major grains began to climb. A small drop in world wheat production combined with the entry of the USSR into the world market with large purchases of grain led to a doubling in world prices for major grains and increasing talk of a world food crisis. This, in turn, provoked a rise in the demand for phosphate, used in fertilizer and produced by Mauritania and Togo in West Africa. As luck would have it, a drought in India and frosts in Brazil led to sharp increases in prices for tea, cocoa, and coffee (all tripling in price between 1975 and 1977). These beverages were important exports for a number of African countries, including Kenya, Malawi, Cameroon, Ivory Coast, Ghana, Tanzania, Rwanda, Burundi, and Uganda.

As we have noted, taxes on exports had become an important source of government revenues in much of Africa. The response of almost all of them to the windfall gains in their export earnings was to spend: they undertook ambitious development projects, expanded education, and increased wages and government employment.[30] As is often the case, the Nigerians provided the most dramatic example of an export-financed expansion—a 3,000 percent increase in state expenditures between 1970 and 1980.[31] Moreover, a number of governments—for example, those of Nigeria, Senegal, the Republic of the Congo, the Democratic Republic of the Congo, and Zambia—went on to borrow from international commercial banks (many of which were eager to lend their excess petrodollars) on the assumption (or hope) that export prices would remain high for the foreseeable future.

Just as the prices of many primary products soared during the first part of the 1970s, most of them plunged during the latter part of the decade. The speculative boom in most minerals lasted only a year or two. International grain production soon expanded to meet the increased demand from the USSR, and prices declined to more normal levels. Favorable weather returned to India and Brazil, leading to an increase in the supply of tea and coffee and an easing in prices. Only petroleum prices remained high (until 1982, that is, when they too dropped sharply). With trade balances deteriorating and budget revenues falling, many African governments protected their economies from painful adjustments by tightening economic controls: imposing quotas on imports, allocating funds directly to foreign exchange, adding subsidies and regulations, and fixing domestic prices below market clearing rates.

These policies of state-led growth and increasing controls produced conditions that could not be sustained economically. The growth of African states required increasing revenues. High taxes on agriculture provided a number of governments with revenues in the short term. But in the long term, that taxation discouraged expanded production and investment in agriculture (and often led to smuggling), slowing overall economic growth, undercutting the government's revenue base, and requiring increasing foreign-exchange expenditures on food imports.

Similarly, regulations on private investment in industry and services discouraged investors from risking their capital. As a result, jobs and growth in those sectors rose slowly if at all, and tax revenues remained limited. In those countries reliant on mineral exports, government often neglected, rather than exploited, agriculture, but the result was the same: slow growth and a revenue base dependent on the world price of mineral exports. Finally, the expanding access to education meant that there was a growing number of graduates seeking jobs in the modern sector. Many African governments initially responded to these pressures by offering public employment to all graduates, further increasing the size of the state sector.

By the early 1980s, with growth slowing, export revenues declining, import costs rising, and budgets increasing, governments found themselves seriously strapped for cash. Many were unable to finance their current expenditures (much less any new investments) or to service a large burden of external debt owed to private banks and foreign aid donors. Some governments, like that of Benin, were flat broke and stopped paying the salaries of their civil servants.

From Unsustainable Development to Economic Reform

The 1980s saw the dismantling and partial replacement of the state-led approach to development. Facing severe economic crises by the early 1980s, African governments sought increased aid and debt relief. They turned to the International Monetary Fund (IMF) and World Bank for help, and the era of stabilization and structural adjustment commenced. During the 1980s and 1990s, most African governments adopted stabilization programs approved and financed by the IMF aimed at reducing domestic inflation and closing the gap in their balance of payments. Stabilization policies typically included exchange rate adjustments, reductions in government deficits (usually through decreases in expenditures), and controls on credit. Once inflation was under control and the gap in the balance of payments closed, investment would rise, incomes and jobs would increase and absorb a portion of the rapidly expanding numbers of literate but unemployed young people, and growth would gradually resume.

But it didn't happen. Stabilization programs, when they were fully implemented (which was not always the case), restrained domestic demand for imports. But they failed to regenerate investment and growth. By the mid-1980s, it was clear that more fundamental institutional and policy changes were needed, including reforms in prices, in regulatory regimes, in public services, and in policies and institutions involving agriculture, education, and finance. Programs of structural and sectoral adjustment intended to address these more fundamental problems were designed and funded by the World Bank and other aid donors and agreed to by most African countries during the 1980s and early 1990s. Administrative controls over imports were reduced, and controls on prices of many goods, on wages, and on interest rates were reduced or removed. Tax systems were reformed and some barriers to trade reduced. But the implementation of economic reforms was uneven, with governments continuing to absorb a large proportion of GNP, maintaining sizable fiscal deficits and high trade barriers, and resisting privatization and reform of the civil service. Moreover, some reforms were rolled back in the face of opposition by patronage networks with a vested interest in the economic policies and institutions of the state.[32]

Not surprisingly, the hoped-for increase in investment did not occur. Economic conditions in most countries continued to deteriorate in the 1980s. Africans and others began to look beyond economic policies to the political causes for continuing economic decline.

Politics and Development in Africa

The economic policies that influenced development in Africa at first meshed nicely with the political preferences of African leaders and soon became embedded in the politics of the region. Within a decade of independence, the democratic political institutions put in place by the departing colonial powers had been discarded by military coups or undercut by constitutional changes that banned opposition political parties and suppressed or controlled most organizations in the country, including unions, cooperatives, professional associations, and youth and women's groups. The centralization of power in the hands of Africa's autocrats was justified as a means of ensuring national unity in what were mostly poorly integrated, ethnically diverse countries. It was argued that avoiding divisive and time-consuming policy debates would help ensure political tranquility and rapid growth.

However, the increasing control over economic resources by governments lacking both transparency and accountability led not only to faulty policy choices but, inevitably, to the diversion of many of those resources for political ends—primarily patronage or policies favoring influential groups—or for corrupt personal uses by powerful politicians who were soon called "Big Men."

> Big Men can provide their followers with access to the state's resources. "Jobs for the boys" in the civil service, government

boards and public corporations can be furnished by legal or illegal means. They can . . . channel low-interest loans and contracts from public agencies to their friends and allies. . . . Some patrons will also supply their clients with opportunities for illegal gain from public office; or, at least, they may allow illicit practices to go unpunished for fear of losing support. Corruption is one such opportunity—accepting or extorting bribes for decisions or actions taken in a public capacity. Others include theft of public property, the illegal appropriation of public revenues (fraud) and nepotism.

Secondly, strongmen and/or other Big Men reward their clients by granting preferential access to resources which, though outside the public sector, are subject to governmental regulation or influence. For example, an aspiring businessman is required to obtain a license to establish a transport company, a taxi service or a distributorship for a certain commodity. He must have a permit to import various items or get foreign exchange from the central bank. Indeed, even to purchase land, he may have to satisfy a land board. All these allocations of nongovernmental benefits can become counters in the game of factional manoeuvre.[33]

The widespread use of public institutions as vehicles for patronage weakened the capacity (limited in any case at the time of independence) of those institutions to perform effectively and imposed a further drag on development in most of Africa. The state had in many countries become the major vehicle for gaining access to economic resources. Its leaders, employees, and clients had become the richest and most influential political force in African countries, one that not surprisingly supported existing policies and institutions.[34]

Demands for political reform from outside and inside African countries began to mount at the end of the 1980s and early 1990s. In 1989, the World Bank first urged the importance of "good governance" (transparency, accountability, and predictability), albeit for political reasons the Bank never mentioned the need for democratic reforms.[35] Other aid donors, like the United States, Britain, and France, also began to support democratic reforms. And so did an increasing number of Africans, disillusioned with the economic performance of their governments, impressed by the wave of democracy sweeping the former Socialist states of Eastern Europe and the Soviet Union, and taking hope from the statements of support for democratic reforms from external powers.

African leaders acceded to these demands in varying degrees, usually depending on the intensity of internal and external pressure. Some—for example, the presidents of Benin and Zambia—agreed to constitutional changes and elections and, as a result, lost their positions. Others, like the presidents of Ivory Coast and Kenya, agreed to partial changes and managed to retain power in multiparty elections in which opposition movements were unable to organize quickly enough or to collaborate effectively. By 1996, most countries had held national and local elections. In most of the region there were fewer human-rights abuses and more political rights, increased press freedom, and rapid growth in the number of nongovernmental organizations. In effect, many governments had become more transparent and accountable, with some limits placed on executive power.

But like economic reforms, political reforms were often partial and fragile, and varied in extent from country to country. Freedom House identified seven African countries as "fully free" in 1996, seventeen as "partly free," and twenty as "not free."[36] Military dictatorships continued in several of Africa's largest countries, including Nigeria, Sudan, and the Democratic Republic of the Congo.[37] And in many countries, even the newly democratic ones, the new parliaments, judiciaries, and the media remained inexperienced and weak. The residue of past policies and political behavior—including the practice of patronage, the plague of corruption, and the consequent weak capacity of African states—was still widespread in the middle of the 1990s.

In effect, the earlier unsustainable development model has been dismantled and partially replaced with economic and political reforms inspired by another "model" of development based on free markets, private investment, and governments that are capable and relatively clean (the latter being ensured, it was thought, by the accountability of those same governments to the governed through democratic processes). However, the new and partial nature of the economic and political reforms in many countries, the limited constituency supporting the economic reforms, and the weakness of the new political institutions raised uncertainties about their long-term durability. And these uncertainties, plus remaining problems of corruption and political instabilities in a number of countries, in turn generated questions as to whether the hoped-for significant increase in savings and investment necessary to support sustained growth and consolidate a powerful constituency for the reforms would occur. In fact, by the mid-1990s, savings rates remained low. And while investment levels had recovered from declines in the 1980s and early 1990s, they too were still low—below the peak of $5.5 billion for all of the region reached in 1982.[38] Per capita growth rates had become positive for most

African countries, but for most of these, growth rates were still too low. And while a number of Africans and others took hope from these small signs of economic progress, some worried that the region had replaced an economically unsustainable development model with one that could eventually prove to be politically unsustainable if the pace of economic progress failed to accelerate.

Aid and the Africans

In our discussion of African economic performance and the factors influencing it, we have thus far left out the role of foreign aid. A detailed discussion of the economic impact of that aid will come in the following chapter. Here, it remains for us to examine briefly a key aspect of foreign aid and development: the impact of the policy and institutional environment in African countries and the political relationships between African governments and aid donors on the performance of that aid.

There is little dispute that the economic policies adopted by African governments during the 1960s and 1970s inhibited the ability of aid to contribute to their development, just as they inhibited development itself. Aid projects aimed at expanding agricultural production were stymied by the low prices farmers received for their produce. These prices were often fixed by government marketing boards or were a consequence of overvalued exchange rates and the inflow of competitive imports. Aid-financed primary health care projects in rural areas were often shorted by governments, whose main priority was expanding technically advanced medical facilities for urban elites. Education projects that expanded the number of graduates were compromised when those graduates could find no employment.

While the policy environment was important for the success of aid, even more important were the strengths or weaknesses of the governments receiving it. A look at the process by which aid was managed by Africans shows why this is the case. Based on published studies of public administration and management, available materials on the aid process within African governments, and conversations with officials, the following picture emerges of the aid process in much of the region.[39] A ministry of planning or planning commission is responsible for producing a development plan, usually including projects for funding by aid donors. The ministry of planning is also often responsible for finding the aid to fund those projects. In some cases, this ministry is theoretically responsible for managing and distributing aid funds to spending ministries (for example, ministries of health or agriculture) and for coordinating aid donors. (In certain countries, like Botswana, the ministry of finance includes this planning function.)

In reality, planning ministries have been among the weaker ministries in African governments. In addition to problems with basic data and the lack of personnel adequately trained in planning techniques, the planning function itself became discredited in many countries during the chaotic 1970s and 1980s. Furthermore, planning ministries rarely had the authority or power to coordinate spending ministries effectively or the will to coordinate the forty or more foreign donors operating in their countries. Thus, the planning function typically proved an inadequate mechanism for ensuring discipline and coherence in the use of government resources, including those provided by aid donors.

What about the budget process in African governments? Among the more powerful ministries in most African countries (indeed, in most countries anywhere) is the ministry of finance. In theory, this ministry usually manages the government's budget and its expenditures—often including aid. But this, too, has not always been the case in much of Africa. In a number of countries, budgetary processes have functioned poorly, with secret, off-budget expenditures (Mobutu's Zaire was outstanding in this regard), deficiencies in basic data (for instance, how much was owed to foreign creditors) and sloppy record keeping, unreliable tax administrations (customs revenues, for example, were often pocketed by customs officials), and poor coordination and discipline within government generally. For example, individual ministries and state-owned enterprises in a number of governments were authorized to borrow directly from abroad without prior approval from the ministry of finance. In some countries, such as Mozambique for many years, the entire government budget was a state secret.

Exacerbating these weaknesses, aid donors during the 1960s and 1970s began to deal directly with spending ministries as they prepared and implemented their projects. An aid donor typically conceived a project (often based on the development priorities prevailing in the donor's capital) and proposed it to the appropriate spending ministry. The minister, who almost always agreed, would then take the proposal to his or her finance minister for approval. Approval was rarely withheld, especially since donors were already willing to fund the project. However, approval often meant the allocation of government resources as its contribution to the project (and the implicit commitment of future government resources to maintain it). These pressures from donors influenced the

overall spending and investment priorities of African governments regardless of their preferences or plans. And they led to implicit commitments to maintain projects regardless of future revenues. (When government revenues and foreign exchange dropped during the late 1970s and
the 1980s, so did the funding of aid projects, often leading to their collapse.)

Once a project was agreed to, the aid donor frequently funded a "technical advisor" (usually its own national) in the spending ministry to oversee the project. At times, donors created separate units in spending ministries (or even independent of them) to manage their projects. These
were techniques for circumventing the institutional weaknesses of bureaucracies and for moving significant amounts of money quickly. African governments at times welcomed foreign "technical experts" or officials of aid agencies within their ministries, since they viewed those
individuals as their "agents" with the aid agencies themselves, capable
of generating more aid.[40]

The aid for structural and sectoral adjustment that became popular in
the 1980s (of which, much more in the following chapter) strengthened
ministries of finance vis-à-vis spending ministries because adjustment
programs were typically negotiated with finance ministers and the funding provided to them. However, project aid continued to be provided
to spending ministries and involved direct relations between them and
donors. Also in the 1980s, as we shall see, the number of donors increased, and the amount of aid spent on "technical assistance" rose. Both
of these changes put added pressures on senior African officials to spend
time arranging visits by donor officials and to use productively the many
foreign consultants present in their ministries, often for short periods of
time only.[41]

Managing the aid they received was only one of the challenges confronting the many governments that actively sought assistance from
abroad. They also had to manage their relationships with major donors.
In theory, aid was provided needy governments to help them develop
their economies. In practice, governments providing the aid almost always had a political agenda as well. (We shall explore these agendas in
detail in the case studies on aid donors.) Julius Nyerere pointed to this
challenge.

The English people have a proverb which says: "He who pays
the piper calls the tune." How can we depend upon foreign gov-

ernments and companies for the major part of our development without giving to those governments and countries a great part of our freedom to act as we please? The truth is that we cannot.[42]

In much of the period covered by this study, the policy agendas of major aid donors related primarily to the Cold War competition between the West and the Socialist bloc for influence in the region. But there were other international political agendas as well: the competitions between the USSR and China for the leadership of socialist-oriented governments, between the two Chinas for recognition as the legitimate representative of the Chinese people, between the two Germanys for the same legitimizing recognition, between Israel and the Arab states for recognition and diplomatic support in the United Nations and elsewhere, and— muted but at times vigorous (at least, on the French side)—between the United States and France for influence in Africa. Africans learned quickly to exploit these various competitions to extract aid while avoiding political concessions to those providing it.

One can identify three broad strategies adopted by African governments in managing their relations with aid donors during the first two decades of independence: "switching" (that is, playing off one side against the other), "balanced benefaction,"[43] and "reliance/penetration." Switching was adopted by several African presidents at independence— most notably Kwame Nkrumah of Ghana and Sekou Toure of Guinea, and later Siad Barre of Somalia and Mengistu Haile Mariam of Ethiopia. Surprisingly, few others actually switched from one side of the Cold War to the other, perhaps because donors distrusted the leader doing it,[44] and consequently tended to provide him low levels of aid and other support. Many leaders hinted at switching sides in the Cold War (and if they were credible leaders of large countries, this alone could inhibit political pressures from donors), but few ever did.

There was a considerable amount of switching between other diplomatic competitors in Africa, for example the mass decision in 1973 to break diplomatic relations with Israel (and lose the accompanying aid) in the wake of war with Egypt. If this switch involved an expectation that Africans would be generously rewarded with aid from the newly oil rich Arab countries or with low-priced oil, they were mistaken.

More widely practiced and more rewarding was a policy of balanced benefaction, practiced by a number of Anglophone countries, most notably Kenya and Tanzania. They persuaded as many donors as possible to provide assistance so that political pressures from any one donor could be ignored. If pressures became too insistent, aid from that donor could be rejected without significant loss of revenues.

A third strategy was adopted by a number of Francophone countries— relying on a main aid patron, France, but penetrating the French political system to influence its policies from inside. Africans were relatively successful in this strategy, receiving large amounts of aid from Paris and managing to influence French policy and even personnel decisions of importance to them.[45] One observer of France's Africa policies remarked on the "interpenetration of French and African politics, rather reminiscent of Israeli politicians' forays to New York and Capitol Hill. The difference is that France has to deal with 19 Israels of varying power and determination."[46]

Two changes in Africa and the world greatly diminished Africans' abilities to pursue strategies designed to maximize aid flows and minimize attendant political pressures. One was their own deepening economic crisis in the 1980s, making them desperate for more aid to finance their widening balance-of-payments gaps. The other was the virtual elimination of the USSR and its allies from aid competition by the early 1980s. This was evident in Moscow's refusal to admit Mozambique to the Council for Mutual Economic Assistance in 1981 because membership would have implied the provision of large amounts of aid. The Soviets' refusal of an urgent request in 1982 for a new aid program from the new "radically oriented" government of Jerry Rawlings of Ghana was another indication of the winding down of the Cold War in Africa.

While the Africans had in the past been successful in fending off pressures from aid agencies urging economic-policy reforms, in the 1980s this was no longer the case. They were in more urgent need of aid and had no sources except Western donors and Western-funded multilateral aid agencies. The strategies employed at the height of the Cold War were not entirely abandoned. Africans at times attempted to play off bilateral aid donors as well as the World Bank and the International Monetary Fund against one another when their policy advice differed (Kenya and Tanzania became well known for this maneuver). However, donors pressing for economic-policy reforms in Africa cooperated among themselves for the very purpose of limiting the abilities of African officials to manipulate them, as we shall see in subsequent chapters. There was still considerable "reliance/penetration" behavior, with Francophone Africans urging France to protect them from economic-policy reforms pressed by the World Bank. And the more sophisticated and influential Africans attempted to play off different elements of government bureaucracies within donor countries against one another. A story circulated around Washington during the 1980s that President Mobutu of Zaire had threatened the Peace Corps with expulsion and then offered to rescind that threat if the U.S. Treasury would help ease the economic reforms urged upon him by the IMF.[47] These and other strategies provided a measure of independence from aid donors in the 1980s and 1990s even though the bargaining power Africans enjoyed from the Cold War had greatly diminished.

Conclusion

Let us sum up briefly the African side of the aid effectiveness equation. The same policies and weak institutions that inhibited development also made aid in support of it less effective. The weakness of their institutions affected the way Africans managed the aid—or failed to manage it. Their eagerness for aid and their institutional weaknesses led to "donor driven" identification, design, and implementation of aid projects; donors decided which countries received aid and how much. This has also been largely the case in aid-funded economic-reform programs, though Africans have to an extent resisted implementing programs to which they reluctantly agreed, or have at times influenced the nature of those programs to their advantage—through their aid patrons or through playing off different aid agencies. Still, the design of reform programs has remained largely in the hands of the aid agencies funding them, and there we must look for an explanation of their effectiveness. But first we must examine in detail the amount and impact of aid in Africa.

Chapter Three

Aid and Development in Africa

The question with which this book began—"Why, with so much aid, has there been so little development in Africa?"—took it as given that there had been "much aid." Is this true? The first task of this chapter is to answer this question. We then turn to how foreign aid is supposed to help development. We conclude with an assessment of how effective aid has actually been in supporting development in Africa.

So Much Aid?

Foreign aid is defined here as a transfer of concessional resources from one government to another or from a government to an international aid agency or a nongovernmental organization (which, in turn, transfers those resources to poor countries). The resource transfer must either be a grant; or, if a loan, it should carry a grace period, interest rate, and repayment terms that provide a grant element of at least 25 percent. And the resources must be provided with the ostensible goal of promoting economic development in a less-developed country. This is the definition used by the Development Assistance Committee (DAC) of the Organization for Economic Cooperation and Development (OECD) for "official development assistance" or "ODA." Excluded from this definition are private transfers of concessional resources (for instance, private contributions to NGOs for relief or development work abroad), military aid, credits for the promotion of a donor country's exports, public resource transfers between well-off countries (for example, U.S. aid to promote peace in Northern Ireland or democratic change in Russia), international bribes, tributes, or funding for covert action against another government or foreign organization.

Foreign aid comes in a number of forms. It can be provided in cash as a grant or loan. It can come in the form of food, clothing, medicine, or other commodities, provided on concessional terms. It can also come in the form of debt cancellation. Most aid has been in the form of monetary grants or loans. The main nonfinancial economic aid has been food, typically drawn from surplus agricultural production in aid-giving countries. The major bilateral source of food aid had long been the United States, although the amount of U.S. food aid has decreased in the 1990s with falling levels of surplus production. Total food aid worldwide was $800 million in 1996, representing 1.5 percent of all ODA. (Because food aid is a relatively small proportion of total aid, we shall have little to say about it in this book.)[1]

Debt forgiveness involves reducing or extinguishing a liability on the part of a borrower to a creditor. By implication, debt forgiveness constitutes a grant of the resources that would have been spent in servicing the debt. The real value of those resources is equal to the present value of the amount of the debt that would have actually been repaid in the absence of debt reduction or cancellation. (The amount of the debt likely to be repaid can equal zero. For example, the U.S. government has in the past forgiven debt owed it by Egypt, calculating it as a zero resource transfer on the assumption that the debt would never have been repaid.)

For some countries, including a number in Africa, their nominal international debt is high relative to the size of their economies and is considered an important obstacle to their future growth. Further, overall debt forgiveness by bilateral aid donors is still relatively small—$2.8 billion in 1996, or 5 percent of total ODA.[2] And multilateral aid agencies like the World Bank, to which much of the debt is owed, do not forgive debts owed them. Thus, the issue of reducing African debt burdens remains an urgent one. However, it also remains beyond the purview of this study.

Foreign aid can finance several distinct types of activities. It can be used to fund discrete investment projects—for example, the construction of a road or a school or an industrial plant. It can pay for technical assistance—expert advisors or training for nationals of the recipient country. Project aid has been by far the most common form of foreign aid and remains so today. However, foreign aid can be provided as "program aid"—a transfer of concessional resources to another government for budget or balance-of-payments support or in exchange for agreed sets of activities to be undertaken by that government, for example, adopting economic-policy reforms. An early example was the U.S. Alliance for Progress in Latin America, in which recipient governments agreed to reform land tenure or tax systems in exchange for the aid. Finally, although governments and international organizations are the recipients of nearly all foreign aid, a limited but increasing amount of aid is provided to nongovernmental organizations, both "northern" (that is, based in developed countries) and "southern" (indigenous to developing countries), for work on development-related activities. The DAC estimates that government aid provided to NGOs amounted to nearly $1 billion in 1996.[3] (Although NGOs are increasing in importance as sources and implementers of aid projects, they still handle a relatively small proportion of total aid. We shall leave consideration of the overall effectiveness of their aid in Africa to others.)[4]

In 1996, foreign aid worldwide totaled nearly $55.5 billion.[5] A third of that—nearly $17 billion—went to the countries of sub-Saharan Africa. Figure 1 shows the history of total aid to Africa since 1970.[6]

Aid to Africa rose slowly until the middle of the 1970s and then began a sharp ascent with increases in aid worldwide, the intensification of the Cold War in eastern and southern Africa, and the greater emphasis on using aid to help the poorest countries, many of which were in Africa. The total level of aid to the region ceased to increase for several years in the early 1980s. In the wake of a major drought in Ethiopia in 1984 and the worldwide focus on the worsening economic crisis in the region, aid again rose sharply, peaking in 1990. Aid flows have trended downward thereafter as donors have shifted funding into countries of Eastern Europe and the former USSR and have decreased their overall levels of aid.

The Donors and Recipients

Turning to the sources of aid, as of 1996 there were at least forty major bilateral and multilateral donors active in the region and many smaller governments and NGOs providing aid. Five donors disbursed over $1 billion: France ($2.5 billion), the European Community ($2.0 billion), the International Development Association (IDA) of the World Bank ($2.5 billion), Japan ($1.3 billion), and Germany ($1.3 billion). The United States and the United Kingdom contributed just over $600 million each.[7] In addition to the twenty-one members of the DAC and to numerous UN agencies, other sources of aid to Africa include Arab governments and multilateral aid funds, Israel, China, and Taiwan. Govern-

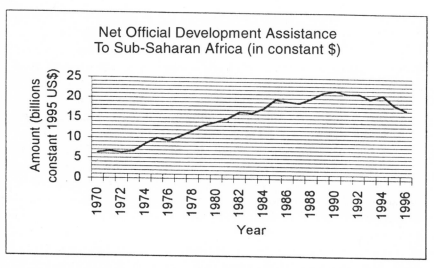

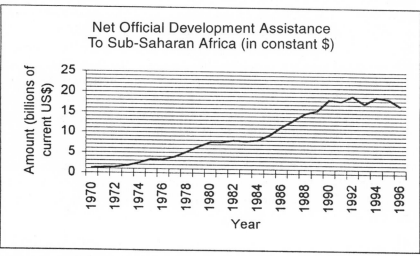

Figure 1. Aid to Sub-Saharan Africa, 1970–1996. (*Source:* Development Assistance Committee data)

ments believed to be providing aid for which data are rarely available include Libya, Iraq, and Iran. One of the newer donor governments in Africa is Korea, whose aid to Africa totaled just over $5 million in 1993.[8] The countries of Eastern Europe and the USSR were past sources of aid to African governments, but their aid terminated with the end of the Cold War, though some of the successor states—for example, the Czech

Republic—are in the process of initiating new aid programs in Africa.[9] And from time to time, still other developing countries, such as Brazil or India, have provided aid, particularly to countries where they have a significant expatriate or emigrant population or where their language is spoken. Not all of these donors are active in every African country. But in the larger African countries, like Kenya or Zambia, it is not unusual to find forty or more aid agencies funding projects and programs, often together with hundreds of NGOs.

Moving from a profile of aid donors to aid recipients in Africa, nearly all countries in the region receive some official development assistance. Those receiving the largest absolute amounts of aid have tended to be the most populous countries or the favored diplomatic partners of major aid donors or, since the 1980s, those with the more ambitious reform programs. Table 1 shows the countries receiving the largest amount of aid in Africa over the past several decades.

The discussion thus far has given an overview of aid to Africa. But to assess whether the aid has been large relative to African economies, we must turn to two ratios that establish the relative size of aid flows: aid as a proportion of GNP and aid as a proportion of total national investment. Over the past five decades, it has been unusual for foreign aid to exceed 1 or 2 percent of any country's gross national product. At its peak from 1955 to 1957, U.S. aid to Korea reached 10 percent of the GNP of that country but remained this high for only two years. Of the major world recipients of aid in 1989–90, in only three countries (Egypt, Jordan, and Bolivia) did aid exceed 20 percent of GNP, while the average ratio of aid to GNP for sub-Saharan Africa at that time equaled just over 22 percent.[10] In 1993–94, foreign aid was equivalent to 5 percent or more of the GNP of forty out of forty-seven African countries. In sixteen of those countries, it contributed 20 percent or more of their GNP. More-

Table 1. Top Five Recipients of Aid to Africa

1970	1980	1990	1995
Nigeria	Tanzania	Kenya	Zambia
DRC[a]	Sudan	Tanzania	Ivory Coast
Kenya	DRC[a]	Mozambique	Mozambique
Tanzania	Kenya	Ethiopia	Ethiopia
Ghana	Zambia	DRC[a]	Tanzania

Source: Development Assistance Committee, *Development Cooperation* (Paris: Organization for Economic Cooperation and Development, various years).

[a]Democratic Republic of the Congo, formerly Zaire.

over, the relatively large aid flows to sub-Saharan African countries have
not been transient. For thirty-five of these countries, aid has equaled 5
percent or more for at least a decade and in some cases, for more than
two decades, often with aid as a percentage of GNP increasing over that
period. The extreme case was Somalia, where in 1990 foreign aid equaled
a whopping 237 percent of GNP. (This percentage included relief aid.
The more "normal" ratio of aid to Somali GNP was usually over 100
percent between 1977 and 1990. Mozambique's aid-to-GNP ratio was
over 50 percent between 1987 and 1993. These two have been the highest in the world.)[11] See table 2 for details.

Figures of aid-to-GNP ratios for 1996 suggest that these percentages
have begun to decline but remain above 10 percent of GNP in many
countries and are still among the highest in the world.[12] If there are any
lingering doubts of the relative importance of aid throughout much of
sub-Saharan Africa, one final set of figures should erase them. Investment is one of the keys to sustained growth and development. Investment
is usually what foreign aid is intended to finance. In 1992–93, aid
equaled 50 percent or more of investment in twenty-nine African countries, and in thirteen of those countries, aid was equivalent to more than
100 percent of investment. And although data on investment is incom-
plete, in most of these countries for which there is a time series, high
ratios of aid to investment have continued over decades.

There can be little argument that the answer to the first question in
this chapter—"Has there been so much aid in Africa?"—is a decisive yes
for most of the region.

Aid and Development

We must now ask how foreign aid is supposed to help development.
There is a large literature on foreign aid and development, reflecting the
evolution of thinking over the past several decades.[13] We will not attempt
to review it here. We shall simply describe four broad categories of activity in which it is generally agreed that aid is supposed to promote development.

Capital Formation

Investments in physical and human capital are a major element in foster-
ing economic growth. In the 1950s and early 1960s, mainstream development economists considered the major constraint on growth in poor

Table 2. Aid Dependence in Africa, 1970–93

	Aid as a Percentage of GNP—Number of Years		
	5–10%	10–15%	15%+
Benin	15	6	2
Botswana	9	5	10
Burkina Faso	3	9	12
Burundi	4	9	11
Cameroon	13	0	0
Central African Republic	5	8	11
Chad	3	9	12
Congo	15	6	0
Democratic Republic of the Congo	4	0	0
Ethiopia	7	1	9
Gambia	5	2	16
Ghana	4	5	0
Guinea	0	3	5
Guinea (Bissau)	0	0	19
Ivory Coast	5	0	0
Kenya	12	4	2
Lesotho	3	14	7
Liberia	5	3	1
Madagascar	9	3	4
Malawi	4	11	9
Mali	1	7	16
Mauritania	3	1	20
Mozambique	4	1	9
Niger	8	7	9
Rwanda	1	18	5
Senegal	10	8	6
Somalia	0	0	21[a]
Sudan	9	7	3
Swaziland	21	2	0
Tanzania	5	8	9
Togo	10	8	6
Uganda	7	1	6
Zambia	6	3	8
Zimbabwe	9	1	0

Source: World Bank data.

[a]For 14 of these years, aid was equal to or greater than 100 percent of GNP.

countries to be a lack of investable funds, resulting from low levels of domestic savings and limited foreign investment and commercial lending. Foreign aid was seen as a means of easing that constraint and so, permitting a higher level of capital formation and more rapid growth than would otherwise be possible. In the 1960s, economists added the limitations on foreign exchange (and so, on the ability of a country to import needed capital goods and expertise for investment purposes) as another important resource constraint that foreign aid could ease.[14] From the beginning of sizable aid flows in the 1950s and continuing to the mid-1990s, a significant proportion of aid has been provided to finance investment projects aimed at expanding infrastructure, social services, and agricultural and industrial production.

Development Ideas and Technologies

Another element in development, as we observed in the previous chapter, involves technological innovations that make land, labor, or capital more productive. Such innovations typically arise out of basic and applied research in areas critical to the development of poor countries. Since the 1960s, aid has been used to fund a substantial amount of development-related research in both developed and developing countries and by international research organizations, particularly in the areas of agriculture and health. It is worth mentioning too that aid has also funded research on the process of development itself, and the findings have contributed to evolving views of specialists and practitioners on the problems of development and their solutions. Aid-funded research played a role in the increased concern in the 1970s about the distributive effects of development and led to the adoption of policies targeted at poverty alleviation. Research by the World Bank provided the intellectual underpinnings for the emphasis on economic-policy reforms in the 1980s. As we shall see in more detail below, aid-funded research has played a role in sectoral policies and programs, for example, heightening awareness among African officials of the consequences of rapid population growth or environmental degradation.

Economic and Political Reform

With the increased emphasis in the 1980s on the critical role of economic policies in supporting or inhibiting development, development specialists came to regard foreign aid as a useful tool in promoting economic-reform programs in developing countries. Aid could encourage a dialogue with recipient governments on development problems and their solution. It could finance economic-reform programs (for example, the costs of preparing and implementing reforms). Or, where governments were resistant to reforms, aid could be offered as an incentive for governments to adopt reforms. In the 1990s, when development specialists turned to the problems of politics and governance as obstacles to development, aid was also used as an incentive to persuade governments to adopt political reforms and as a source of financing for particular aspects of those reforms, for example, elections. In 1997, several major aid donors, including the World Bank, began to condition their aid on efforts to reduce corruption on the part of recipient governments.

Strengthening Government Performance

Development specialists recognized early on that the "absorptive capacity" of government played a key role in the efficiency and effectiveness with which national resources were managed. Aid could ease this constraint through "institution building" with technical assistance to fund advisors to government agencies to assist them to organize themselves and carry out their responsibilities and to finance the training and education of developing-country nationals. Technical assistance remains an important and growing component of foreign aid today. It has risen from a total of $4.8 billion per year in 1980 (or 18 percent of total aid that year) to $14.1 billion in 1996, or 25 percent of total aid worldwide.[15]

Overall Impact

An assumption in most discussions on foreign aid is that if it is large enough and effective in achieving its specific objectives, it will spur development in the countries receiving it without significant negative effects. Many aid advocates, especially those concerned with development in Africa, argue that since development is lagging in the region and needs are great, more aid should be provided. Others, like the World Bank, take a more systematic approach. The Bank calculates the amount of aid countries require on the basis of "gap analysis." This approach involves identifying, first, a target level of growth over a time period and, second, the probable level of domestic savings and other anticipated sources of investment multiplied by the additional output of capital anticipated (or the incremental capital output ratio) from additional investments. Third, the difference is calculated between what is projected to be available and its output in terms of growth and what is needed to achieve the growth target. This is the "gap" to be filled by foreign aid.[16]

In fact, there has been considerable controversy over the macroeconomic impact of foreign aid—whether significant amounts of aid depress saving rates,[17] encourage the expansion of government into the economy, push up prices and real exchange rates, create problems of aid dependence, and have other negative consequences. These issues remain unresolved and, as we shall see below, are a serious source of concern in Africa.

Aid and Development in Africa: Impact

If there has been so much aid and so little development in Africa, what impact has foreign aid in fact had there? This question really comprises three levels of inquiry. The first involves the impact of aid-funded research on ideas about how development occurs and the dissemination of those ideas by aid officials in dialogues with their African counterparts or officials from other aid agencies. A second part of the question involves the performance of aid-funded projects and programs in the areas of capital accumulation, technical assistance, and economic and political reform. A third part involves the overall impact of aid on recipient economies and societies, especially where aid flows have been significant in size.

An Overview of Aid's Development Impact in Africa

Let us summarize briefly the impact of aid on African development, to be elaborated in more detail below. In the wake of independence in the 1960s, most Western governments initiated aid programs in Africa. They encouraged African governments to plan their countries' development and, often, urged the adoption of policies encouraging industrial growth—policy preferences already strongly present in the region. Donors provided substantial sums for infrastructure and social services, especially education—again coinciding with African priorities at the time. Aid donors used their resources and their advice in effect to reinforce the "unsustainable development model" (described in the previous chapter) that expanded the role of the state but discouraged the production and investment necessary to sustain both economic growth and the state itself.

In retrospect, the ideas of development during the 1960s were simplistic, and the emphases on government planning—at least in the case of Africa, where governments were exceedingly weak—and on industrialization (in these highly agrarian countries) were misplaced. However, projects in infrastructure and social services funded by Western aid donors were appropriate to the region's urgent requirements at the time (even if some, as we shall see, were inappropriate in design to conditions prevailing in the countries receiving the aid).

The 1970s saw rapid increases in aid, particularly during the latter half of the decade. The focus of Western aid discourse shifted increasingly to poverty alleviation with a priority on projects to develop rural areas. The focus on rural development (and by implication, agricultural development) was appropriate to Africa, where 90 percent of the population were small farmers and where agriculture produced a significant proportion of national income. But unfortunately, there was a tendency among donors to emphasize redistributive goals while downgrading the importance of growth in the overall development equation. And the design of projects in rural development was often faulty, with high rates of failure based on excessive institutional complexity, lack of knowledge on the part of aid agencies about African smallholder agriculture, and inattention to the often adverse policy environment and weak public institutions that were charged with helping to carry out the complicated projects. Additionally, the rapid rise in aid in the latter half of the decade eased pressures on African governments to adjust to the deterioration in their terms of trade brought on by increases in prices of petroleum and manufactured goods and the collapse in most other primary-product prices.

With the economic crisis in Africa in the 1980s, there was a major shift in aid donors' attitudes toward development; discourse now focused on the role of economic policies as impediments to growth and on the importance of stabilization and structural adjustment reforms. After at first denying the need for policy reforms (and the appropriateness of donors' insisting on them), many African officials came to accept their importance by the end of the decade. Foreign aid was now used in large part as balance-of-payments support for economies suffering from import strangulation and governments committed to economic-reform programs. The aid was used, in effect, to dismantle the unsustainable development model adopted by most African governments and to urge its replacement with a neoclassical economic vision of free markets, private investment-led growth, and minimal government intervention in the economy.

However, aid agencies at first underestimated the extent of needed reforms and then overestimated the abilities and willingness of African governments to implement them. Moreover, donors' leverage in persuading (or forcing) Africans to implement economic reforms turned out to be less than expected when donors themselves proved unwilling to withdraw aid for African's noncompliance with their commitments to reform. Reforms were typically implemented only partly, and their success in restoring growth to the region remained limited.

The limitations on the extent of reforms and the continuation of low growth rates in most of Africa led aid agencies to look for other causes of lagging growth. At the beginning of the 1990s, much attention was paid to the quality of governance in African countries, with a number of aid agencies pushing hard for democratization in the hopes of promoting cleaner, more responsible and predictable governments and, so, improved growth. However, the relationship between democracy and growth lacked a strong theoretical or empirical basis. Donors' policies were in many ways experiments and to a considerable degree reflected their own values as much as their notions about what was needed to spur development. By the mid-1990s, efforts to condition aid on democratic reforms had only mixed success, and the impact over time of democratic reforms on growth was still uncertain.

A second emphasis in thinking on development in the 1990s was on strengthening the capacity of African governments to manage their economies. This was not a new idea but a return to an old one and based on the urgings of Africans and the increasing weaknesses of their governments. The problem was a real one and one too long neglected by donors. But how to address it effectively with aid was still far from clear. Finally, during the 1990s, donors began to adopt or expand a wide variety of socially oriented aid activities, including conserving the environment, addressing gender issues, poverty lending, strengthening civil society, and others involving social, cultural, and behavioral change in African societies. These new activities were typically added to donor portfolios on top of already existing activities. Moreover, the expanding sectoral scope of donor activities was no longer integrated into a broad development paradigm but was rather largely a series of efforts to address discrete problems, often of concern to influential groups within donor countries. These new activities were undertaken as aid levels were beginning to decline.

Conclusions on Aid and Development in Africa: A Preview

This brief overview suggests several broad conclusions about the impact of aid in Africa that we shall elaborate in the remainder of this chapter. These include the impact on development ideas and discourse, the effectiveness of projects and economic-reform programs, the impact of technical assistance on African governmental capacity, the overall impact on growth and poverty, and the political and economic side effects of foreign aid on development, including aid dependence and its consequences.[18]

1. The understanding on the part of aid agencies of African development problems has evolved considerably since the 1960s, based on the growth of their technical expertise in a number of areas and of their expanding local experience and knowledge. But even with the expanding understanding of development in Africa, a considerable portion of aid agency programs remain experimental, including those encouraging policy reform and democracy, and those intended to help strengthen the capacity of African institutions and to support beneficial behavioral change in African societies.

2. Related to learning on the part of aid agencies is their contribution to learning on the part of their African counterparts as well as on the part of other aid agencies. Several aid agencies have had some success in their dialogues with their African counterparts over the decades of this study in raising key development issues, helping to inform themselves and their African counterparts about the extent and causes of such problems and identifying solutions. This impact of elaborating and transferring knowledge and ideas on development is one that is difficult to quantify, especially as it is often not tied to specific aid-funded activities. The consequences of dialogue are likely to appear only in the long term. Yet, dialogue remains a key element in aid effectiveness (in that it would likely not take place in the absence of aid), and evidence suggests that it has contributed to an improved appreciation of the development process on the part both of aid agencies and African officials.

3. However, even as the understanding among aid donors of African development problems has grown more sophisticated, their capacity to design and implement aid programs and projects to address the complex challenges of development in Africa has lagged, along with the effectiveness of their aid interventions. This is not surprising, given the difficulties of bringing about change in foreign countries and the bureaucratic and political constraints on the policies, projects, and programs of aid agencies themselves.

4. As a result, aid-financed projects and programs in Africa have for the most part been among the least effective in achieving their goals and sustaining their achievements of any in the world, and there is some evidence that aid projects became less effective in the 1980s and 1990s even as the level of aid rose. Fixed-capital formation (for example, road construction) and the expansion in social services were among the more ef-

fective activities. Agricultural- and rural-development projects and efforts to strengthen African institutions were among the least effective aid interventions in Africa. Agricultural research had a generally disappointing payoff. Economic-reform programs were mixed in their outcomes and among the least effective of any region in the world. And aid in the form of technical assistance and training to strengthen the capacity of the African public sector, while enjoying early success, decreased in effectiveness even while it increased in size during the 1980s and 1990s. Indeed, the large amounts of technical assistance during these decades may have actually contributed to the weakening of African public agencies and become an obstacle to economic progress in the region.

5. Turning to the overall impact of aid in Africa, most of the econometric studies of the relationship of aid to growth have found that aid has had no significant impact, either positive or negative, on economic growth in the region. In terms of reducing poverty, we can say little based on direct evidence of the incidence of poverty or the distribution of income in individual African countries over time. The data is too weak in quantity and quality (including time series data) to permit significant conclusions. We can say that aid has indirectly helped reduce poverty in Africa by contributing to the financing of infrastructure, education, and health throughout much of the region.

6. However, there is also evidence that the large amount of aid over an extended period of time may have had significantly negative economic and political effects in a number of countries. The assumption, in short, that more aid is necessarily better for development may not hold.

Let us examine these conclusions in more detail.

Development Discourse and the Transmission of Ideas

Development takes place in an intellectual environment that includes ideas of what development is and how to promote it. These ideas have been the product of thinking and research in universities and research institutes, plus the learning from the experience of development practitioners in the field, both local and foreign. They are a key part of the broader dialogue on development between aid officials and experts from developed countries and those in developing countries.

It is clear that several aid donors—in particular the World Bank and the United States—have had an important impact on African thinking on development. This is most evident in the area of economic policies, where in the early years of independence, aid agencies urged African governments to take an active role in planning their development and supported their emphasis on industrialization. The United States, for example, often required a government to have a development plan as a condition of its aid and offered assistance in the development of such a plan. In retrospect, these ideas appear misguided, taking too little account of the weaknesses of the bureaucracies whose actions they were intended to influence. These views changed, and in the 1980s, the World Bank took the lead (with the support of a number of other aid agencies) in urging Africans to expand their private sectors and reduce government controls over economic activity. In addition to its discussions with African officials, the Bank offered courses in economic development at its headquarters in Washington, seminars in Africa, and conferences on a variety of development topics in an effort to influence African thinking on development. We cannot measure the impact of these efforts, but they likely contributed to the sea change in African development discourse evident in the 1990s. At the beginning of the 1980s, the role of the private sector in development was rarely mentioned—indeed, the idea of capitalist development was an anathema to many Africans. The state was still the principal vehicle for economic progress. The reverse was true in many African circles by the middle of the 1990s.

Another area where there has been a sea change in African thinking is in the impact of rapid population growth. Again, at the beginning of the 1980s, it was not uncommon to hear African officials deny that rapid population growth was a problem for their economies. Indeed, there were many governments with pronatalist policies, encouraging large families on the belief that they had a large amount of territory to fill up. By the 1990s, such views appeared rare. The development of detailed statistical data on population and health (including projections into the future and their economic implications), funded with USAID monies, plus a continuing discussion between U.S. aid officials and Africans on the challenges presented by rapid growth in their populations, had contributed to these changed attitudes and in a number of African countries led to reversals in government policies on family planning.

Not all the aid agencies studied here conducted extended development dialogues with African officials. A number were too small or lacked the presence or influence to do so. Where such a dialogue occurred, there is evidence that it had a significant impact on the thinking of Africans and often, on the policies they adopted. At times, that impact was negative, particularly when the ideas urged by aid officials were inappropriate to African conditions—for example, in the 1960s when foreign experts often lacked experience of the region. At other times, the ideas put forth by aid donors were important in pointing to key development problems, like faulty economic policies, even though the solutions proposed by donors were not fully accepted by African officials. Nevertheless, it is clear that both donors and recipients of aid have learned a great deal over the past three and a half decades—and surely more than would have been the case in the absence of a development dialogue between the two. This is an important aspect of the impact of aid in Africa.

Aid Projects and Programs

Turning to the performance of aid-funded projects and programs in Africa, there have been some outstanding individual successes—for example, the eradication of river blindness in parts of West Africa, the contribution of aid-funded family-planning services to the decline in fertility in Kenya, and more broadly, the contribution of aid to the expansion of infrastructure and social services in many African countries.[19]

At the same time, aid projects throughout much of Africa have failed to reach their objectives nearly as often as they have succeeded, a higher rate of failure than in any other region of the developing world.[20] Moreover, aid-funded projects in Africa have tended to prove the least sustainable of any worldwide. To elaborate on these points, let us refer to several of our earlier categories of aid-funded activities—capital formation, technological innovation and dissemination, policy reform, and institution building—bearing in mind that individual aid-funded projects and programs can include elements of all of these categories.

Capital Formation

A significant proportion of foreign aid in Africa has been allocated to the expansion of infrastructure and social services, including the construction of physical facilities and the provision of equipment, supporting an increase in roads, ports, public utilities, communications networks, schools and universities, and health clinics and hospitals. Expanding these facilities, very limited in most countries at independence, was critical to development in the region and contributed to the improvements in literacy, longevity and health of the average African described in the previous chapter.

However, these positive contributions of foreign aid have also had their drawbacks. There have been numerous criticisms of aid-funded infrastructure as overdesigned and overpriced, reflecting in part the intrusion of the commercial interests of donor countries in financing large, expensive projects, to be undertaken by business enterprises in their own country. Educational and health systems supported by aid donors have also been criticized as inappropriate to local needs. Health services have tended to be primarily curative and concentrated in urban areas, while the more serious and widespread health problems were found in rural areas and could often be prevented by proper hygiene and nutrition. Education, especially at the university level, has problems of irrelevance to local African needs (with its concentration on social sciences and humanities when the more pressing needs are for graduates in engineering, the sciences, and business), high cost, and declining quality.

The sustainability of aid-funded investments in infrastructure and social services has often proven to be limited. Any traveler in Africa is painfully aware of the poor condition of the road systems, and much of aid in the 1990s for infrastructure has been for the rehabilitation of past construction rather than the creation of new transport and communications facilities. Schools, hospitals, and health clinics are also often run down and lacking in books and medicines. These problems of maintenance are common in much of the developing world but are especially acute in Africa for several reasons: one involves the weakness of African governments. Organizing and managing the upkeep of assets of any kind can be challenging. A schedule of maintenance must be established and workers adequately trained and organized to follow it. Machines must be serviced regularly to remain operative. Spare parts or books and medicines must be ordered and distributed on a timely basis. Weak organizations find it difficult to plan and implement complicated tasks of this type.

Adding to the administrative problems of maintenance has been the shortage of budgetary resources suffered by most African governments over the past two decades, and the diversion of public resources for private gain evident in numerous government agencies in the region. Finally, foreign aid may have unintentionally worsened the problems of maintenance and sustainability in Africa. Aid donors have usually insisted on funding new projects rather than financing the recurrent costs of past projects. And they have often required African governments to put up counterpart funds to help finance their new projects. These are reasonable requirements where small amounts of aid are concerned. But where there are large amounts of aid and large numbers of aid donors, combined with scarce budgetary resources in recipient countries, these requirements can create perverse incentives for officials eager for more aid and new projects to divert budgetary resources from funding the maintenance of existing activities to providing the counterpart funds necessary to attract the additional aid.

Aid has been allocated not only to fund infrastructure and social services. It has also been provided to agriculture and industry—in the form of credit, equipment, advice, and training. Projects in agriculture in Africa have had a particularly poor record of success and sustainability. For example, efforts to improve the productivity of the livestock sector have failed in the past due to a lack of understanding of the culture and practices of livestock owners, particularly nomads. "Integrated rural development" projects, popular in the late 1970s and early 1980s, which sought to reduce poverty and boost the incomes of the rural poor in Africa through multiple aid-funded activities (e.g., in health, education, sanitation, transport, and agricultural production) proved particularly ineffective. Aid agencies were little informed about the preferences, constraints, and techniques of Africa's small farmers. Moreover, the projects were usually far too complicated for African bureaucracies to manage. And where aid donors established separate, expatriate organizations of their own to manage these projects, those organizations often collapsed for want of a bureaucratic home within African governments once the aid was terminated and the expatriates gone.

Aid has also been provided in support of industrial development in Africa, though in smaller amounts than aid to agriculture. Aid for industry has included the construction of turnkey factories, turned over to governments to manage, as well as loans and grants to governments to establish or expand industrial enterprises. Aid in this area has been among the least effective, with state-owned enterprises (whether aid-funded or not) tending to suffer from the same problems of capacity as other government agencies.

Technology Development and Dissemination

The aid-funded development and dissemination of new technologies that lead to a more productive use of resources have not played the role in economic progress in Africa that they have in other parts of the world. This is most evident in the area of agriculture. For example, improved crops and agricultural techniques that brought dramatic increases in agricultural production in much of Asia and Latin America have not for the most part benefited sub-Saharan Africa. Some of the improved crops (for instance, wheat) are little grown in the region. Other advances in agricultural technologies do have potential benefits for African farmers but have yet to be adapted and disseminated.[21] The principal reason relates to the familiar problem of organizational capacity. It is frequently the case that, to be productive, technological advances must be adapted to local conditions. That adaptation requires local organizations capable of research over a sustained period of time. In most developing countries, these are universities or specialized research institutes. While there are now numerous universities in Africa and not a few research institutes of all kinds, few have proven capable of undertaking the long-term research and producing the results needed to develop or adapt locally usable, productivity-enhancing technologies. As with other organizations, they have often suffered from limited resources, poor leadership, and weak management. A similar set of problems has limited the effectiveness of agricultural extension services.

Further limiting the ability of agricultural research to benefit African farmers was the adverse policy environment, described in chapter 2, that prevailed for so long, in which governments often imposed high taxes on agricultural production (especially commodities for export) and permitted exchange rates to become overvalued, thus discouraging expanded production and encouraging the importation of foodstuffs. Reforms in agricultural pricing and exchange rates have reduced these disincentives to agricultural investment and growth, and there is some evidence farmers have begun to respond with expanded production.[22]

Economic-Policy Reform

Aid agencies have been significantly involved in nearly all of the economic-reform programs in sub-Saharan Africa over the past fifteen years. We saw in the previous chapter that the era of aid for economic-policy reform began in the early 1980s. Since that time, most African countries have agreed to one or more stabilization or structural-adjustment programs supported by the IMF and World Bank,[23] encompassing exchange rate devaluations; trade liberalization; reductions in budgetary deficits; reductions or removal of price controls, and regulations on trade, investment and labor practices; privatization of state-owned enterprises; educational, health, and financial-sector reforms; and reforms of the civil service.

While most countries have agreed to wide-ranging reforms, they have often failed fully to implement and maintain many of those reforms. A

1994 study by the World Bank, assessing adjustment programs in twenty-nine African countries during the 1980s, found that most countries had implemented some reforms, that a handful of countries had implemented a significant number of reforms, and that overall performance in implementing reforms remained disappointing—more so than in other parts of the developing world. The most frequently implemented types of reforms include currency adjustments, elimination of controls on prices and interest rates, and the reduction of tariffs on imports (though not of nontariff barriers to trade). A number of countries have made efforts to simplify investment regulations. But certain types of reforms have lagged: in the civil service, in privatization of state-owned enterprises, and in the financial sector.

What explains the pattern of aid-financed economic reform in Africa? And why have reforms not been more extensive and more fully implemented? Three factors help answer these questions. One is African governments' ability to manage complicated reforms. It is relatively easy to design and implement a currency realignment. It is far more complicated to privatize public enterprises or to reform financial institutions. The assets, liabilities, and market value of public enterprises must be evaluated, potential buyers must be informed and bids sought, a decision to sell must be made and ownership transferred. Obtaining accurate information, evaluating alternatives to privatization, and fairly and effectively implementing the sale of state-owned enterprises are all challenging for governments with weak institutions. Reform of banking systems also presents complex problems of assessing and recovering nonperforming assets, of recapitalizing, of changing or retraining staff (or of selling off the bank to private investors), and of establishing regulations and effective regulatory bodies that can monitor bank performance.

A second factor is politics. The impact of a currency devaluation is diffuse, affecting many people but few so much that their livelihoods are threatened. However, privatization and civil-service reforms eliminate jobs; government employees, understandably, usually resist. Government employees are among the best organized and most influential economic interest groups in African countries, and their opposition has played a key role in the reluctance of governments to implement reforms. Resistance to financial-sector reforms is also political: banks in many countries have provided political elites access to loans that were often poorly secured and never expected to be repaid. Effective reforms of banks would cut off that access and could result in demands for the repayment of loans. The opposition of political elites to bank reforms has been a key factor in the slowness with which they have been implemented.

A final explanation for the pattern of reforms involves the aid donors themselves. The World Bank, the IMF, and bilateral aid agencies signaled that they would reward governments adopting reforms and penalize governments refusing to adopt reforms. It is hardly surprising that African governments, desperate for aid and the access to debt rescheduling that came with a World Bank– or IMF-supported reform program, agreed to adopt economic reforms even if support for them inside and outside government was weak. But it soon became clear that donors were reluctant to terminate their aid when reforms were not fully implemented. (We shall explore the reasons for this reluctance in the section on World Bank aid to Africa.) Thus, donors themselves created incentives for Africans to agree to, but not fully implement, reforms.[24] Not surprisingly, Africans chose to avoid the administratively and politically more difficult reforms, described above.

Governmental Capacity

Foreign aid seeks to strengthen organizations in developing countries by providing for the education and training of local individuals and by advising government agencies on policies, programs, organization, and management. Efforts to strengthen African institutions may be divided into two periods: the period shortly after independence (roughly 1960 to the mid-1970s) and the period after 1975. In the earlier period, aid was used in a number of the poorest countries—for example, Botswana, Lesotho, and Swaziland—to ensure the continued functioning of government agencies after independence. It financed regular budgetary expenditures until governments could expand their revenues and provided teachers for schools and universities and expatriate experts to help manage government agencies and advise African officials until Africans were ready to take over those responsibilities. And it financed higher education abroad for large numbers of Africans who were to return home to take up positions of responsibility in their countries. In short, technical assistance in the early years of independence was focused on creating and strengthening the institutions of governance in Africa.

However, evidence suggests that many African government agencies are weaker today than in the past. An assessment of national capacities by experts on behalf of the African governors of the World Bank in 1996 came to a striking conclusion: "Almost every African country has witnessed a systematic regression of capacity in the last thirty years; the majority had better capacity at independence than they now possess."[25] Yet there were more aid-funded technical assistants in Africa than ever before, as many as eighty thousand by the year 1987.[26] During the 1980s alone, between $40 billion and $50 billion in aid was spent on technical assistance in Africa, a quarter of total aid to the region.[27]

Aid donors have found efforts to strengthen African institutions among the least effective of their activities. Indeed, evidence suggests that technical assistance has become part of the problem of institutional weaknesses, not the solution. For example, a study of technical assistance by Elliot Berg concluded, "Almost everybody acknowledges the ineffectiveness of technical cooperation in what is or should be its major objective: achievement of greater self-reliance in the recipient countries by building institutions and strengthening local capacities in national economic management. Despite 30 years of a heavy technical assistance presence and much training, local institutions remain weak and this type of assistance persists. Deficiencies in technical cooperation are not the sole or even the main explanation for this situation, but they contributed significantly to it."[28]

Problems with technical assistance in Africa have been several—some having to do with the nature of the organizations the assistance was supposed to help, others with the nature of the assistance itself. First, of all the problems of African development, the extent and causes of organizational weaknesses are the least understood and the means of addressing them effectively the least developed. It is clear that these weaknesses extend beyond the need for training or expertise on the part of staff. They are, generally speaking, part of an entrenched system of behavioral incentives created by the use of government agencies for the political and personal goals of political elites and government officials. However, the specific causes of organizational weaknesses vary from country to country and by agency and are often difficult for outsiders to perceive or influence. In fact, relatively little is known about the functioning of particular African public agencies—how decisions are made and by whom. For example, it is widely recognized that African political leaders, in their efforts to achieve ethnic balance in government, assign representatives of certain groups to particular ministries and that those ministries often draw a large percentage of their staffs from that particular ethnicity. Those ministries often come to be seen as representing the interests of that ethnic group as well as fulfilling the responsibilities assigned to the ministry itself. Other African leaders have followed a policy of frequently shifting cabinet ministers so that no one would gain enough power or enough of a political base in a particular ministry to act independently of the president. In these cases, if decisions are made at all, they are made by the career staff of ministries. Professor Claude Ake lifted a veil on the functioning of government agencies while reminding us of how little we know about it: "The state in Africa has been a maze of antinomies of form and content: the person who holds office may not exercise its powers, the person who exercises the powers of a given office may not be its holder, informal relations often override formal relations, the formal hierarchies of bureaucratic structure and political power are not always the clue to decision making power. Positions that seem to be held by persons are in fact held by kinship groups."[29]

Technical assistance has been managed by aid donors in a way that has not only lessened its effectiveness but also, in some cases, weakened African institutions. Donors offer (or frequently, require) technical assistance as part of their projects whether or not African officials need or want it. Project designs are often highly complex and technically beyond what African governments can manage on their own, requiring foreign technical assistance. African officials accept the complex designs and the accompanying technical assistance as the price of aid. In other cases, donors in a hurry to spend their monies have preferred not to rely on the performance of African officials; rather than cutting back on aid, they place their own nationals in government, in effect, to oversee its expenditure. This practice undercuts African officials and often leads to a collapse of the aid-financed activity after expatriate officials depart.

Another problem involves the equipment and training that comes with technical assistance. Sometimes African officials seek technical assistance—not because they want it but because they want the opportunities for patronage that it brings. Expatriate experts often come with funding to hire local staff. Training often means travel abroad for Africans on attractive per diems. These resources can be used to reward clients by African officials supervising the technical experts, creating perverse incentives for Africans to seek to expand rather than to reduce technical assistance.

Third, donors (unintentionally) encourage the use of technical assistance as a result of adjustment programs that restrict expenditures on important services, forcing governments to seek foreign-funded experts to do jobs that their own citizens could handle but the governments can no longer pay for. Many of the teachers in Mozambique, for example, are expatriates—not because Mozambicans could not teach but because the government cannot afford to pay them.[30]

To sum up, technical assistance aimed at strengthening African institutions has over the past several decades been among the least effective of aid-funded interventions. But more troubling, it appears in some cases to have become counterproductive—too much aid has been combined with too little understanding of the institutional problems it was intended to address.

Aid and Overall Economic Growth in Africa

Despite the relatively large flows of foreign aid to African countries since independence, econometric studies correlating aid with growth have found no significant relationship (either positive or negative) between the two.[31] Findings are similar in studies examining aid and growth worldwide. But given the relatively large amounts of aid provided to African countries over an extended period, these results are, at first glance, surprising.

However, taking into account the unsustainable development "model" pursued by Africans, described in the previous chapter, these results are less astonishing. The policy and institutional weaknesses that prevented growth in African countries also limited the effectiveness of aid in promoting that growth. This conclusion is partially borne out by one of the econometric studies referred to above. This study, undertaken by World Bank staff and covering fifty-six countries worldwide (twenty-one of which were in Africa), found that aid had a positive impact on growth in countries with good fiscal, trade, and monetary policies. There was no such effect in countries with poor policies.[32] Most of Africa falls into this latter category. The ineffectiveness and unsustainability of aid projects and programs discussed above provide an additional explanation.

Foreign Aid in Africa: Side Effects

Development advocates tend to assume that if a little foreign aid is good for development, more is better. Implicit in this notion is a view of foreign aid as primarily a means of easing the resource constraints on development. But the experience of aid and development in Africa suggests that in certain circumstances, more aid is not necessarily better, especially in countries where politics and policies inhibit growth, where government institutions lack the capacity to manage it well, and where the aid itself is poorly designed and implemented. And relatively large flows of aid over an extended period may have negative effects even in the best-managed of countries. In this section, we assess situations in which more aid may actually have inhibited development, including the provision of large amounts of aid by multiple poorly coordinated donors, negative economic and political side effects, and the problem of aid dependence.

The Sum of the Parts

We have already referred to the large number of aid donors operating in most African countries, each with its own goals, administrative requirements, and high-level visitors who want to see as many senior officials as possible. The multiple demands of donors place a considerable administrative burden on government agencies. But this is not the only problem arising from the multiplicity of donors. The main problem is the lack of adequate coordination of their aid interventions by donors.

In fact, donors have managed to coordinate themselves reasonably well in one area of activity—policy reforms. Led by the World Bank, aid donors have recognized that coordination is crucial if they are to avoid being played off against one another and to persuade reluctant African governments to accept painful reforms. Donor representatives within African countries have also made ad hoc efforts to coordinate (or at least exchange information on) their projects. Such efforts have not prevented the occasional disaster, such as the eighteen separate aid-financed water systems in Kenya (without interchangeable parts), each provided by a different donor.[33] The most serious weakness in coordination appears at the level of the overall development program of a country. Donors typically finance projects and programs they identify as consistent with their own goals and expertise and provide levels of aid consistent with their own capacity and priorities. The negative impacts of the current system are three: one donor's interventions can undercut another's; uncoordinated projects can distort investments and government development priorities (as with the water projects in Kenya); and large, uncoordinated inflows of aid can place demands on government budgets for counterpart funds, limiting funding available for other uses, often far into the future. The problems, identified above, of too much technical assistance in Africa are a direct result of too many donors funding that assistance with too much money in an uncoordinated fashion.

The problem of too little aid coordination derives as much from the reluctance of African governments to take the initiative in coordinating the donors as from the difficulties of donors acting in a coordinated manner themselves. The reluctance on the part of the Africans arises from the weakness of bureaucracies, from fears of being "ganged up on" by donors working together, and from the incentives for individual ministries to resist central coordination (which might result in less aid than they would receive by dealing directly with aid agencies). Another factor is the eagerness of governments for the aid, making it difficult to reject particular offers (which is often part of coordinating those providing the aid).

Both donors and African officials are concerned about problems of coordination in Africa. And the World Bank has begun to try to coordinate other donors in "sectoral assistance" programs. It is too soon to assess this effort. One question is whether other donors will agree to a World Bank–led coordination effort at the sectoral level.

Economic Side Effects of Aid

There are two principal economic side effects of large flows of foreign aid. One involves a "soft budget constraint"; the other is the "Dutch disease."

A number of analysts have suggested that the large quantity of aid has provided many governments with a soft budget constraint—in effect, permitting them to continue with fiscal and other policies inimical to development because foreign aid has eased the financial pressures on them to reform. There is some direct evidence of this effect in Tanzania, where one study found that aid eased financial pressures on that government at a time when such pressures might have led it to discontinue unwise policies.[34]

The major instance of a soft budget constraint facilitating such a delay was the effort on the part of the fourteen Francophone countries of the franc zone (sharing a common currency tied to the French franc at a fixed rate and backed by the French treasury), whose currency was clearly overvalued during the 1980s, to avoid devaluing the CFA franc. Continued balance-of-payments support from the French government and the World Bank delayed the necessary adjustment by easing an otherwise unmanageable gap in the balance of payments. The Bank recognized this problem but, under pressure from the Africans and the French government, continued to provide assistance while an effort was made (primarily by the Ivory Coast) to reduce the gap in the balance of payments by depressing domestic prices. For predictable political reasons (specifically, civil servants resisted large decreases in their real wages or elimination of their jobs), this effort failed. The Bank finally ceased program lending to CFA countries, and eventually the economic costs of maintaining the overvalued CFA franc forced a devaluation. (See chapter 6 for more details.)

More broadly, it seems likely that the surge in foreign aid to African countries during the late 1970s did enable them to put off the painful reforms necessary to improve trade balances and to spur their economies. The continuation of large aid programs in support of economic reforms that were only partially implemented during the 1980s may have had the same impact—of dampening the financial pressures for reform. However, there is relatively little empirical research on this issue, and it is difficult to do more than recognize it as a potential problem.

The Dutch Disease

"Dutch disease" is the inflation and real appreciation in exchange rates that can arise from large increases in foreign exchange, whether from sudden increases in export prices and earnings, from sizable inflows of commercial capital or foreign direct investment, or from surges in foreign aid.[35] Such windfalls in foreign exchange, if they are spent on domestically produced goods in sectors where employment and capacity utilization is high, can increase the price of those goods and contribute to general inflation. Inflation, in turn, leads to a real appreciation in the exchange rate, discouraging exports and encouraging imports. A major case of the Dutch disease can undercut a country's development. This is a widely observed effect of windfall foreign-exchange earnings in oil-producing countries.

Some economists and government officials in donor countries as well as in Africa have speculated that large flows of foreign aid may be causing a real appreciation of exchange rates, when what is required are real depreciations in exchange rates to restrict imports and stimulate exports.[36] In theory, most aid has been provided to finance imports rather than to purchase domestically produced goods, lessening its impact on domestic price levels and the exchange rate. However, some expenditures on local goods (including services and accommodation for field representatives) have been unavoidable, with the consequent multiplier effects of those expenditures domestically.

Relatively little empirical work has been done to ascertain the extent of the Dutch disease in the region, perhaps because of its methodological challenges. One assessment of aid in Ghana—one of the more likely candidates, with the surge in foreign aid during the first half of the 1980s accompanying its stabilization and structural-adjustment programs—did find evidence of the Dutch disease.[37] The lack of research prevents us from generalizing on the incidence of the problem. However, there is some reason to believe that the Dutch disease may not be so serious in Africa as the amount of aid might suggest. The flows are large but in most countries have reached their current levels over an extended period. This suggests that economies have had time to adjust to the impact of aid on domestic demand (while creating a dependence on that aid). Moreover, during much of the 1980s, there was considerable underutilized capacity in African economies that would help dampen the impact of aid-financed local expenditures. Here again, there is a need for more empirical work.

Political Effects of Aid

As a transfer of resources from a government or international institution to another government, foreign aid is unavoidably a tool of statecraft. It is at a minimum a symbol of a relationship between two political entities. As such, it can have a political impact on the government receiving it independent of the purposes for which it has been provided. The focus of this section is not the diplomatic or political objectives of the governments or international organizations providing the aid (which are discussed in chapter 4) but the potential impact of aid on the domestic politics and diplomatic relations of recipient countries—a topic that has received almost no attention in the literature on foreign aid.

Foreign aid is not an automatic element in the relationship between governments that are better off and those that are less well off. Rather, it is provided voluntarily by governments or international institutions to other governments.[38] It thus goes beyond diplomatic recognition (in which one government acknowledges another as a legitimate member of the international community of states) and typically signals that an aid-giving government places a special value on its relationship with the government receiving its aid. Much like a state visit, foreign aid symbolizes a measure of approbation by the donor of the recipient and vice versa. Furthermore, rising aid levels are often interpreted (and intended) to symbolize warming relations (that is, increased approbation), while falling aid levels are often seen as a sign of cooling relations or displeasure by donor or recipient with the other. Most diplomats and persons in the aid business in donor and recipient countries have observed or experienced this aspect of aid.[39]

What is the political impact of the foreign approbation associated with aid on the governments receiving the aid? On the one hand, it can undercut the legitimacy of that government at home and abroad if the aid is interpreted as a symbol of control by the donor. The recipient government may be viewed by its own people as a puppet of the donor. African governments have been well aware of this problem and have often sought to deal with it in ways described in the previous chapter. On the other hand, foreign aid can also bolster the legitimacy of those governments receiving it. In the years immediately after independence, African governments were eager to strengthen their legitimacy by emphasizing the symbols of statehood and their rule. They sought diplomatic relations with as large a group of countries (particularly the more powerful countries) as they could. The government of Ghana, for example, set up fifty embassies abroad, far more than could be justified on the basis of traditional economic and political links (and far more than could be afforded). Great powers were often urged to set up embassies in African capitals. African governments joined regional and international organizations, and their leaders' participation in those organizations—for example, speeches at the UN General Assembly—were widely publicized within their countries to symbolize their international acceptance and importance. They sought state visits to major world leaders. These activities affirmed the "juridical statehood" of African governments to their own people and to other governments and peoples—as well as the importance and international acceptability of their leaders.[40] Foreign aid, especially from prominent or powerful foreign governments or international organizations, served these same purposes.

Foreign aid has helped bolster the legitimacy of African governments in several other important ways. Africans gaining power at independence promised their peoples a rapid improvement in their standards of living. Often, African leaders justified restrictions on political and civil rights on the grounds that they were necessary to ensure rapid development. They thus set for themselves a test of their legitimacy—economic performance. Foreign aid was supposed to finance development. But more than that, it became a symbol of development—or at least, of development to come—indirectly supporting governments' promises to deliver a better standard of living for its people. No one has captured this dimension of foreign aid better than Julius Nyerere, former president of Tanzania.

Our Government and different groups of our leaders never stop thinking about methods of getting finance from abroad. And if we get some money, or even if we just get a promise of it, our newspapers, our radio, and our leaders, all advertise the fact in order that every person shall know that salvation is coming, or is on the way. If we receive a gift we announce it, if we receive a loan we announce it, if we get a new factory we announce it— and always loudly. In the same way, when we get a promise of a gift, a loan, or a new industry, we make an announcement of the promise. Even when we have merely started discussions with a foreign government or institution for a gift, a loan or a new industry, we make an announcement—even though we do not know the outcome of the discussions. Why do we do all this? Because we want people to know that we have started discussions which will bring prosperity.[41]

What, then, can we say about the past impact of foreign aid on the legitimacy of African governments? It likely contributed to the legitimacy of a government by symbolizing the approbation and often active support of that government by a foreign power. And the more powerful the donor, the greater the potential impact of its approbation. For regimes whose legitimacy was relatively strong, this symbolic function of foreign aid was not terribly important. But it is likely to have been quite important to regimes whose domestic and international legitimacy was weak— typically the more inept, corrupt, or repressive regimes.

Former president Mobutu of Zaire, for example, led one of the world's most corrupt and incompetent regimes. He had little legitimacy at home except with the political elite who circulated in and out of his government. However, he was clearly eager to be seen with the leaders of important countries and to receive aid from their governments. That aid helped for a time to confirm his international acceptability and friendships with powerful countries in the eyes of other governments that might have been tempted to distance themselves from him, isolate him diplomatically, or support efforts to overthrow his regime. And more than once, Mobutu was able to parlay support from the United States into keeping the French or Belgians from cutting him off or even acting to remove him. He used support from the French and Belgians for the same purposes vis-à-vis the United States. And the support from these governments helped him maintain a modicum of relations with African governments (whose leaders were reluctant to criticize him in public but were not hesitant to do so in private). It was no accident that after the United States and Belgium ceased their support (leaving only the French behind him), Mobutu was forced out of power by Laurent Kabila in 1997 with substantial military aid from the neighboring governments of Rwanda, Uganda, and Angola.

The implication of this analysis is that foreign aid, when provided to a regime whose legitimacy is weak, can prolong the life of that regime. Where that weak legitimacy derives from faulty governance or poor economic performance (as it often does), those problems can continue and worsen as an indirect effect of aid, especially where it is large and comes from major powers (or important international organizations). It is possible though difficult to prove that foreign aid, provided by a major power to a corrupt or incompetent regime, encourages poor governance, by giving the regime a sense of security based on its relationship with the major power. It is hard to view as entirely coincidental that several of Africa's collapsed states—Liberia and Somalia—and several of the worst-governed states (the former Zaire and Sudan under President Numeiri) were also among the largest recipients of U.S. aid over an extended period.

Aid Dependence

The relatively high levels of foreign aid over a prolonged period in much of Africa have provoked statements of concern on the part of donors and unease on the part of recipients about their dependence on the aid. There is, however, little rigorous work on the nature and impact of that dependence.[42] A first question is what *dependence* on foreign aid really means. Do relatively large inflows of aid always create dependence? A common-sense answer is that high levels of aid over a short time—for example, in response to food shortages caused by a drought—do not normally create dependence. But high aid levels over an extended period—let us say, five years—can influence national expenditure and investment patterns. Indeed, they can become an essential part of those patterns (i.e., not easily replaceable), making a decrease or termination in that aid potentially politically or economically disruptive. It is at this point that a country could be said to be dependent on foreign aid.

Such dependence need not be a bad thing. If the aid is used to generate development and so, reduce the need for it (as it was in Botswana), then dependence on aid for a period can be highly beneficial. What must be of concern to donors and recipients alike, however, is the extended period during which many African governments have already become reliant on aid, with little growth and little prospect of that reliance diminishing significantly. Indeed, African governments continue to plead for increased aid, by implication further extending their dependence.

There are two major problems with dependence, one potential and one real. The potential problem arises from the inevitable uncertainties associated with state-to-state transfers of resources. These are voluntary, and there is no guarantee that they will continue indefinitely. Indeed, there are signs that such transfers are beginning to decline. The greater a government's and country's reliance on such transfers, the greater the potential disruption should that aid decline rapidly or disappear entirely. It could be argued, for example, that foreign aid (especially balance-of-payments and budget support) has financed many of the activities of African governments and, through a multiplier effect, the incomes and consumption of a significant proportion of those employed not just in the modern, formal sector but in the informal, urban sector that often relies on the formal sector. The disappearance of that aid could leave government services unfunded and significant numbers of public employees without incomes, bring about a serious recession in highly aid-dependent countries, and possibly lead to hardship and even political turmoil. Table 3 gives an indication of the dependence of African governments on foreign aid. Unfortunately this data is only available on a limited number of countries, but clearly, on the basis of these figures, the potential disruption for many countries in Africa could be significant if aid were eliminated or substantially reduced.

Another aspect of aid dependence that must be of greater concern is its impact on the initiative and accountability of recipient government officials—the creation of an "entitlement mentality." Where foreign governments and international institutions finance a significant proportion of government expenditures, particularly investment expenditures, and where many of the decisions on investments are left to those foreign governments and institutions, a diminution of the sense of initiative, respon-

Table 3. Aid as a Percentage of Government Expenditures

Country	Percentage	Country	Percentage
Gabon	7.5	Lesotho	46.5
Zimbabwe	11.9	Zambia	54.5
Seychelles	13.3	Sierra Leone	56.3
Mauritius	14.1	Guinea	71.5
Botswana	18.3	Chad	75.6
Cameroon	22.7	Ghana	77.4
Kenya	33.9	Malawi	96.9
Ethiopia	40.1	Madagascar	101.4

Sources: World Bank, *World Tables* (Washington, D.C.: World Bank, 1995); World Bank, *World Debt Tables* (Washington, D.C.: World Bank, 1995).

Note: These figures cover various years in the 1990s depending on the availability of data.

sibility, and accountability on the part of recipient government officials to their own populations is almost inevitable. We cannot measure this essentially psychological consequence of aid dependence in Africa. But it is easy to observe. Several examples from my own experience illustrate it. In December 1994, I traveled with the U.S. national security advisor to several African countries. In most countries, there were meetings with cabinet ministers. In one country, a set of meetings took place one morning on the veranda of the U.S. ambassador's residence. A series of ministers appeared one after another, each with a list of projects he wanted the United States to finance. One wanted a road. Another wanted something else. There was little talk of the broad development strategies of the government, its accomplishments, or any issues that did not involve foreign aid. It was not, "Here is how we are addressing our development challenges and how you might help." It was just a set of pleas for money.

A year later, I was visiting another African country and had occasion to sit in on a meeting of ten or so of the country's main aid donors. They were exchanging their views and trying to create a common position on relatively minor issues involving the government's policy toward the media. It was clear from the meeting not only that the donors (one of whose members had dubbed them the "board of directors," presumably of the country itself) were deeply engaged in influencing the political as well as the economic policies of the government, but that both public officials and private individuals and groups had begun to appeal to this grouping for support on their issues. It seemed evident that the accountability of the government to its people was gradually being replaced by accountability to its major aid donors.

A final anecdote involves a seminar in Washington in 1996 in which two of the African participants, in a discussion of foreign aid, made strikingly different statements. One, an ambassador from an East African country, upon hearing that U.S. aid to Africa was likely to fall, complained that it was unfair, Africa needed more aid, how could the United States abandon the region. The other individual—a government official from South Africa—argued that his government did not need to be told how to spend its money from foreign aid donors; and if the latter's preferences did not coincide with his government's, it was better not to have the aid. The differences in the two attitudes was striking: one was the attitude of a government used to seeking and receiving significant amounts of aid, almost regardless of its use; the other—much more rare—was of an African government unaccustomed to aid and willing to reject it where it was deemed inappropriate.

These stories and many others like them suggest that aid dependence has had an impact on the attitudes of many African elites, diminishing their sense of responsibility for their own future, their initiative in gaining that future, and their accountability to their populations for shaping the policies leading toward it. Much more research is needed on this aspect of aid dependence, if only because it may be among the most negative but important side effects of large flows of aid over an extended period of time.

Summing Up

This chapter has provided a general overview of the problems of the developmental effectiveness of aid in Africa—which are substantial. We already know that aid donors had the major say over which countries they aided and how the aid was used. We must now ask, why, if aid donors have had so much influence over whom they have aided and how their aid has been used in Africa, has their aid not been more effective? It is to this question that the remainder of this book is addressed.

Appendix A

Table 4. Net Aid Flows to Sub-Saharan Africa (Annual Averages, Millions of Current Dollars)

Donor	1970–74	1975–79	1980–84	1985–89	1990–94	1995–96
France	363	571	1,032	1,798	3,073	2,565
Italy	19	16	178	987	674	341
Japan	16	100	251	669	964	1,218
Sweden	46	185	251	400	572	427
United Kingdom	118	202	343	450	621	615
United States	158	261	703	897	1,204	842
EDF[a]	188	419	628	1,060	2,036	1,872
World Bank	89	311	612	1,365	2,158	2,360
Other	626	2,354	3,784	5,180	7,192	7,365
Total	1,622	4,419	7,782	12,807	18,295	17,603

Source: Development Assistance Committee data (provided by DAC staff).
[a]European Development Fund.

Table 5. Net Aid Flows to Sub-Saharan Africa (Billions of Dollars)

Year	Current $	Constant 1995 $
1970	1.2	6.3
1971	1.3	6.7
1972	1.4	6.3
1973	1.8	6.7
1974	2.5	8.5
1975	3.3	10.0
1976	3.2	9.3
1977	3.9	10.4
1978	5.2	11.8
1979	6.5	13.2
1980	7.5	14.0
1981	7.6	14.9
1982	8.0	16.5
1983	7.7	16.3
1984	8.1	17.5
1985	9.4	19.7
1986	11.4	19.2
1987	13.0	18.8
1988	14.8	19.9
1989	15.5	21.4
1990	16.2	21.9
1991	17.9	21.1
1992	19.2	21.3
1993	17.3	19.9
1994	18.9	20.9
1995	18.5	18.5
1996	16.7	17.2

Source: Development Assistance Committee data.

Appendix B

The Challenge of Evaluating Aid

There are several significant problems of methodology and data in assessing the developmental effectiveness of aid. The methodological problems apply to efforts to evaluate the impact of aid generally. The data problems are especially severe in Africa. The methodological problems include defining "effectiveness" of aid; isolating the impact of an aid intervention; determining the counterfactual (that is, what would have happened in the absence of the aid); and estimating the fungibility of aid—the substitutability of aid resources for other resources available to recipients, making the identification and evaluation of what the aid actually finances problematic. Finally, as with almost any study in Africa, there are problems with the extent and reliability of data. Let us examine each of these challenges briefly.

There is no generally accepted definition of what constitutes aid "effectiveness" in promoting development. Many studies of effectiveness focus on the impact of aid on overall growth. But it is difficult to establish this relationship (for reasons elaborated below), and in the many cases where aid is but a small portion of total available resources, the effort may not be justified. Other approaches—implicit in many of the implementation reports and impact studies of aid donors—focus more narrowly on whether aid projects and programs have achieved their stated objectives and sustained those achievements. These are the easiest assessments to make. Some approaches also assess the appropriateness of the particular objectives or broader aid policies in which they fall. A few impact studies examine any negative impacts of the aid project or program. These are among the most challenging and costly assessments to make, given the complexity of assessing indirect impacts and the length of time often needed before a fair judgment can be made.

Aid-financed projects and programs typically have immediate goals (i.e., the output of a particular project or program, for example the construction of a rural road), intermediate goals (strengthening the marketing of agricultural products), and ultimate goals—promoting agricultural development or alleviating rural poverty. It is not difficult to determine whether the immediate goals of a particular project have been achieved, for example, whether a road has been constructed or not. Beyond these goals, however, it becomes increasingly difficult to determine the impact of aid among the numerous other factors affecting economic, social, or political conditions. Thus, claims of success or failure must often be qualified, the more so as the number and complexity of the goals increase and the time between the aid-financed activity and the desired outcome grows. And yet it is the broader, longer-term goals that are the most important and most require evaluation.

A related problem is the counterfactual. Attributing particular changes to foreign aid assumes that an aid intervention was the cause of those changes. In the absence of controlled experiments (usually absent in aid programs), it is difficult to prove that events would have been different if aid had not been provided. Evaluators attempt to deal with this problem through collecting good baseline data before an aid-financed activity is undertaken and then, based on assumed trends absent aid, compare data gathered at the completion of a project. But good baseline data is not always available or easily measurable and can be expensive and time consuming to generate. The theory that would permit accurate projection of trends in the absence of aid is also frequently lacking. These methodological problems do not prevent us from assessing the impact of aid on the various levels of goals, but they do remind us that many assessments are suggestive rather than definitive.

The third methodological problem, related to the problem of the counterfactual, is the potential "fungibility" of aid. Aid resources intended to finance a particular project—let us say again, the construction of a rural road—may actually end up financing indirectly other activities if the recipient had intended to finance the road even without the aid. Thus the additional expenditures permitted by the aid resources may in reality fund the building of a bridge, the importation of new Mercedes limousines, a buildup of foreign-exchange reserves, or any of a host of other activities. Fungibility is always a potential problem, and studies of it provide mixed results. There is evidence that much of foreign aid does, in fact, finance what it is intended to, particularly where the quantity of aid is large relative to the economy of the recipient country.[43] In any case, evaluators tend to ignore the issue of fungibility, assuming that what the aid is intended to finance is, in fact, what it is financing. There is usually no other practical way of dealing with this problem when undertaking evaluations.

Finally, we face a problem of data in assessing the effectiveness of aid. This problem takes two forms. First is the availability and reliability of statistics on economic, social, and political conditions in aid-receiving countries. This is a severe problem in sub-Saharan Africa and one that has worsened with the deterioration in government statistical services. There are considerable uncertainties about such basic information as population size and growth, the distribution of income, incidence of disease, agricultural production, and so on. Data on income distribution and household expenditures over time is so limited that it does not permit us to draw any significant conclusions on the impact of aid on income distribution.

A second problem of data is somewhat different. It involves the quality of evaluative materials available for assessing the effectiveness of aid. Literally thousands of aid projects and programs may be under way at any one time in Africa. Only a small percentage of them—probably not more than 15 or 20 percent—are ever evaluated for impact.[44] Most aid agencies do audits of projects to ensure that funds have been spent as intended. Many do completion reports to ascertain if the immediate goals of the project have been attained or to analyze the final rate of return of the

project. "Impact evaluations," involving a broader look at the consequences of the project (often including side effects), undertaken some
time after the project is completed, are far less numerous but are potentially the most useful. They are also often the most expensive and usually
involve the greatest degree of subjectivity. Evaluations of all kinds of projects and programs undertaken by different donor agencies usually em-
ploy distinct approaches, vary enormously in quality and, so, rarely prove
comparable, except at a broad level of generalization. But even given
these caveats, there is enough data—statistical and evaluative—for us to
draw some important conclusions about aid's impact in Africa.

Chapter Four

Foreign Aid: The Donors

Each government with a foreign-aid program must make three key decisions: which countries to aid, how much aid to provide, and what the aid finances. These decisions are made primarily within annual budget and programming processes (though unanticipated needs and opportunities may also trigger decisions) and are informed by the objectives that the aid program is intended to serve. Promoting economic development in recipient countries is typically only one of the objectives for which aid is given and not always the predominant one. Others include advancing political and security concerns, gaining commercial advantages, and achieving cultural goals. Domestic and bureaucratic politics also frequently play a role in aid decisions.

Different agencies within the donor government typically represent these various interests, including ministries of foreign affairs for political and security objectives, ministries of trade for commercial objectives, and, at times, the offices of prime ministers and presidents—usually for security or political purposes. Aid agencies, established by most aid-giving governments with the mission of promoting development abroad, are the principal proponents of developmental concerns. Aid agencies behave in goal-oriented ways to further development as a result of the socialization of staff and leadership of the agency, and the personal and professional incentives to which the staff and leadership respond.[1] These agencies are independent organizational entities or are located within foreign-affairs ministries, usually as a discrete bureau or department. (In most countries with independent aid agencies, those agencies have some association—formal or informal—with their ministries of foreign affairs.)

Because the overall goals of aid programs are broad and typically involve multiple objectives, both the policies and key decisions on the allocation and use of aid are frequently the result of negotiations involving aid agencies and other government agencies. The greater the autonomy of aid agencies in making these decisions, the more likely the aid will be allocated on developmental criteria. And the more developmental criteria are used to determine which countries receive the aid, how much they receive, and how they use it, the greater the probability that the aid will be effective in promoting development in those countries.

But allocative choices are only one aspect of what influences the developmental effectiveness of aid. Being able to identify appropriate development policies, projects, and programs; to design and implement projects and programs that achieve their goals; to learn from experience; and to influence constructively the thinking of other aid agencies and recipient government officials on development issues are other elements affecting the effectiveness of foreign aid. The greater the capacity of aid agencies to accomplish these tasks, the more likely the aid is to be effective developmentally. The autonomy and capacity of aid agencies are thus key factors in determining the developmental effectiveness of foreign aid.

The remainder of this chapter elaborates these concepts. We first examine in detail the various goals for which foreign aid is deployed by donor governments. We then develop the concepts of autonomy and capacity and describe their components and the factors that affect them. We next present several hypotheses involving the effectiveness of aid that this book will test. The chapter concludes by describing the framework to be applied to each of the eight case studies that follow.

The Goals of Foreign Aid

Nearly all aid-giving governments have as one of the stated goals of their aid programs promoting development abroad, reflecting the humanitarian values and economic interests of their publics. However, most governments also pursue other goals with their aid, including diplomatic, commercial, and national cultural goals. Let us examine these other motives in more detail.[2]

Diplomatic Objectives

Governments frequently wish to pursue "high diplomatic politics" with foreign aid by providing it in exchange for important foreign-policy objectives, such as gaining diplomatic recognition, establishing military bases, obtaining a supportive vote in the United Nations, or bolstering a preferred regime through the economic and political support that aid brings.

Foreign aid can be used for "low diplomatic politics," in pursuit of less pressing but useful goals. For example, aid may be the entry price for maintaining a cordial relationship with a recipient government, particularly when other foreign governments are also providing aid. This has been the case in much of Africa, where so many foreign governments were willing to provide aid for diplomatic and developmental reasons. Specifically, aid may be provided to enhance the access of diplomats to government officials. U.S. ambassadors in African countries complain that their "phone has stopped ringing" when they have little aid to distribute.[3] (Americans are not alone. I have heard ambassadors from other countries make the same complaint.) Finally, aid may be provided as pure political symbolism. For example, an aid program may be initiated or increased for a country on the occasion of a state visit by that country's president, to signal that the visit was a success.[4] Or it can be cut to show the displeasure of the donor government with the recipient.

Commercial Motives

Aid in support of commercial goals can take several forms. The most common one is requiring that funds be spent for goods and services produced in the donor country. Almost all bilateral donors of aid "tie" at least a portion of their aid in this way. DAC statistics indicate that roughly one-quarter of bilateral ODA is currently tied or partially tied.[5]

But tying aid is only one way of promoting commercial interests in donor countries. Concessional resources are sometimes combined with government credits at near commercial rates to provide export subsidies in the form of "mixed credit" financing packages for exports—for example, in international competition for large infrastructure projects—airports, dams, or ports—or for major purchases of commodities, for example, airplanes, telecommunications, or railway equipment. There are also cases (we do not know how many) in which governments use their aid to entice (or bribe) recipient governments to undertake infrastructure projects built by firms from the donor's country that are of low priority, inappropriate, overdesigned, or overpriced.[6] A more subtle manifestation of the commercial influence over aid has been the preference on the part of donor governments in the past for large, capital-intensive (and therefore export-intensive) projects, a practice often criticized by development specialists.

Cultural Objectives

A number of governments also provide aid to promote appreciation of, or adherence to, their religion, language, or particular values. These cultural goals usually have a strong appeal to the public in the aid-giving country and are emphasized for that reason. They are manifested in the selection of recipient countries, for example, favoring those in which the donor's culture, religion, or language is already established. Cultural goals can also be reflected in what the aid finances, for example, promoting the use of a particular language in the school system, or the adherence to a particular religion through channeling funds through local churches or mosques.

The allocation of foreign aid to achieve objectives other than development may be quite effective—but the effectiveness of aid in pursuing goals other than development is beyond the scope of this book. And providing aid for nondevelopmental goals does not necessarily mean that development will be undercut. The use of aid to promote diplomatic, commercial, or cultural objectives can coincide with development needs of recipient countries. But this result is fortuitous. There are innumerable cases, in Africa and elsewhere, in which development and commercial or diplomatic goals have collided rather than coincided—in which governments chosen to receive the aid have had a poor policy environment, weak or corrupt institutions, or lacked a commitment to the economic betterment of their peoples, or where aid-funded projects were remunerative commercially for enterprises in the donor country but of low priority for the recipient country.

The Analytical Framework

The approach of this study to analyzing the performance of aid donors is an "agency-centered" one, focusing on the autonomy and capacity of the agencies responsible for managing foreign aid to promote development abroad.

Autonomy

Autonomy refers here to the ability of an organization to make policy and allocative decisions to achieve its mission and purposes.[7] The mission and purposes are usually specified in laws and regulations, and the agency is held accountable to the executive and (in democratic systems) to the legislature and public for realizing them. This, at least, is the theory. In practice, as James Q. Wilson has observed, "No agency has or can have complete autonomy, but all struggle to get and keep as much as they can."[8] Most public agencies find themselves from time to time forced to pursue policies, allocate resources, or take actions not fully congruent with their goals. When this situation occurs with frequency and affects a significant proportion of allocative decisions, we can say that the autonomy of an agency is limited.

Two major channels through which the autonomy of public agencies is circumscribed are the way they are funded and the way they are "governed." Few public agencies are self-financing. Some public lending agencies receive revenues from loan repayments; but, unlike private firms, they are rarely able to retain those earnings and are required to return them to the government treasury. Most public agencies rely on decisions from ministries of finance or agencies responsible for governmental budgets for their annual funding levels. In democracies, they also depend on periodic action by their legislatures to appropriate those funds. Budgetary authorities and legislatures usually require evidence of past agency performance—or at least, the expenditure of past funds—as a prerequisite of agreeing to new funding. At times, they also use their authority over funding to urge or force an agency to adopt particular policies or to allocate the funding in a given manner. Major factors determining the extent to which legislatures attempt to exert significant influence over executive-branch agencies include the nature of the political system and the strength of party discipline. When executive-branch officials and legislators go beyond assessing agency performance and begin to direct agency decisions, they have gone beyond holding the agency accountable and have begun to circumscribe its autonomy. If policy and allocative decisions are sharply constrained by legal or regulatory restrictions, agency autonomy can also be constrained.

Finally, an organization's autonomy can be limited or expanded by its allies and constituents. Other public agencies and private interest groups, including nongovernmental organizations, lobbyists, informal networks of influence, and even powerful individuals, can constrain (or support) an agency's autonomy. Foreign governments can also be a source of direct and indirect pressure on or support of public agencies where their interests are at stake. The means and extent of influence of these groups will depend on the nature of the political system in which they work. Finally, in a democracy, the public—if concerned or aroused on an issue—can influence policy and allocative choices by public agencies.

Although the objects of pressures from other government agencies, legislatures, private domestic interests, and foreign governments, public agencies are not passive entities. Not only do they have their own goals and interests, but they often behave inside and outside government as advocates for those goals as well as for their budget and staffing levels and at times for an expansion in their size and mandate and occasionally to protect their very survival. Agencies may actively seek alliances and constituencies inside and outside government, for example, by financing programs of other government agencies or of supportive private interest groups. They may also seek to influence public opinion on their behalf, where that is legally and practically possible, and to cultivate key individuals in the media who are sympathetic to their causes. In short, while public agencies are influenced by their political environments, they also have their own interests and often attempt to mold their environments to their benefit.[9]

The question arises, how do we assess the degree of an agency's autonomy? As with many concepts in political science, autonomy is easier to describe than to measure. The approach of this study of individual aid agencies will be twofold: to examine the factors, described above, that support or constrain the ability of individual aid agencies to make allocative and policy decisions; and to examine the pattern of actual decision-making. Because there is no realistic way to quantify agency autonomy, no such attempt will be made here.[10]

Capacity

The freedom of public agencies to make policy and allocative choices on development criteria is only one of the ingredients of effective programs. The capacity to identify and design policies, projects, and programs and implement them to achieve overall purposes is the other major ingredient.[11] What are the major factors that affect these activities? Several frequently arise in the literature on the performance of public agencies: clear overall mission and goals and policies appropriate to achieving them, a "technology" (i.e., instruments and knowledge) that is effective in realizing the goals, an organization, staff, and processes appropriate for achieving those goals and policies, and the ability to monitor performance and adapt to changing circumstances, as well as program successes or failures.

Let us first consider goals. These are usually stated in legislation, in government white papers, or in other public documents that justify the existence of the agency. The goals provide direction for the selection of policies and programs as well as a basis for evaluating the performance of an agency. Also important is that they constrain agencies, setting boundaries on their functions and activities.

An important characteristic of goals is their number and specificity. The fewer the number and greater the specificity of agency goals, the easier it will be for an agency to choose (and limit) the number of tasks it performs, to realize them effectively, and to show how it has achieved them. (At the same time, the fewer its goals, the more limited its "customers" and support constituencies among the public are likely to be.) However, the goals of public agencies are rarely very specific but rather are usually multiple and are sometimes contradictory. The multiplicity of goals can create conflicts inside and outside agencies over which has greater priority. Moreover, when goals are couched in vague terms—for example, "promoting the long-run security" or "supporting sustainable development" of a country—it is difficult to know or demonstrate when any one of them has been achieved, since many of them are not easily measurable. These problems, very common in aid agencies, lead to familiar patterns of bureaucratic behavior: the displacement of a focus on achieving goals with a focus on process, the emphasis on "inputs" (often, how much money is spent) rather than "outcomes" to demonstrate program success, and a tendency toward overoptimism or exaggeration of achievements and a defensiveness about failures. (This latter tendency is most evident where public agencies and programs are under particularly critical scrutiny from their publics or legislatures.) Agency goals need not be fixed over time. They can shift as a result of changing conditions (for example, their realization or a decline in their relevance), learning on the part of the agency, changes in leadership, and the need for constituency building.

Additional important elements in determining an agency's capacity for effective programs are its internal processes, its staff, and its organization. Public agencies usually try to create orderly and regularized policy and programming processes, often involving the identification of priority objectives, programs to achieve those objectives, evaluation, and feedback mechanisms. Ideally, an agency will also have adequate financial resources and staff who are technically qualified to implement programs effectively. And it will have an organization appropriate to its activities, which may include decentralized decision-making in field offices if its activities are undertaken in places distant from its headquarters location.

Analyzing Aid Agencies: Hypotheses

It is often assumed by experts on foreign aid that one of the principal impediments to the effectiveness of that aid is its allocation on political and security grounds rather than on developmental criteria.[12] This assumption contains two hypotheses: one is that the main cause of the poor performance of aid in promoting development is its allocation for other purposes—in other words, that the autonomy of aid agencies is significantly constrained. A second hypothesis is that the principal source of constraints on aid agency autonomy is the ministry of foreign affairs that wishes to pursue political and security goals with the aid. The case studies included in this book will provide the basis for testing both of these hypotheses.

There are a number of components of "capacity" of aid agencies, the impact of which we shall explore in this study. One of them involves the organization of the agency—in particular, whether it has a field staff with delegated authority not only to design and implement programs and projects but to commit funds to finance them. The importance of such field missions has been something of an article of faith among certain aid agencies—particularly USAID. We shall want to test whether the existence of field missions with extensive delegated authorities has made a difference in the effectiveness of aid in Africa.

Another hypothesis put forth by several astute observers of foreign aid is that the nature of the bureaucratic processes in which that aid is programmed (typically involving a considerable degree of preplanning and control over the design and implementation of the aid) is inappropriate for the types of tasks the aid is expected to achieve, which tend to be experimental, involve a considerable degree of uncertainty, and require a high degree of flexibility to implement effectively.[13] We shall also examine this hypothesis in our case studies.

A further hypothesis emerging from current debates on aid is that the effectiveness of the aid has been limited as a result of the lack of "ownership" of its activities by recipients and their limited participation in shaping and managing it.[14] This view implies that aid donors should transfer greater authority over decisions on how the aid is used to those recipients. We shall evaluate this hypothesis in light of the experience of several aid agencies examined here.

Applying the Framework to Aid Agencies

This study examines the aid agencies of six governments and two multilateral aid agencies: those of the United States, France, Britain, Sweden, Japan, and Italy, and the World Bank and the European Development Fund of the European Commission.[15] The common analytical framework in which these agencies are examined has five sections. It begins with a review of the three essential decisions all governments or multilateral development agencies have made on their aid to African countries—which countries to aid, how much aid to provide, and what to finance with the aid—and how and why these decisions have changed over time.

A second section will examine the effectiveness of aid in promoting development in Africa. This will include two or three categories, depending on the aid agency. The first category is the allocation of aid by country. Did the aid agency provide significant amounts of its resources to African governments that were poor development partners? Aid (for diplomatic purposes) to governments such as the Democratic Republic of the Congo (that is, the former Zaire) has clearly been ineffective. Second, to what extent did the agency's aid projects and programs achieve their goals and prove sustainable? Third, to what extent did the aid agency contribute to a development dialogue with the Africans? Did it provide intellectual leadership in development discourse?

The third and fourth sections of the framework will analyze the autonomy and capacity of the bilateral or multilateral aid agency and the factors influencing those attributes. Factors influencing the autonomy of aid agencies include organizational location and coherence. Are they independent or part of another agency? Are responsibilities for managing development aid fragmented or located in a single organization? The influence of other agencies over aid allocations and policies, the role of the legislature, the influence of private organizations and networks, and the impact of public opinion are additional factors to be analyzed. The factors influencing capacity include the existence and clarity of aid agency goals or development doctrine, programming processes, staffing and organization—particularly whether the agency has a field organization and if so, with what authorities. The fifth section will relate these attributes to effectiveness.

Chapter Five

The United States

The United States was the first country to make foreign aid an important tool of its foreign policy. It began providing significant amounts of economic assistance to Greece and Turkey in the wake of the withdrawal of British support and in the face of a Communist-supported insurgency in Greece and Soviet pressures on Turkey in 1947. Shortly after initiating aid to these two countries, the Truman administration announced a major assistance program to support European recovery—the Marshall Plan. And in 1949, President Truman proposed a Point Four aid program to provide modest amounts of technical assistance to needy countries. These programs marked the beginning of the era of foreign aid and reflected the two major motivations for U.S. aid: containing Communism and promoting development.

As independence for African countries approached in the late 1950s, the U.S. government feared that the withdrawal of European control from the region would expand the arena of competition with the USSR and its allies. It also foresaw that the new countries would have extensive economic needs and that there were opportunities to support successful development there. Motivated both by its diplomatic concerns and its development mission, the United States prepared to expand the small aid programs it had already put in place in Liberia and Ethiopia to the newly independent countries.

Which Countries to Aid?

The United States, like other donors operating in Africa, has had to decide which countries to aid. Since the early years of African independence, successive U.S. administrations have shown a preference for providing some aid to each independent country in the region. These preferences have reflected the diplomatic goals of the foreign-policy establishment. U.S. aid has also been concentrated in a dozen or so countries, reflecting preferences of both the diplomatic and the development communities. These preferences have at various times been facilitated or constrained by pressures from Congress and the availability of budgetary resources.

As African countries gained their independence, the United States usually moved to establish a diplomatic mission in each capital. With few U.S. economic interests or historical ties to the countries where they were posted, ambassadors were eager to have an aid program to enhance their access and influence with the government. Moreover, Africa was seen in Washington as a new arena of Cold War competition with the USSR, and officials wanted to be positioned to encourage the new governments to remain supportive of the West and of the United States in the UN. As one student of U.S. aid in the early 1960s observed, "Every American ambassador, even the ambassador to the Upper Volta, finds it useful to have an aid program, which he justifies on political grounds. It makes it easier to talk to the minister of finance, and it promotes good relations with other government officials."[1] Finally, other developed country governments were establishing aid programs in these countries, and the former colonial metropoles were continuing aid programs initiated before independence. African governments expected, sought, and required aid from foreign powers accredited to them. At the same time, Africa was the newest development challenge for the U.S. aid community. It was a region at an early stage of development with what seemed excellent prospects for achieving significant economic progress. By 1963, the United States Agency for International Development had established aid programs in a total of twenty-nine African countries.

However, the initial concerns in Washington about Soviet gains in Africa soon wore off, with the overthrow and murder of Patrice Lumumba of the Congo (whose radical rhetoric and appeal to Moscow for military help in the wake of Belgian intervention in his country had alarmed Washington) and the unpredictability and independence of Sekou Toure of Guinea and Kwame Nkrumah of Ghana—two self-proclaimed socialists who had sought aid from Moscow upon gaining independence in the late 1950s. By 1963, Congress was complaining about the large number of U.S. aid programs in Africa, a region still regarded as primarily a European responsibility.

In an attempt to quell these and other criticisms, President Kennedy commissioned a report on foreign aid by General Lucius Clay. Kennedy appointed Clay because he hoped that an outspoken critic of aid would find merit in it and say so in his report. However, the report concluded that "these new countries value their independence and do not wish to acquire a new master in place of the old one. . . , [that] we are trying to do too much for too many too soon, that we are overextended in resources and undercompensated in results, and that no end of foreign aid is either in sight or mind."[2] The report recommended that the United States fulfill its existing aid commitments and then reduce the size and number of its programs in Africa.

Several years later, another report commissioned by President Johnson echoed these views. It urged that the number of programs in Africa be reduced and that aid be concentrated where it would be most effective in supporting development. Congress subsequently voted to restrict the number of aid missions, and by the early 1970s, there were only ten operating in the region.[3] (Small amounts of food aid and relief funds were provided to most African countries despite the closure of aid missions there.)

However, in 1972, after several years of serious drought in the Sahelian countries, Congressmen Charles Diggs, the first African American chairman of the Africa Subcommittee of the House Foreign Affairs Committee, introduced a bill in Congress proposing a Sahelian Development Program that would not only provide relief to the Sahelian countries but create a long-term, regional development program as well. Diggs's bill eventually became law and opened the way to reestablishing aid missions in Senegal, Mali, Burkina Faso, Niger, Chad, and Mauritania—countries with little economic or strategic interest to the United States, but among the poorest countries in the world.

At this time, development policies in the United States also shifted, to emphasize poverty reduction and working in the world's poorest countries. Since many of those countries were located in Africa, there was now a justification for expanding the number of programs there. From this time on, the number of U.S. aid programs in Africa increased to include all friendly countries. By the early 1990s, the United States had programs in forty-three African countries, with USAID field missions in over thirty.

However, the end of the Cold War and budgetary politics in Washington once again changed the political context of decision-making on aid. The rationales for aiding the more repressive, incompetent, and corrupt regimes ended. Aid to the Democratic Republic of the Congo (formerly the Congo and later, Zaire), for example, was discontinued in 1992. Efforts to reduce the federal budget deficit during the first half of the 1990s led to an overall reduction in aid and a consequent fall in aid to Africa, forcing USAID to close nine of its missions in the region.

How Much Aid to Provide?

Even more than decisions on which countries to aid, decisions on how much aid to provide shed light on the policies and priorities influencing foreign aid. During the early 1960s, Cold War concerns played a major role in determining the size of aid flows to individual African countries. Upon coming to power, Kwame Nkrumah of Ghana and Sekou Toure of Guinea, despite their "socialist orientation," sought aid from Washington. President Kennedy, who saw their requests for help as a political opportunity, in 1962 responded with $65 million to help finance the Volta dam in Ghana, with $10 million for assorted activities in Guinea, and, in the wake of political instabilities there, with $84 million in the strategically positioned Congo. (Total U.S. economic assistance to Africa that year was only $226 million.)[4] A large Soviet offer of aid to Ethiopia in 1961 also led to a boost in U.S. aid to that country, from $8 million in 1960 to $42 million in 1961.[5]

Once it became evident that neither Nkrumah nor Toure was about to become a pawn of Moscow and pressures from Congress to reduce aid to Africa grew, the overall level of aid began to fall and the number of countries aided decreased. However, in the mid-1970s, two factors led aid to Africa to rise once again. One was the increasing emphasis on using aid to alleviate poverty. The other was a renewal of Cold War tensions in the region.

In 1974, the sudden Portuguese decolonization in Angola and Mozambique left Marxist-oriented governments in both countries. These governments promptly sought and received military and economic support from a newly assertive USSR. These Soviet-supported governments and the ongoing civil war in Rhodesia (in which a white-led regime had unilaterally declared independence from Britain in 1965 only to be challenged by a black-led insurgency) were seen by Washington as threatening the stability of the entire southern African region. In the late 1970s, the United States increased its economic assistance to southern Africa to symbolize its engagement and to help stabilize friendly regimes by spurring economic development.

In 1974, Emperor Haile Selassie of Ethiopia was deposed by a military coup led by Mengistu Haile Mariam. The new government was highly critical of the West and the United States in particular. In the wake of an invasion from Somalia, it sought military aid from Washington. But Washington refused, citing the poor human-rights record of the government. Mengistu then turned to Moscow for help and received a massive supply of arms and other assistance. The Soviets had finally established a close relationship with Ethiopia (something they had long coveted), but Washington saw the new relationship as an escalation of the Cold War, provoking Zbigniew Brzezinski, then director of the National Security Council, to make his much-quoted remark that "detente was buried in the sands of the Ogaden." Washington responded to the Soviets in Ethiopia by stepping up its aid to neighboring countries, including Somalia and Kenya. U.S. aid to southern Africa and the Horn continued to rise during the late 1970s, reaching 75 percent of total U.S. aid to Africa by 1980 (compared with only 15 percent in 1970).

Two other changes in Washington occurred in the 1970s that were to have a substantial impact on the size, distribution, and use of aid. One was the rise of African Americans as a political force supporting higher levels of aid to Africa and a distribution of that aid to countries in need. The first manifestation of a more assertive and influential African American voice in U.S. Africa policy was the Sahel Development Program, proposed by Congressman Diggs. This program did not lead immediately to an increase in overall aid to Africa. Rather, it was financed largely out of a decrease in aid to oil-exporting Nigeria that followed the quadrupling in petroleum prices in 1973. But the new program did establish the principle that economic need was a legitimate basis for U.S. aid.

Further strengthening that principle was a major change in development policy that took place in the early 1970s, referred to briefly above. During much of the 1960s, U.S. aid worldwide emphasized the expansion of infrastructure and education, reflecting the ideas of development and the role of aid in supporting it prevalent at that time. But in 1973, Congress passed an authorization bill with "New Directions" in foreign aid—emphasizing the goal of reducing poverty worldwide.[6] This legislation established that more aid should be allocated to the poorest countries and should be provided for projects that attacked the problems of poverty directly, particularly in rural areas, where most of the poor lived. The legislation added a development rationale to the renewed strategic rationale for increasing U.S. aid to Africa.

U.S. aid to Africa continued to rise in the 1980s, increasing from $541

million in 1979 to $1.5 billion in 1985. (This latter figure included sub-
stantial funding for drought relief for Ethiopia.) The level of aid remained
around $1 billion per year for the rest of the decade. During the latter
part of the 1980s, major recipients still included politically important
countries, like Sudan (which had been the first Arab country to support
the Camp David Accords between Egypt and Israel), the Democratic
Republic of the Congo, Somalia, and Kenya. Another group of countries—those implementing economic-reform programs (the major thrust
in development policies during the 1980s)—received lower but still significant amounts of aid, including Senegal, Ghana, Cameroon, and Malawi.

By the beginning of the 1980s, there were signs that the Soviets were
no longer willing to compete with the West for influence or strategic
position in Africa. Moscow had turned down a request from Mozambique to join the Council for Mutual Economic Assistance and a request
from the government of Ghana for a new aid program. By 1986, there
were other signs that the Cold War in Africa was beginning to wind
down. Chester Crocker, assistant secretary of state for Africa from 1981
to 1988, has observed that "Moscow's gradual reappraisal of its African
policies" was first visible in 1986.[7] Events in the region also contributed
to a lessening in the urgency of Cold War competition, particularly the
successful resolution of the civil war in Rhodesia, the election of a new
government there, and the granting by the British of independence to
that country—renamed Zimbabwe—in 1980. At the same time, the region's Marxist governments (and their Soviet backers) in southern Africa
and the Horn were under increasing military and economic pressure.
The Marxist government in Angola was challenged by a United States–
and South African–backed insurgency there. The Marxist government
of Ethiopia was similarly besieged by a long-running civil war in which
the province of Eritrea demanded its independence. And the Marxist
government in Mozambique was beginning to face a South African–
backed insurgency within its borders as well. These conflicts were costly
to the Soviets and to their African partners. The Soviets had other problems: a bloody conflict in Afghanistan and deepening economic problems
at home. Moscow not only commenced to reassess its support of its African clients but began in 1988 actively to collaborate with the United
States to resolve conflicts in the region.

With the winding down of the Cold War, one might have expected to
see a decline in U.S. aid to Africa. But it continued its climb. This in-

crease was a result of other factors that had now become important in foreign-aid decision making. One was the prevailing views on development policy that still favored aid to the poorest developing countries but also emphasized the importance of economic reforms. Moreover, the deepening economic crisis in Africa also created a rationale for increased aid. Several prominent organizations—the Council on Foreign Relations and the Overseas Development Council—gave visibility to this crisis in a major study that recommended increased aid in support of policy reforms in Africa.[8] In the wake of the drought in Ethiopia and the deepening economic malaise in Africa, a UN special session on Africa's economic problems was convened in 1986. It endorsed a Program of Action for African Economic Recovery and Development that would combine policy reforms by Africans with increased foreign aid.

The 1985 drought in Ethiopia and the increasing international attention to African economic problems helped to put the region on the U.S. political agenda. But without a domestic political constituency for aid to the region, it seems likely that the growing pressures to reduce the federal budget deficit, the decrease in the Cold War competition in Africa, and the need on the part of the administration for aid resources to buttress its priorities elsewhere in the world would have likely led to a decrease in that aid. (There was in fact an effort in the mid-1980s to transfer $300 million of funds originally intended for Africa to Central America to support friendly governments there.) By the mid-1980s, African Americans as well as NGOs working on relief and development were far better organized and influential politically than they had been in the 1960s when U.S. aid to Africa decreased in the wake of an easing in Cold War fears.

In 1987, an informal alliance of the Black Caucus and others in Congress, NGOs working in Africa, and key administration officials supported a proposal floated by InterAction (the U.S. NGO umbrella group) to create a separate Development Fund for Africa (DFA) within the U.S. bilateral aid program. The new fund would help maintain congressionally determined aid levels to Africa, prevent "raids" on Africa monies to fund activities in other parts of the world, and provide the administration with an exceptional degree of allocative flexibility. (Development assistance monies were increasingly constrained by congressional earmarks, often determining allocation by country as well as the uses of that aid. The DFA would be free of such earmarks.) In return, the administration would allocate the funds for Africa primarily to achieve developmental goals and would create a system for reporting to Congress on the impact of that aid. In 1988, the Development Fund for Africa was passed by Congress in the foreign-aid appropriations bill.

The DFA soon became a symbol of U.S. support for African development, with the supporters of a greater engagement in the region (primarily the Congressional Black Caucus and NGOs) successfully advocating annual increases in the level of its funding. Thus, the DFA rose from $500 million in 1988 to $800 million in 1991 (when Congress uncharacteristically appropriated more than the $560 million the administration requested). The target for DFA funding for subsequent years was $1 billion, and the House of Representatives actually appropriated that much in fiscal 1992. The Senate, with no African American members or others with an active interest in Africa (apart from the chairman and ranking minority member of the Africa Subcommittee of the Senate Foreign Relations Committee) agreed to only $800 million for the DFA that year, as requested by the administration, and this became the final figure.[9]

The end of the Cold War may not have had an immediate impact on overall levels of aid to Africa, but it did affect which countries received it. Except for humanitarian relief, aid to several favorites of the past—Sudan, Somalia, Liberia, and Zaire in particular—was terminated. By 1996, the leading recipients of U.S. aid in Africa were South Africa, Mozambique, Ethiopia, Uganda, and Ghana—all countries implementing economic or political reforms or both.

The election of the first Republican-controlled Congress in forty years in 1994 changed the domestic political landscape of foreign aid. Now in power were conservative politicians, often with little knowledge or experience of foreign aid or foreign policy in general and with few ties with development-oriented NGOs. Several new chairmen of congressional subcommittees dealing with foreign aid began to ask why, with so few economic and national interests in Africa, the United States continued to provide the region with so much aid.[10] The Cold War, which might have tempered their skepticism about foreign aid, and about the importance of U.S. engagement in the world, was over. Eliminating the federal budget deficit was a high priority for the new Congress. Overall bilateral aid levels were cut substantially—from $7.7 billion in 1993 to $5.3 billion in 1996. Funding for the Development Fund for Africa dropped to a little more than $600 million in 1995 and the fund itself was not reauthorized (though the administration continued to use it as a presentational category for its aid). Total U.S. bilateral aid to Africa (which included food aid) fell from $1.2 billion in 1993 to $1 billion in 1996.

The easing in budgetary pressures in 1997 and 1998 and the lessening of congressional enthusiasm for cutting programs led to a stabilization in overall foreign-aid levels and a slight increase in aid to Africa. But by 1998, it seemed unlikely that the administration would propose, or Congress agree to any time soon, a return to the higher levels of the early 1990s.

What the Aid Finances

Even though diplomatic concerns had much to do with which countries received U.S. aid and how much, decisions on what the aid actually financed were usually left to USAID. The determination of overall policies reflected prevailing ideas of aid's role in development. Decisions on projects and programs in individual countries were usually the outcome of negotiations between the USAID mission in the field and USAID headquarters in Washington, with the former typically proposing and the latter assenting or amending, depending on agency policies, on available budgetary resources, and, increasingly with time, on congressional earmarks and directives.

Evolving concepts of the role of aid in development set out the broad parameters of USAID's policies. In most cases, these policies were applied to USAID activities worldwide. As mentioned earlier, during the 1960s, it was believed that foreign aid could help fill the gap between the (usually low) level of domestic savings and the target level of investment as well as the gap between actual foreign-exchange earnings and the larger amount needed to fund desired investments. To help estimate that gap, governments in developing countries were expected to produce development plans and strategies. Indeed, U.S. aid was at times conditioned on such plans and often financed the technical assistance needed to create them. Foreign aid would help fund investments that the private sector would not finance, such as physical infrastructure and the expansion of social services. Financing of infrastructure and social services— particularly education—fit in well with developmental needs of the newly independent states of Africa.

U.S. policies on development aid shifted during the 1970s to emphasize the alleviation of poverty, targeting the poor in the world's poorer countries. In Africa as elsewhere, this meant a sharp reduction in funding for infrastructure (except rural roads, for example, if they could be shown to benefit the poor). It meant a shift away from higher education toward support of primary schooling. And it meant work in rural areas, where most of the poor resided. In addressing the problems of rural development, USAID, along with other donors, began to finance "integrated rural development projects"—large projects made up of multiple activities (such as roads, primary education, rural water, agricultural extension services) designed to raise particular rural areas quickly from impoverishment.

The 1980s saw another shift in U.S. development policies, once again similar to changes implemented by other donors. The focus was once more directed at promoting rapid economic growth as a result of the serious problems of debt and economic recession experienced in much of the developing world. USAID increasingly allocated its aid in Africa to programs of policy reform. Aid for such programs rose from virtually none in 1980 to nearly half of all U.S. bilateral assistance to the region by 1983.[11]

By the 1990s, other priorities arose for the use of U.S. development aid, including promoting democracy, protecting the environment, microenterprise lending, micronutrient research, female reproductive-health services, child survival projects, and activities aimed at increasing gender equality. These priorities were not the result of a new aid and development paradigm. Rather, most of them were the consequence of pressures directly on USAID from organized outside groups or powerful individuals within the administration or in Congress (often responding to pleas and pressures from organized interests). Congress often included "earmarks" in aid legislation or directives in legislative reports to USAID to undertake particular types of activities at specified levels of funding.

Congressional earmarks and directives were not new. Congress had long required that bilateral aid be spent in broad categories of activities, including agriculture, education, and population and health. What was new in the 1980s and 1990s was the proliferation and narrowing of such earmarks and directives. The result was frequently that USAID missions submitted laboriously prepared budget proposals to Washington of the projects and programs they would like to undertake in their particular countries and then were told that they would have funds to finance only certain types of projects (often not the ones they wanted to finance) because of the legislative restrictions emanating from Congress or other commitments by the administration.

While USAID bureaucrats were masters of designing the types of projects they wanted to fund and then presenting them as fitting into the various categories Congress had imposed,[12] congressional restrictions did have an impact on the agency's flexibility in shaping projects and programs to fit local needs. It was in part an effort to limit the application of these restrictions to U.S. aid in Africa that led to the creation of the DFA. That proved effective but only for a time. By the 1990s, the restrictions on aid to other parts of the world were so tight that USAID itself began to extend them to Africa. (For example, funding for population programs in Africa could be counted against the overall earmark for population. This created incentives to fund more population activities in Africa than USAID mission directors wanted in order to expand the amount of less restricted aid in Latin America or Asia.)

To what extent did these broad shifts in policies and the increasing restrictions on what USAID should fund affect the agency's projects and programs in individual countries? USAID, like any large bureaucracy, is slow to implement fundamental changes. Yet broad policy changes did influence what the agency did in particular countries. Despite complaints from USAID officials in the 1970s that terminating most infrastructure projects was inconsistent with the needs of African countries, proposals for such projects from USAID's field missions were turned down in Washington, and so their number diminished. Meanwhile, the number of rural development projects grew. In the 1980s, projects supporting policy reforms increased dramatically, as we have seen. At the same time, expenditures on agricultural projects fell. In the 1990s, despite complaints from USAID mission directors and economists (who preferred the flexibility of programs aimed at policy reform to the complicated process of designing projects, procuring services, and implementing projects), projects in the agency's priority areas expanded.

A glance at the USAID program proposed for Zambia in 1997 gives a sense of the portfolio of activities the agency was funding in Africa. The program was to total just over $20 million—a medium-sized U.S. aid program in Africa. Most of the activities were projects (primarily funding technical assistance) rather than cash transfers in support of economic-reform programs. Funding for technical assistance, for example, included advice to the Zambian Privatization Agency and the Zambia Communications Authority to help create a regulatory framework. Training and management advice were provided to small and medium-sized Zambian businesses. Technical assistance and pilot projects involving rural credit, the dissemination of new technologies, and promoting community engagement in wildlife management were among the projects in the area of rural development. Activities involving a redesign of the health information system, malaria prevention, family planning and HIV/AIDS awareness, skill training for health providers, and creating a reporting process were among the health interventions. Finally, there were small projects involving civic education, training for journalists, advice on legal reform, and funding for election monitoring.[13] The breadth of this portfolio reflects the trend, evident in the United States and in other donors as well, toward expanding the types of aid-financed activities and the move away from macroeconomic or sectoral policy reform. It also reflects the large proportion of activities that involve behavioral change on the part of Zambians, including such things as community wildlife management, HIV/AIDS awareness, and civic education.

The Effectiveness of U.S. Aid

What can we say about the developmental effectiveness of U.S. aid in Africa? How much aid did the United States provide to Africa's more corrupt and incompetent governments? To what extent did USAID's projects and programs achieve their objectives and remain sustainable? And to what degree did USAID provide intellectual leadership in development in Africa?

The first point to make involves the allocation of aid to several of what have become "failed states" (wherein governmental authority has collapsed because of civil conflict or gross political incompetence and corruption). Two of Africa's collapsed states—Somalia and Liberia—have been among the largest recipients of U.S. aid. And the Democratic Republic of the Congo--failed, but not destroyed by civil conflict—was until the 1990s consistently among the largest recipients of overall U.S. aid in Africa. The Sudan, another major recipient of aid in the past, is ruled by a brutal and repressive dictatorship and plagued by civil war. Aid was provided these governments primarily for diplomatic reasons, and, while there are no assessments of what has become of the aid projects funded in these countries, there can be little doubt that few of them have succeeded or been sustained.

In these states, aid may have unintentionally encouraged the misrule that led to collapse or to civil conflict. It was provided in significant amounts (compared with the levels of aid for other African countries) over an extended period of time regardless of the corruption, repression, or incompetence of the rulers. The aid symbolized support and approbation of the government and was often sought and accepted for that reason, far more than the resources it brought.[14] U.S. aid to these four countries totaled just under $5 billion from the end of the Second World War to 1995, or just over one-fifth of a total of $22 billion in U.S. aid to Africa.[15]

Most of these countries would have received some U.S. aid even if they were not important diplomatically, but the amount would have been much smaller given the poor quality of political leadership and their weak commitment to development. (U.S. aid to Liberia before Sergeant Doe's coup in 1980 averaged about $14 million per year. In 1981, it rose to $55 million and remained just over $60 million until the middle of the decade.) The effectiveness of this aid from a diplomatic perspective is beyond the scope of this book. But its effectiveness in promoting development in these countries must be judged to have been limited or even perverse.

The second element in this assessment of U.S. aid to Africa involves the developmental effectiveness of the projects and programs it financed.[16] The bulk of USAID's evaluations of its work in Africa tell a story much like that in the overview in chapter 3 of aid's effectiveness in Africa generally. USAID projects in Africa have usually proven less effective in achieving and sustaining their objectives than projects in other parts of the world. Projects have been most effective when there was a known, proven technology for realizing their objectives. They were least successful when they involved a complex set of activities or behavioral or institutional changes on the part of Africans. A summary of selected project evaluations will illustrate these general points.

Exemplifying the problems of complex interventions were the rural-development projects popular in the late 1970s.[17] In Senegal, for example, one evaluation found that "the effort to administratively integrate a variety of rural development activities in a single project exceeds the administrative capacity of the host country. It also seems clear that USAID does not have the institutional capacity to implement projects of that nature."[18] Livestock projects were USAID's "least successful investment," largely due to an "uncritical acceptance of the American range management model."[19] Among the other reasons for these failures was overoptimism on the part of U.S. planners, "planning without facts" due to the lack of information on African agriculture, failure to take account of the weaknesses of the African organizations with which the United States chose to work, and the inability of USAID to make midcourse corrections in its projects when the assumptions on which they were based proved unrealistic.[20] These judgments were repeated in most of the evaluations of agricultural projects in Africa. They were also reflected in projects involving natural-resource management—for example in Rwanda and Gambia. In the former case, an evaluation found, among other things, that "developing appropriate NRM (natural resource management) technologies is a complex undertaking requiring site-specific applied research."[21] The evaluation of a forestry project in Gambia found that it "failed to have any positive effect on the environment, the adoption of sound forest management policies and practices, or the socioeconomic well-being of targeted beneficiaries."[22] The main reason for these failures was that the technologies introduced were inappropriate to physical, economic, and social conditions in Gambia.

USAID's projects in Africa confirm the observation that where goals were relatively simple and technologies were known (or learned quickly) and brought tangible benefits to Africans in a relatively short period, they had greater success and sustainability. Among the best-known successes was the effort (in collaboration with several other donors) to eradicate river blindness in seven countries of West Africa.[23] The incidence of river blindness was sharply reduced in 90 percent of the area covered by the project, with benefits not only for the health of Africans but for the productivity of agriculture in these fertile river valleys. The project benefited from clear and simple goals, from a period in which donors could experiment and learn how to address the problems of river blindness, sustained support by multiple donors, and concrete benefits to Africans.

Aid-financed efforts to inoculate children against diseases, according to one evaluation that covered programs in six countries (including one in Africa), have coincided with a reduction in childhood mortality. And though a USAID evaluation was "unable to determine the portion of mortality reduction directly attributable to health services for mothers and children . . . or specifically to A.I.D.'s Child Survival Program," it did suggest, on the basis of circumstantial evidence, that "A.I.D. can take credit for a meaningful share of the progress made in countries where the agency has made a substantial contribution."[24] The immunization program in Malawi, part of a multidonor activity, achieved an 80 percent coverage rate nationally. Unfortunately, the spread of new strains of malaria meanwhile caused the child mortality rate to increase.

Family-planning programs have had mixed results, reflecting several important factors in aid's effectiveness. The program in Kenya has helped contribute to the significant reduction in fertility in that country, evident in the 1990s.[25] Key to this success was the commitment of the Kenyan government to reducing population growth and—for reasons that are still being studied—the change in the attitudes of Kenyans, both in urban and rural areas, toward fertility. USAID's efforts to create a database on population and health conditions in Kenya and its dialogue over a period of time with the government over the implications of population growth for long-term development helped convince the government of the problems created by a 4 percent rate of annual population growth. The family-planning services set up by USAID were in place when the demand for contraceptives surged.[26]

However, the impact of family-planning projects in Africa has not been uniformly positive. In Ghana between 1968 and 1991, their impact was "practically negligible." The number of family-planning delivery points increased later, and the use of family-planning devices grew. Nevertheless, there have been limited reductions in fertility in Ghana. The lack of political commitment on the part of the government and the intermittent availability of family-planning services were among the reasons for the relative ineffectiveness of this project.[27]

USAID is the lead donor in Africa in promoting democracy. While there is a dearth of evaluative materials on the impact of these relatively recent programs (begun only in the 1990s), it is clear that funding elections and election monitors (which usually cost in the millions or tens of millions of dollars) has helped ensure relatively free and fair electoral outcomes. Again, these interventions involved the application of familiar technologies to a discrete problem with a concrete (and immediate) outcome.

Most of the projects aimed at behavioral or institutional change in Africa have had poor results. But one exception to this generalization should be mentioned for the lessons it provides. An evaluation of the USAID program in South Africa between 1986 and 1993, based on extensive interviews with South Africans,[28] found that U.S. aid had been highly effective in building black leadership and strengthening community institutions. The assessment states, "Through USAID/South Africa's education and training projects and through its funding of numerous black-led NGOs, disadvantaged South Africans were able to acquire the knowledge, skills, certificates, and leadership and management experience that are critical" to assuming power.[29] This program's limited goals and the scope it gave its grantees to manage funding for their organizations contributed to an unusually effective program, suggesting that "social engineering" and activities to strengthen institutions can be effective where aid officials have clear objectives and where recipients are actively engaged in managing the aid-funded activities.

As for economic-policy reform (a priority of USAID in Africa during the 1980s and early 1990s), the pattern seems much like that described in chapter 3: individual successes (for example, removal of price controls and subsidies and a reduction in taxation), especially where reforms were administratively simple and powerful interests did not oppose them.[30] An evaluation of six economic-reform programs in Africa avoided comparing successes and failures but warned, "Policy reform involves a highly complex set of political, economic and social changes with winners and losers in both the public and private sectors. . . . A.I.D. must carefully consider the costs of adjustment and be prepared to analyze thoroughly and deal creatively with the sociopolitical effects of the changes it is supporting."[31]

Even many relatively effective projects in Africa are not sustainable over the long term. In Malawi, the willingness or ability of the government to finance a childhood inoculation program was in doubt once foreign aid for it ended. Evaluations found that other health programs were more sustainable if the beneficiaries felt them worthwhile (in particular, for them) and, often, if they were willing to pay part of their costs. Sustainability of education programs also depended on the recurrent costs of the programs to government and the availability of jobs for graduates.

Let us turn to the question of the degree to which USAID contributed to the discourse on development in Africa. Several of the agency's evaluations refer to the impact of the agency's studies of development problems on the thinking of African officials about development in their countries. For example, USAID has undertaken a number of studies of population growth, including fertility surveys and future projections of population growth, and the probable impact of that growth on the demand for government services. Indeed, among the most comprehensive data on social conditions in Africa are the Demographic and Health Surveys, funded by USAID and often covering several decades of data on population, fertility, family planning, mortality, and health of mothers and children. An evaluation of the population program in Kenya observed, "It was the Kenya Fertility Survey that revealed in 1977–78 that Kenya had the highest fertility in the world and that its annual population growth rate was nearly 4 percent. These results alarmed the Kenyan leadership and contributed directly to the increase in political commitment to family planning."[32] It is understandably difficult to convince a government official that he or she has a problem until reliable data is available to demonstrate incontrovertibly that the problem exists.

Another USAID evaluation cites eleven areas—from the relationship between structural adjustment and poverty and the role of agriculture in development to the adoption of a new strategy for preventing malaria—

in which its studies and reports have led to a "paradigm shift" in the way African policymakers view issues. Even taking into account the tendency for aid agencies to exaggerate positive impacts, it appears that well-executed studies financed by USAID, especially ones in which African officials have been involved, have led to changes in thinking on the part of Africans and to better-informed policy choices.[33]

Let us summarize this discussion of the developmental effectiveness of U.S. aid in Africa by asking how the choice of countries to receive the aid and the policies to guide how it was spent influenced its effectiveness. A significant amount of aid has been wasted, from a development point of view, in several countries that were favored diplomatic partners of the United States, including Zaire, Somalia, and Liberia. The governments of these countries ceased to function, and their economies ultimately collapsed, largely due to their own repression, incompetence, and corruption. The United States did not cause the poor governance that led to economic and political failures in these states but may have helped prolong it. It is worth noting here that not all U.S. diplomatic favorites in Africa ended up as collapsed states. Kenya, for example, was a favored recipient of U.S. aid during the 1980s and has avoided major civil strife. It is also worth pointing out that with the end of the Cold War, the incompatibility of diplomatic and development goals in Africa has greatly diminished, with aid funds more often allocated on developmental criteria.

To what extent have the overall development policies governing the use of U.S. aid in Africa influenced the effectiveness of that aid? Several general points can be made on the basis of the materials in this section. The policies emphasizing infrastructure and education prevailing in the 1960s were appropriate to the development needs of Africa at that time and, in the words of one study, "contributed measurably and significantly to human capital accumulation" and to physical capital accumulation as well.[34] The region was greatly lacking in these basic foundations of development. The emphasis on development planning is more controversial. The idea seemed an unobjectionable one: governments ideally need to play a role in guiding the development of their economies to ensure balanced and equitable growth. However, African governments in these early years lacked the basic capacity for such planning and were increasingly politicized. The emphasis on planning may have hastened (and helped to rationalize) the impulse toward centralized control of economies already evident in most of the region.

The development policies adopted by the United States and other aid agencies during the 1970s, emphasizing direct action to alleviate poverty in Africa, in particular rural-development projects, were inappropriate to the region. The United States and other donors knew too little about African smallholder agriculture at this time to design reliably effective projects, and the projects they did design were beyond the capabilities of recipients to implement. Moreover, donors, including the United States, ignored the economic-policy environment for agriculture in Africa that itself discouraged expanded production by smallholders as well as others.

The development policies of the 1980s, emphasizing policy reform, were appropriate in targeting serious obstacles to growth. But the reform programs themselves often overlooked the difficult political environment in which the policies they sought to change were embedded, as well as the capacities of African governments to implement administratively complex policy changes.

By the 1990s, the United States no longer had a "development paradigm" around which to shape its aid policies. Rather, it had a set of activities it was prepared to fund, and those activities often arose from political pressures from NGOs and restrictions from Congress. What impact did the growing number of earmarks and directives from Congress have on the effectiveness of aid? The impact cannot be observed in particular projects or sets of projects. Child inoculation projects, for example, are generally regarded as successful in reducing the incidence of childhood mortality in the region. But there are several troubling consequences nonetheless. One involves the inoculation programs. Recall that an evaluation worried about the sustainability of the programs and whether the government of Malawi would eventually pick up the cost. Requirements for aid agencies to fund particular types of activities at high levels (or to provide governments with designated amounts of aid regardless of their development performance) can produce a "moral hazard" in which recipient governments assume that aid will be forthcoming for those projects and that therefore they have no need to assume responsibility for them. This may be a consequence of the high levels of child-survival monies that Congress has required USAID to spend.

Another possible consequence of congressional directives and earmarks is that more monies than can be effectively used are spent on required activities. One sign of this problem would be pipelines of unspent monies. (While data on USAID's pipelines are not publicly available, large pipelines of unspent funds for population and child-survival programs in Africa were, in fact, of concern to USAID's managers when I served in the agency.)

Analysis

Since it was created in 1961, USAID has been the principal bilateral aid agency of the U.S. government, responsible for shaping policies, proposing budgets, making allocative decisions, and managing a worldwide foreign-aid program. It is headed by an administrator appointed by the president and has its own personnel and programming systems. USAID takes "foreign-policy guidance" from the secretary of state but submits its annual budget to both the secretary of state and the Office of Management and Budget (the U.S. government's budget agency).

USAID and the Department of State have been the two principal agencies involved in foreign-aid decisions within the U.S. government. The economic agencies—for example, the Department of Commerce and the Export-Import Bank—have rarely played a role in policy or allocative decisions involving foreign aid, in contrast to other governments in which these agencies have had a much more important role. (The influential role of the Department of State has likely served to limit the influence of the other agencies over aid programs.)[35]

Decisions on the allocation by country of U.S. aid and at times on the use of that aid are usually the result of a series of negotiations between USAID and Department of State officers in the field and bureaus and policy-level officials of the two agencies in Washington. These negotiations take place in the preparation of annual budget submissions to OMB and to the Congress as well as over the reallocation of aid for unexpected needs during a fiscal year. In many cases, the views of USAID and State officials are not greatly different on aid levels for individual countries. Ambassadors and USAID mission directors tend to want as much aid for their countries as they can get. The views of officials of the two agencies in Washington are not normally greatly different either, except when the Department of State feels there are compelling political reasons for providing aid to a particular government while USAID believes that the development rationale is weak. Where such differences cannot be negotiated out, they are "escalated" to more senior officials. If the political reasons are sufficiently compelling to command the attention and support of the secretary of state, the Department of State's views usually prevail. This was more commonly the case during the Cold War than at present, when compelling security issues in Africa are far more limited, leaving USAID with increased autonomy over decisions on which countries are aided and by how much.

The increased autonomy of USAID vis-à-vis the Department of State has undoubtedly contributed to efforts on the part of that department, together with key members of Congress, to force a merger of USAID into the State Department. A proposal for such a merger surfaced within the administration in 1994, supported by senior State Department officials. It was defeated by USAID and its various allies inside and outside the administration. But it was then picked up by Senator Jesse Helms, chairman of the Senate Foreign Relations Committee, who repeatedly attempted to pass legislation requiring such a merger. By the end of 1997, those attempts had failed, but the issue of the organizational location of USAID promised to remain a contentious one, both within the administration and in Congress.

During the 1980s and 1990s, Congress played an increasingly influential role in U.S. aid to Africa. For nearly all government agencies, the Senate and House of Representatives are responsible for passing two kinds of legislation: authorization bills permitting agencies to function and expend funds, and appropriations, providing the monies that can be spent. In the case of foreign aid, Congress had failed since the mid-1980s to pass authorizing legislation. The need for periodic authorizing legislation can be waived (provided existing authorization legislation does not lapse). And because foreign aid has been relatively unpopular among the American public, many members of Congress have avoided voting for it whenever possible, making the passage of not-absolutely-necessary authorizing bills difficult. But monies do need to be appropriated every year, or programs will come to a halt. And it has been through the appropriations process and other oversight mechanisms that Congress has increasingly constrained bilateral foreign aid.

Beginning with the "New Directions" aid legislation in the early 1970s, Congress appropriated bilateral aid in several broad functional accounts, including agriculture and rural development, population and health, and human-resource development. Funds appropriated for these accounts had to be spent for activities falling within these sectors. But within these broad categories and restrictions, the administration retained considerable flexibility in deciding how much funding to provide particular countries and for what purposes. The Reagan administration in 1981 faced a Democrat-led Congress. Among the issues on which the Democrats in Congress and the Republicans in the administration differed sharply were policies on abortion and the implications of those policies for population and family-planning programs abroad. The administration was strongly opposed to abortion and to funding any agency, domestic or international, that had anything to do with it (even if U.S. funds were not involved in abortion-related activities). NGOs active in the family-planning field feared that the administration would cut drastically or even eliminate funding for family planning abroad. To protect aid for family planning, these groups urged sympathetic members of Congress to write an "earmark" into aid appropriations that would compel the administration to spend a certain amount of funding for these purposes, whether it wanted to or not. An earmark for population activities encouraged other NGOs to press members of Congress for other earmarks (written into law) or "directives" (preferences for spending particular amounts for given purposes) included in committee reports that administration officials regard as virtually the same as an earmark.[36]

By the mid-1990s, there were earmarks and directives setting aid levels for certain countries (e.g., Israel, Egypt, and some of the countries of the former Soviet Union) and for the way aid was used, for example, child survival and basic education, microenterprise, protection of parks in peril, protection of neotropical birds, HIV/AIDS prevention, dairy development, polio eradication, environmental health, promotion of the use of micronutrients, funds for specific activities at a number of universities, and a range of other activities reflecting the personal predilections of key members of Congress, their staffs, and, often, NGOs and special-interest lobbies. And while the Development Fund for Africa was set up to provide the administration with maximum flexibility to determine the use of its aid in Africa (ironically, with its own level set as an earmark), earmarks and directives increasingly constrained the use of those resources as well. By the mid-1990s, earmarks and directives covered nearly half of development assistance resources and could not be met without using a significant proportion of monies for Africa. Reflecting on the constraints imposed by earmarks, Congressman Lee Hamilton, former chairman of the House International Relations Committee, remarked on the politics of the earmark for population programs:

> There is a very intense, well motivated, special interest group that looks upon those population account figures as the most important part of the bill. . . . They want to lock that money in, and most Members are sympathetic to that. . . . The difficulty comes not with any one of these earmarks but the multitude of them. . . . So that when you are trying to administer this program

at the country level, you find yourself all locked up, with scores of restrictions and earmarks as to how the money can be spent. . . . You don't have the kind of flexibility you need.[37]

As noted earlier, a constituency for aid to Africa took shape within the Congress during the 1970s, led by the Subcommittee on Africa of the House Foreign Affairs Committee and supported by the Congressional Black Caucus (CBC). The CBC's primary interest in Africa had been to end the apartheid regime in South Africa. But the caucus also paid attention to issues of aid—primarily the response to relief needs (to ensure that response was generous and timely) and the overall level of aid to Africa. CBC members supported high levels of aid through action in Congress and pressures on administration officials. While those pressures were influential in Democratic administrations, they were far less so in the Republican-controlled Congresses of the mid-1990s.

Outside of the Congress, NGOs and public-interest groups with an interest in foreign aid or in Africa have become numerous and an active constituency for foreign aid for development generally. It is worth spending a moment examining this broader constituency, for its activities affect the size and direction of aid to Africa. Organizations with an interest in foreign aid include those delivering aid-funded services such as disaster relief or development-related work, for example, family planning or environmental conservation abroad. There are also universities undertaking foreign-aid funded research or training, as well as civic associations like the Rotary Clubs with health or urban-renewal activities in poor countries. Some NGOs only engage in advocacy on aid-related issues, such as RESULTS, a national organization that identifies one or two issues annually on which its members throughout the country lobby members of Congress for earmarks,[38] or the America-Israel Public Affairs Committee (AIPAC), which is highly effective in influencing issues affecting Israel and, above all, in garnering support in Congress for foreign economic aid, over $1 billion of which is provided Israel each year. There is also a peak association of development NGOs, called InterAction.[39] InterAction and its roughly 150 member organizations make up the core of the constituency for development aid in the United States. InterAction itself has a secretariat, various newsletters, and standing committees. It acts as a source of information for its members on salient foreign-aid issues, attempts to coordinate those members in their lobbying efforts in Washington, lobbies on occasion on urgent development issues, and operates public-education activities on foreign aid. Its member organizations include CARE, Catholic Relief Services, the Council of Jewish Federations, The Hunger Project, Médecines sans Frontières USA, the National Wildlife Federation, Oxfam America, Save the Children, and many others.

Despite their numbers, InterAction and its member organizations suffer from several political weaknesses in their advocacy work. The coalition tends to fragment, with individual NGOs promoting congressional earmarks for their favored programs, especially when aid budgets are being cut. (Although InterAction has attempted to persuade its members to work together to lobby Congress, the organization faces classic problems of collective action and the prisoner's dilemma. It finds it difficult to energize its many diverse members to lobby Congress actively on broad, common interests like the annual aid appropriation and at the same time to keep member organizations from breaking ranks to lobby for earmarks for their particular interests. While InterAction has had increasing success in coordinating its members on major advocacy campaigns, its success has been far from complete and is not assuredly permanent.)

While InterAction and its member organizations may be larger, more sophisticated, and better organized than most of their counterparts in other aid-giving countries, they wield considerably less influence than many interest groups focused on U.S. domestic policies. Some of its members are unaccustomed to acting as advocates for aid and development, and others have proven reluctant to do so. When organizations have been willing to lobby, they have often had persuasive arguments to present to administration officials and members of Congress and their staffs in support of higher aid budgets and other issues. But thus far, they have lacked the coherence and the instruments of political pressure that make interest groups effective in the open, fragmented U.S. political system—in particular, funds to contribute to the campaigns of members of Congress, the ability and willingness to use the media to attack and embarrass members who vote against their interests,[40] and the ability to mobilize key elites in the home constituencies of important members of Congress to contact those members directly to lobby on salient issues. The development lobby in the United States is still young. It remains to be seen whether it will be able to imitate the more experienced (and better-financed) domestically oriented lobbies.

In regard to the opinion of the American public toward foreign aid, polls show several things. The American public is one of the least supportive publics of foreign aid of all the major aid-giving countries. Three-quarters of the American public thinks that the amount of foreign aid is too large, and two-thirds believes that it should be cut.[41] Moreover, the support for foreign aid among the general public and, significantly, among political elites (who have been far more supportive of foreign aid than the public), has been falling since the middle of the 1980s, and in a 1995 poll was found to be only 45 percent, the lowest since polling on foreign aid was begun in 1974.[42] The weak and declining public support for foreign aid in the United States has made the aid far more vulnerable to attack and created a much tenser and even hostile political environment in which the program must function than has been the case in most of the other countries considered in this study.

Capacity

The legal instrument that authorizes a bilateral economic aid program is the Foreign Assistance Act, first passed in 1961. This act, now many hundreds of pages long, has been amended numerous times since its original passage. Much of it has little relevance to current U.S. aid programs (involving, for example, restrictions on aid to Communist countries). Efforts to pass simpler, more relevant legislation to replace the 1961 act have failed, most recently in 1994 on the initiative of the administration (but without support from both houses of Congress) and earlier, in 1991, on the initiative of Congress but without the support of the administration. The current legislation is far from ideal, but it has proven difficult to craft new legislation with enough benefits for the administration and members of Congress to offset any costs of change (or simply of voting for a foreign-aid bill) and to create a coalition broad enough to gain passage.

Over the past two decades, successive AID administrators have issued policy documents, given congressional testimony, and made speeches setting forth their priorities for U.S. bilateral aid.[43] As noted earlier, during the administration of President Carter (1977 to 1981), these were focused on direct interventions to relieve poverty and labeled "Basic Human Needs" policies, in line with mainstream development thinking of the time. The Reagan administration eventually identified "Four Pillars" of its aid program: policy reform, reliance on the private sector, a focus on the transfer of science and technology, and support of institutional development in recipient countries. USAID under the Clinton administration published a document setting out five broad areas in which it would concentrate its activities: population and health, environment, democracy, economic growth, and humanitarian relief.[44] As with many previous policy documents, this one signaled a shift in emphasis (toward the first three of these categories and away from the fourth) rather than a fundamental change in orientation or an abandonment of past activities. It also signaled inadvertently that there was no "development paradigm" guiding its work but rather that it would pursue a broad array of activities in developing countries. Indeed, there was little in the area of development that could not be fitted into one of its five categories.

Programming Systems

USAID has one of the most elaborate and time-consuming programming systems of any aid agency. The system has been primarily country-oriented rather than oriented toward achieving crosscutting goals, for example, reducing population growth rates. It has typically required a number of reports and documents, beginning with a country-focused programming plan usually covering five to seven years, which reviews economic needs and conditions in the country and links planned programming with the agency's overall priorities. There have also been country "action plans" and annual budget submissions that provide detailed proposals of projects and programs that are intended to realize broader strategic goals. Finally, there have been a variety of documents associated with the details of specific projects and programs themselves, expected rates of return, technical considerations, and other information. One expert on USAID's programming systems demonstrated the extensive requirements of a project paper (the document describing a proposed project) as they were in the 1970s and 1980s:

> [The project paper will include] (1) the goals or objectives of the project, and the program or sector goals to which the project will contribute, in which the specific purpose of the project must be described, the intended outputs delineated and the required inputs or resources identified; (2) objectively verifiable indicators, including measures of goal achievement, conditions that will indicate at the end of the project that the purpose has been achieved, the magnitude of outputs and type and quantity of implementation targets; (3) means by which the indicators can be verified; and (4) important assumptions concerning the ability to achieve goals and targets, project purposes, and outputs and the means of providing inputs. . . . The project paper also had to assess the project's cost and benefit implications and implementation requirements . . . to include (1) a description of the recipient government's administrative arrangements for im-

plementing the project, and an assessment of the implementing agency's potential for providing leadership, resources, commitment and "grass roots" management; (2) an implementation plan that outlines responsibilities for actions within the implementing agency and describes its relationship with other government organizations; (3) a network chart that shows the scheduling of activities over time and identifies milestones for measuring success or progress; (4) a description and discussion of potential problems or weaknesses about which reforms or policy changes should be negotiated with the government; (5) a description of proposed monitoring and evaluation techniques; (6) an analysis of logistical support required for implementation; and (7) a description of evaluation arrangements including plans for host government collaboration in evaluation, collecting baseline data, supervising progress and training evaluators.[45]

Attempts have been made to simplify programming since the time this description was written, by creating a "strategic-planning process" in which USAID missions identify several broad strategic objectives, subobjectives, results to be achieved, and indicators of those results. It appears from USAID officials that in fact the new approaches have had little if any impact on the complexities of programming. Officials in the field, for example, estimate that fully 80 percent of their time is occupied solely with these processes. And the programming process is only one part of an extensive set of documentation associated with the operation of the agency.

Once a program or project is completed (for projects, this can take as much as seven years), USAID's Center for Information and Evaluation may undertake an impact evaluation of the project, usually together with similar projects elsewhere. The findings of impact evaluations are broadly circulated throughout the agency, but it appears that the impact of those evaluations on USAID officials designing and managing projects and programs has been limited.[46]

Despite the efforts to elaborate systematic programming systems, in 1994 USAID was sharply criticized by the General Accounting Office (an arm of the U.S. government) and other management experts for "serious accountability and control problems."[47] The GAO and others complained that the agency's decentralized field organization had led to a lack of overall policy and program coherence and an inability to measure the impact of its activities abroad. As a result of these criticisms and of the passage in 1993 of the Government Performance and Results Act, USAID began to require its field missions and bureaus to identify not only strategic objectives but measurable indicators of the results of their activities and to enable decision-makers to allocate resources according to performance. "Managing for results" is intended to achieve other goals besides enhancing USAID's accountability to the U.S. taxpayer. It is also intended to increase the focus of agency staff on the outcomes of their activities rather than on the size of their program and project expenditures. As with other aid agencies in this study, professional satisfaction and advancement in USAID has often turned on the abilities of managers to spend available monies. The focus on the impact of their expenditures has been far less, undoubtedly contributing to many of the problems of effectiveness identified here.[48]

At first glance, a focus on managing for results must be applauded. There seems to be little question that the past focus on obligating funds has eclipsed a concern for the impact of those funds, in USAID and in other aid agencies. And yet, this change raises several fundamental questions about the efficacy of programming systems like USAID's for promoting effective development. First of all, are these systems compatible with the nature of the task they attempt to achieve—promoting development, often involving complex changes in foreign societies? And are they compatible with the political realities and constraints on the allocation of foreign aid in the United States—in particular, congressional earmarks and directives?

By the mid-1990s, USAID's portfolio of activities abroad included a broad array of what we have referred to earlier as "complex interventions," often involving social and political as well as economic changes in recipient countries. The means of accomplishing some of these activities are known, for example, the strengthening of family-planning services. But technologies for many of them are not well established, for example, how to strengthen civil society. To develop those technologies and to ensure that aid-funded activities respond to real needs and conditions in recipient countries, those activities need to be designed and implemented flexibly, in concert with local experts and intended beneficiaries. This approach has proven to be incompatible with the control-oriented programming systems of the past and may also prove so with the system of "managing for results" that is evolving.

The second question is also a troubling one. We have already noted the increasing constraints imposed by congressional earmarks. Those constraints can make a mockery of USAID's programming system, in which field managers propose programs and projects they regard as appropriate to the development of their countries. I have observed several years in succession when months of document preparation, presentation, and discussion on the proposed aid budget for a country are at the last minute made irrelevant because a certain amount of money to meet a congressionally imposed earmark or directive or for a purpose judged politically important (or to meet an administration-generated objective) has to be spent in a particular country whether it fits into budget proposals and strategic objectives or not. This is a second serious misfit between programming systems and political realities.

Staffing

As of 1994, USAID had a direct-hire workforce of just over three thousand.[49] (When foreign nationals and personal service contractors are included, the workforce totals over nine thousand.) The staff-to-expenditure ratio of less than $1 million per direct-hire official compares favorably to the staff-to-expenditure ratio of other major aid agencies.[50] USAID staff have the responsibility of setting broad policy and program directions in their countries, often providing technical direction to the design of projects, participating in the programming process, monitoring the management of projects, and relating to government officials, private individuals and groups, and representatives of other aid agencies within their countries if they are posted abroad. They rarely deliver services themselves to recipient governments, except through their involvement in policy discussions. Aid staff are typically "wholesalers" rather than "retailers," making the agency dependent on the various intermediaries with which it works for the implementation (and often the design) of its programs, including contracting firms, NGOs, universities, individual experts, even other agencies of the U.S. government. As a result, USAID staff, even in the field, are often at least one step removed from the direct implementation of their activities.

Organization

Little of what has thus far been described significantly distinguishes USAID from other aid agencies. Most are based on legislation or have published white papers articulating broad goals. Most have programming and evaluation systems. Most rely on intermediaries (contractors, NGOs, universities) to deliver technical advice, other services, or goods. What USAID claims as its most exceptional quality is its field missions. These are in essence offices in the field with a director, program managers, technical specialists, administrative officers, and at times lawyers and procurement officers, located in countries where there are aid programs and responsible for designing and implementing those programs. During the 1990s, USAID had roughly seventy offices or "missions" abroad. What makes USAID's field missions different from the field representatives of other aid agencies is the number of officers it locates in the field and the degree of authority it gives them over the choice, design, approval, and implementation of aid-financed activities in their countries or regions (within the policy and programming parameters set by Washington, described above). According to an evaluation of USAID's field presence based primarily on interviews with officials of USAID and other aid agencies, the field presence brings enhanced influence in recipient countries and accountability to the beneficiaries of projects and programs.[51] The close working relationships USAID officers develop with their local counterparts lead to a "better understanding of local conditions; political and cultural sensitivity; ready access to host-country officials; sustained, day-to-day involvement in the process of policy reform; keeping development on the U.S. government's agenda; and more effective promotion of sensitive issues, such as family planning and environmental protection."[52] USAID's field presence is the organizational strength of the agency most frequently mentioned by its career staff.

Conclusion

While USAID has some important developmental achievements to its credit in Africa, the effectiveness of its aid in supporting development has suffered from problems both of limited autonomy and limited capacity. A significant proportion of the aid has been provided to governments lacking the commitment or capacity to promote development in their own countries, several of which have subsequently collapsed. Aid to these governments has been lost, from a development point of view, and appears likely to have prolonged the policies and behavior that led those countries to ruin.

USAID has also suffered from limitations on its capacity where the agency has tried to bring about policy, behavioral, or institutional changes, especially where the concrete benefits of those changes were not quickly available to those whose behavior it wanted to change. It appears that the factors limiting USAID's capacity were two: cumbersome programming procedures that did not fit well with the types of activities funded; and limitations on technical and local knowledge needed to design and implement those activities. There is still only limited technical knowledge—even after thirty years of effort—on how effectively to bring about institutional changes in foreign countries. Policy changes, it is now recognized, frequently require political changes, especially if they are to be sustained; and donors are still learning about the political dimension of policy reforms. In addition, all these types of interventions require considerable local knowledge and flexibility in their design and implementation, including the ability to terminate them.

USAID's programming systems are based on the assumption that the means to achieve strategic and programmatic goals are known, and applying this knowledge (appropriately tailored to local conditions) will produce measurable results in a given time frame. For much of what USAID does, this may be a fair assumption. But for the projects and programs involving institutional, behavioral, and policy change, this is not an accurate assumption, confirming at least in part the hypothesis presented in chapter 4 that the misfit between the programming systems and the nature of the tasks has limited the effectiveness of aid.

The existence of large field missions with delegated authorities has not ensured an effective aid program, contradicting another of the hypotheses in chapter 4. Why is that? One reason is that USAID officers often serve in a single post for only three or four years, usually just enough to begin to understand another, very different culture—or in Africa's ethnically diverse societies, a mix of very different cultures. In Africa, few USAID officials speak local languages (though most speak some French in Francophone countries), usually essential for a truly intimate knowledge of the local environment. It is also often the case that the extensive reporting requirements to Washington occupy much of the time of officials, preventing them from spending more time learning about the country they serve in or overseeing their projects and programs. Further, those most involved in implementing aid projects are not USAID staff but contractors or NGOs. While the local and technical knowledge of these individuals can be substantial, this is not always the case. And USAID often has little control over who is selected for these responsibilities. They are chosen by the firms and NGOs selected by USAID to implement and, at times, to design its activities.

Finally, it is also possible that a sizable field mission creates its own bureaucratic distractions, further limiting the advantages of its presence in the field. The evaluation of USAID's in-country presence, cited above, makes the following observation: "Many of the large and medium-sized Missions have become mini-AID/Ws [replicating headquarters in Washington] with their own internal bureaucracies. The need for review by, and clearances from, a bevy of procedural specialists tends to constrain the flexibility, quick decision-making and risktaking that decentralization was designed to promote."[53] Another evaluation suggests that "the effectiveness of AID's African missions . . . has been constrained by many pressures. Foremost among these is the pressure to obligate appropriated funds in a timely manner. Other significant constraints arise from pressures to select and package activities in accordance with the current policy climate in Washington; to comply with ever-increasing, complex, and time-consuming documentation, contracting, and procurement requirements. . . . it is simply not practical to engage in extensive analysis or to explore alternative projects in more than cursory fashion."[54] In short, USAID's development work in Africa—though not without important achievements—has suffered from many of the problems of aid effectiveness described in chapter 3. The agency's autonomy—constrained by the Department of State and, increasingly, by Congress—and the process-based limitations on its capacity go far to explain the problems with the effectiveness of its aid in Africa.

Chapter Six

France and Britain

The two principal colonial powers in Africa were France and Britain. Foreign aid for both of them has been an instrument of their postcolonial diplomacy as well as a means of bolstering development in the region. Yet their postcolonial policies, the nature of their aid programs, and the impact of their aid on development have been very different.

France

France has long been the largest single source of foreign aid in Africa. For much of the 1990s, it provided between $2.5 and $3 billion per year to the region. French aid in Africa has its origins in the relationships between Paris and its African colonies during the colonial period. (These colonies include the now independent countries of Benin, Burkina Faso, Cameroon, Central African Republic, Chad, Comoros, Congo [Brazzaville], Djibouti, Gabon, Guinea, Ivory Coast, Mali, Madagascar, Mauritania, Senegal, Seychelles, and Togo.) France's African colonies enhanced the worldwide grandeur of the metropole as well as the glory of French civilization and language. The rhetoric of French colonial policies emphasized the permanence of political ties between France and its territories south of the Sahara and the assimilation of African elites into French society. But in fact, only a small African elite was ever assimilated, and once other African countries demanded and received their independence, it was only a matter of time before Francophone Africans would do the same.

After the Second World War, the government of France began to provide subsidies for the development of infrastructure and education in its African colonies. As decolonization became a subject for discussion in the late 1950s, French officials, intending no doubt to discourage the temptation of independence, rejected the idea of continuing any assistance should those colonies claim their freedom. French president de Gaulle, in a speech before the famous referendum in 1958 in which France's African territories were given the opportunity to choose increased autonomy within a "French Community" or independence, warned, "One cannot conceive of an independent territory and a France continuing to help it."[1]

However, Paris had underestimated the strength of African nationalism. In the 1958 referendum, a majority of the population of one French territory—Guinea—voted *non* to membership in a French Community, opting for immediate independence. Guinea was quickly granted independence by a disappointed and angry French government, which immediately withdrew its officials and terminated its aid. It was not long, however, before other French colonies quietly sought independence from Paris. In 1960, the French government agreed, granted its remaining colonies in west and central Africa their independence, and initiated (or continued) aid programs in all of them.

Which Countries to Aid?

The goal of French diplomacy in Africa has long been to maintain French influence in its former territories—in the words of several French scholars, "to transform a space of sovereignty into a zone of influence."[2] As a result, half of France's bilateral aid worldwide has been concentrated in Africa, and most of that in France's former colonies and other Francophone countries of the region (including the former Belgian colonies of the Congo, Rwanda, and Burundi).

It is important to understand why France sought a zone of influence in Africa. French postwar diplomacy has consistently pursued two major goals: legitimizing France's claim to great-power status, and promoting the prominence of French language and culture. Another, less important motivation has been to ensure that French business interests retain preferential treatment in the markets of France's former African territories.

French governments, going back to the turn of the century, have aspired to the status of a major world power, first as a neighbor to a more powerful Germany in Europe and, after the Second World War, in a world of two superpowers—the United States and the USSR. France's claim to a seat at the high table of world politics has rested in part on its influence beyond its borders through the country's colonial empire, and after that empire was lost, through France's claim to leadership of a bloc of Third World countries—primarily those of Francophone Africa. In *France in Africa* John Chipman observed that "for the last hundred years or so, the importance of Africa to France has been in the fact that France's political leadership has consistently used the nature of France's sway over parts of the continent to help define the power of France."[3]

A second major goal motivating French policies in its former African territories has been cultural: supporting the use of the French language and the acceptance of French culture beyond the borders of France. The French speak of a *besoin de rayonnement,* literally a "need to shine"—an urge to have the glories of French culture and the French language recognized throughout the world and its language widely spoken. While this may sound like cultural narcissism to an Anglo-Saxon ear, it is extremely important to the French (including the French public), and without taking it into account, it is difficult to understand the motivations of French diplomacy, the concentration of French aid in Africa, and the way that aid has been used. Former president Pompidou articulated the *besoin de rayonnement:*

> Of all countries, France has held most profoundly to the export of its language and culture. That trait is truly unique to us. When a Frenchman in a foreign country meets someone else who speaks French, who has read French literature, he has the impression of finding a brother. This the ambition of our intellect, perhaps our genius. Our cooperation [i.e., economic aid] is without doubt oriented and should be oriented fundamentally towards expanding our language and our culture.[4]

France's goal of maintaining itself as the predominant foreign partner of Francophone African governments and ensuring the continued visibility of French language and culture produced a measure of paranoia in Paris about the influence of other foreign governments, above all that of the United States. The United States, as a great power with ample resources, could easily establish a sphere of influence for itself in Francophone Africa if it chose, eclipsing that of France and offering the Africans an alternative foreign partner. French paranoia about American intentions in Africa had been aroused early on by the pressures from President Roosevelt and Congress on the Europeans to decolonize after the Second World War. And when France did grant independence to its African territories, the United States immediately set up embassies and initiated aid programs in most of these countries, confirming some of the worst fears of the French, who reacted subtly but effectively to discourage an expansion in U.S. influence in their former territories, for example, by supporting African governments' efforts to limit the freedom of movement of American diplomats and aid officials. It was not entirely in jest that observers of the African scene during the 1960s used to say (according to Kaye Whiteman, the former editor of *West Africa* magazine) that "the real concealed cold war in Africa was between the Americans and the French."[5] Many French officials have also been leery of the growing influence of the World Bank in Africa, in part because it is often viewed as an "Anglo-Saxon institution," potentially unfriendly to the interests of France and not always fully informed on conditions in African countries. It was clear to the French that if they were to protect their predominant influence, they needed to provide the Africans with substantial amounts of aid, requiring them to concentrate that aid in their former territories.

The concentration of French aid in Francophone African countries has continued over the past three and a half decades despite the recommendations of a series of reviews (commissioned by the French government) that France distribute its aid more in line with its economic engagements abroad. The Jenneneay Report of 1963, the Gorse Report of 1971, the Hessel Report of 1990, and the Fuchs Report of 1994 all recommended that future increases in French aid be provided to countries in Asia and Latin America where France has greater economic interests or which play an important role in world affairs.[6] The French government has consistently ignored the recommendations, and in several cases, it has refused even to publish the reports. During the 1990s, just under half of all French aid was provided to countries of Africa, and three-quarters of that went to the fourteen countries of the Franc zone plus the Democratic Republic of the Congo.[7]

How Much Aid to Provide?

The diplomatic purposes of French aid—the clear and continuing commitment of the French government to maintain its predominant influence in its former African territories—are the primary factors explaining the choice of countries that received it. Those purposes have also been predominant in determining how much aid particular countries have received. Specifically, the influence of two considerations is evident in decisions on the levels of aid to particular countries: the level of aid required to maintain a privileged relationship (which must usually be significantly greater than the aid from alternative sources), and the priority of the country in France's African diplomacy. Foreign aid, as we have already noted, is a little like political campaign contributions: it can facilitate the access of those providing it to those receiving it. And larger amounts of aid, particularly combined with other military, economic, and political ties (as in the case of Francophone Africa), will usually ensure that representatives of the donor government are taken very seriously by the recipient. In Ivory Coast, for example, French aid during the 1990s was usually double all other aid combined.[8] In Senegal, French aid was typically three times larger than the next highest source of assistance.[9] In Cameroon, French aid was almost always the largest, usually by a considerable margin.[10] The same is true for Guinea, Burkina Faso, Mali, and others.

The most important African country for France and its key partner in much of its diplomatic efforts in the region has been the Ivory Coast—especially during the decades when Houphouët-Boigny (who died in 1993) was president. The Ivory Coast was among the larger and more successful economically of France's former African territories and one of the most influential African countries. For a time, France had significant investments in the country and a significant number of expatriates living there. Finally, the president of the Ivory Coast had served as a minister in the French government before the independence period and had close personal and political relationships with a number of French political leaders. France has typically provided over half of total concessional aid flows to Ivory Coast. Other key diplomatic partners for France have been Gabon, Senegal, and Cameroon (as table 6 suggests). None of these is among Africa's poorest countries. The political element in French aid is particularly evident in the level of its aid to Gabon (averaging $100 million per year during the late 1980s and early 1990s)[11]—one of Africa's smallest countries, but because of its oil, Africa's richest country (with an average per capita income of $3,800 in 1995).

France has also on occasion used its aid for symbolic purposes. While it has rarely cut its aid sharply to demonstrate its discontent with recipient governments (except in the famous case of Guinea), it has used its aid aggressively to strengthen relationships with Francophone countries wishing to restore close ties with Paris after periods of hostility. French aid to Mali, for example, remained relatively low during much of the period after independence when a succession of socialist-oriented governments in Bamako were leery of too much reliance on Paris. But with the reentry of Mali into the Franc zone in 1984, French aid quadrupled,

Table 6. Top Five Recipients of French Aid to Africa

1970–71	1980–81	1994–95
Ivory Coast	Senegal	Ivory Coast
Madagascar	Ivory Coast	Cameroon
Senegal	Cameroon	Senegal
Gabon	Central African Republic	Congo
Cameroon	Gabon	Burkina Faso

Source: Development Assistance Committee, *Development Cooperation* (Paris: Organization for Economic Cooperation and Development, 1997), p. A73.

primarily to finance the costs of rejoining the franc zone but also as a reward for Mali's return to the French fold. The same pattern is evident in French aid to Guinea, which increased tenfold between 1984 and 1985, just after the death of Sekou Toure and the ensuing resurgence of France's diplomatic and economic presence in that country.

The Use of French Aid

Diplomatic concerns, so important in the allocation of French aid, also influenced the way French aid was used. Much of the aid was for budgetary support, providing African governments with considerable flexibility in its use. And a considerable portion was for technical assistance and teachers—ensuring French influence throughout African governments and the use of French in the educational systems. Technical assistance and budgetary support amounted to nearly two-thirds of French aid to Africa during the first half of the 1960s.[12] The remainder was provided for a wide range of activities, including projects in agriculture, forestry, fishing, mines, power, infrastructure, health, and research. To give an example, in one year in Guinea, the French government financed activities in the following areas: budgetary support, teachers, scholarships for Guineans to study in France, village well building, soil restoration, teacher education, vocational education, rural credit, forestry, public health, airport management, coffee, rice and fruit production, communications, road improvements in Conakry (the capital), partial financing of state enterprises involving tobacco production, aluminum production and transport, and research by a variety of French institutes in Guinea.[13]

During the 1980s and 1990s, in response to deepening foreign-exchange crises in the region, France again increased its financing for balance-of-payments and budgetary support, often paying the salaries of civil servants African governments could not afford to pay and the external debts (for example, to the World Bank) they could no longer finance. But the deepening balance-of-payments problems were, in fact, a direct result of another French policy—supporting the overvalued CFA franc.

Fourteen African countries are members of a common monetary union with a currency (the CFA franc) tied to the French franc at a fixed rate and backed by the French treasury. By the mid-1980s, it was clear that the CFA franc was seriously overvalued, inhibiting the exports and encouraging the imports of CFA countries, widening their balance-of-payments gaps, causing a serious economic depression, and undercutting the effectiveness of aid in stimulating economic growth. It was also forcing the French treasury to transfer an increasingly large amount of resources to Africa—estimated to reach $1 billion in 1993 alone—to support the CFA franc.[14] Officials from the Treasury, from the Ministry of Cooperation, and other agencies also recognized the need for a devaluation. But the political leadership in both France and Africa continued to resist the idea. While some of this resistance was based on genuine fear on the part of French and African officials about the impact of a devaluation on African economies,[15] much of it appears to have been based on political symbolism and personal interests. A devaluation of the CFA franc could be seen as the beginning of the end of the franc zone and a step by France away from its African clients. It is also pertinent that an overvalued CFA franc made the imports enjoyed by African political elites cheaper, including consumer goods, trips abroad, and education in France for their children.

Three factors finally led to a devaluation of the CFA in January 1994: the termination by the World Bank of most of its aid to Francophone African countries (and so, increasing the financial pressures on France to support them), the death of Houphouët-Boigny of the Ivory Coast, who had strongly opposed a devaluation, and the influence of Prime Minister Balladur, who, in contrast to most French politicians, had relatively few African ties but had recognized the serious financial drain on France of subsidizing the CFA franc. The reluctance of the French government to devalue the CFA franc, despite its increasing cost to Paris and to development in Africa, underlines the continuing preponderance of diplomatic and political factors in France's Africa policies and the impact of those factors on its aid and development in the region.

Developmental Effectiveness of French Aid

From several perspectives, French aid is potentially the most effective development aid in Africa.[16] Not only is France the largest and most influential donor in the countries it aids, but its aid officials are often among the most experienced in Africa. Yet evaluations suggest that French aid has frequently been ineffective.

First, decisions on where to allocate aid and, at times, how it should be used have been driven by diplomatic and political goals, with the result (in the view of the French government itself) that aid has been wasted, has at times encouraged policies and behavior inimical to development, and has inhibited a more professional management of the aid by France. For example, one evaluation by the French government of the impact of its aid in an African country[17]—Burkina Faso—made the following observation:

> The funding of grand and costly projects together with often modest results have equally marked our aid. . . . It is certain that these projects are undertaken as a result of an essentially political decision. . . . But outside political decisions, French aid has been led, through numerous technical studies initiated by its own services and through a poorly controlled decision-making process, to promote, with [African] nationals and others, projects that were highly questionable, notably in the rural sector.[18]

The impact of political and diplomatic interests on the developmental effectiveness of aid is referred to in other evaluations by the French government. An extract from a confidential review of its aid in several African countries observed,

> During the 1980s, the government of France's development aid as well as our military and political assistance for CFA states appears to [have been aimed at] safeguarding political and socioeconomic stability rather than supporting indispensable change. Diversity of views at the Ministry of Cooperation, the weak degree of transparency and the poor quality in the choice, objectives, and conditions for carrying out aid projects largely result from the diversity of agencies involved in our programs. . . . This diversity and lack of transparency in our aid permits a "certain irresponsibility" by Government of France agencies and nationals. . . . France has for too long contributed to the reproduction of social, economic, and political systems that are clientist and predatory, by governments and dominant social groups—as well as accepting lax behavior.[19]

Not surprisingly, information is not available on how much of France's aid (alone or, more commonly, together with other policies of the French government) has had the impact described in these citations. One way to begin to get a sense of the size of France's more "politically oriented" aid is to separate out budgetary aid—the most flexible and the most easily used to finance political favors—from the rest. One study of French aid to Africa in 1986 showed that approximately 10 percent of that aid was in the form of budgetary transfers. (Others have suggested that much of the aid from the Ministry of Cooperation—one of France's two aid agencies working in Africa—is tied to political favors. Aid from the Ministry of Cooperation in 1986 was roughly half of total French aid to Africa.)[20]

In addition to significant amounts of budgetary aid, France provided aid for technical assistance and for projects. One of the principal elements of French aid has been the large amount of technical assistance to former colonies from the beginning of their independence. French *cooperants*—technical advisors, teachers, doctors, administrators—numbered nearly 10,500 just after independence, until starting to decline in number at the beginning of the 1980s, to just over 4,000 by the beginning of the 1990s.[21] In addition to paying most of the cost of their services, France often provided them with funds to spend to ensure the success of their particular activities. Reflecting on the pervasive presence and influence of the *cooperants* together with French officials in Francophone Africa, a senior French aid official once remarked to me, "In Africa, we asked the questions, and we gave the answers."

In 1994 an evaluation of technical assistance, commissioned by the Ministry of Cooperation, found that while *cooperants'* advice and services had been valuable, they had some serious disadvantages. Because assistance was provided over an extended period at a very low cost to African governments, it masked the real expense of the services it delivered, encouraging Africans, for example, to expand higher education beyond their priority needs or their own resources. (The cost of education in Francophone Africa has been exceptionally high, equal in one estimate to a lifetime's earnings for graduates.[22] Because students do not pay for higher education and even receive living expenses, the cost to the government is especially high and draws off large amounts of funds from primary education, which is widely recognized as the highest priority for poorer, less literate countries.) Further, French assistance also encouraged the expansion of university faculties—for example, literature—not necessarily appropriate to local needs. The study found that French *cooperants,* in effect managing many governmental activities, encouraged the hiring and promotion of Africans who were often neither adequately prepared or experienced to assume the real responsibilities of their jobs. Finally, the report found that the volume and continuation of French technical assistance contributed to an avoidance of needed reforms and of an adjustment of expenditures to available resources on the part of African governments.[23]

Let us turn to evaluations of other aid-funded activities in Africa. The Caisse Française de Développement (CFD)—another of France's aid agencies active in Africa—undertakes a number of evaluations each year of its projects in Africa and elsewhere. A survey of the summaries of the findings of these evaluations in *La Lettre de l'évaluation* (published by the CFD) and its monthly report, *Projets de développement* (beginning in January, 1996), shows a pattern of attaining the physical goals of the projects (e.g., the rehabilitation of infrastructure or refinancing of an enterprise), combined with inadequacies on the institutional side—especially the management by African institutions responsible for helping to implement the project. A telecommunications project in the Ivory Coast illustrates this pattern. The objective of the project was to double the telephone service in a cost-effective and financially sustainable manner. The physical goal was more than realized. But the project suffered from delays and cost overruns, and its commercial objectives were not met. As a result, the new capacity was underutilized, while the local management continued to be weak.[24] In another case, in which the CFD undertook to rehabilitate the Water and Electricity Utility of Chad, the physical goals of rehabilitation were attained within the budget planned. But the project proved to be nonviable because of institutional weaknesses of the utility, including financial management and maintenance of facilities.[25]

Finally, the contribution of France to the broader discourse on development in Africa appears to have been limited. There were few significant studies or reports by French development experts on African development that broke new ground or had a significant influence on major aid donors or on African governments, and French experts played a relatively small role in debates on structural adjustment, democratization, or capacity building among aid agencies and their African counterparts.

To sum up, the limits on the developmental effectiveness of French aid in Africa involve both problems associated with support of the political status quo in many of its recipient countries and problems of design and implementation of aid activities themselves, especially where the success of those projects relied on the performance of African institutions. The French played little role in the broader development discourse in the region.

The Future of French Aid

At the annual Francophone-African summit in 1990, French president Mitterrand warned that in allocating its aid in the future, France would take into account the evolution toward democracy on the part of its African partners. This statement was seen at the time as a watershed in French policies (in particular, aid policies) vis-à-vis Africa, signaling that France was willing to base its aid on the performance of recipient governments in the political realm even at the cost of souring relationships with particular African leaders or of destabilizing regimes. But subsequent events proved that this was not to be. France continued to aid African governments—for example, Togo, Cameroon, and Gabon—whether they were making real progress toward democracy or not. In the wake of a military coup in Niger in 1996, France first stopped its aid and then resumed aiding the new military regime. French aid has continued to support a diplomacy of predominance and stability.

Other signs of change in French aid also proved chimerical. A long planning exercise that took place within the French government in 1995 proposed wide-ranging reforms in France's foreign aid, including a full-fledged merger of the Ministry of Cooperation (long responsible for aid to France's former colonies, primarily in Africa) with the Ministry of Foreign Affairs, ending the special treatment afforded Francophone African countries. (The head of the Ministry of Cooperation has, in fact, long reported to the Minister of Foreign Affairs. But Cooperation has remained a separate organization, and the deputy minister who heads it has retained a measure of independence.) However, in 1995, African leaders and French officials continuing to favor the privileged diplomatic and aid relationships for Francophone Africans (which the Ministry of Cooperation had come to symbolize), together with officials from the Ministry of Cooperation who opposed the merger for their own bureaucratic reasons, combined to persuade President Chirac to turn down proposals for reform. Chirac announced at the Franco-African Summit in 1995 that "as long as I'm president, there will be an independent Ministry of Cooperation."[26] He went on to say that "France has no intention of disengaging from the field of development, or modifying the privileged character of its relations with certain African countries." Later, in 1997, the newly elected Socialist government declared that in Africa "the time of the networks is over" and that France needed to "normalize its relations with Africa" and promised a rethinking of the organization and functioning of its aid agencies.[27] In February 1998, the Socialist government approved a reorganization of France's aid bureaucracy. The new arrangements did not (as previously promised by the Socialists in the 1997 election) involve the merger of the CFD and the Ministry of Cooperation and other aid programs into a single aid agency. Rather, the Ministry of Cooperation would be "absorbed" into the Foreign Ministry, with the Cooperation minister retaining his portfolio and the right to sit in on cabinet meetings. The changes were accompanied by commitments to impose stricter financial and political controls on aid to Africa and to condition that aid more on the performance of recipients. It is not clear how real or extensive these changes are. What is clear is a heightened sensitivity on the part of the Socialist government to criticisms of French aid in Africa for being ineffective, incoherent, politically driven, and corrupt.

The constraints on France's budget for assistance are tightening, and these too may have contributed to a restiveness about the country's aid in Africa. Like other members of the European Union, France had to conform to the Treaty of Maastricht if it was to participate in the European Monetary Union. The members of the European Union agreed to cut their budgetary deficits to no more than 3 percent of GNP by 1998, when the common currency would be established. For nearly all member states, this meant years of cutting government expenditures, including expenditures on foreign aid. The French government, in implementing its budget in 1995, cut the budget of the Ministry of Cooperation by a modest $10 million (out of $1.4 billion total). This cut followed a small reduction in the ministry's budget the previous year and has been followed by small cuts in subsequent years. These reductions are not sizeable in any one year and tend to be less than cuts in other forms of French aid. But they have contributed to a significant decline in the level of French aid to Africa during the 1990s—by $1 billion between 1994 and 1996[28]—and they signal that aid to Africa is not untouchable and may well continue to fall in the future.

Analysis

Autonomy

The most important factor explaining the strong diplomatic and political orientation of French aid in Africa is the high priority relationships with its former African colonies have held for successive French presidents. And ensuring that aid and other policies support those relationships has been the advisor to the president on African affairs, a post created by President de Gaulle and occupied by a series of influential individuals, beginning with the late Jacques Foccart, with his considerable expertise and extensive personal contacts in Africa.[29]

Another factor in the strongly political orientation of French aid in Africa has been the highly fragmented nature of France's aid programs.

The two principal sources of French aid to Africa are the Ministry of Cooperation, which provides grants for activities largely in the social sector as well as budgetary support, and the Caisse Française de Développement, which provides concessional credits for projects in agriculture, infrastructure, and industry.

The Ministry of Cooperation has long had as its principal focus France's former colonies in Africa and the Caribbean—nicknamed *le champs* by the French. (That field has now expanded to include all members of the Lome Convention in Africa, the Caribbean, and the Pacific, but the primary focus remains on Francophone Africa.) The ministry is headed by a political appointee (often with little experience in development or in Africa) and frequently takes its instructions from the African advisor to the president. The French government is the only one in this study that has an advisor to the president on Africa, reflecting the importance it ascribes to its relationships in the region and providing the Africans with a direct channel of communications to the president. The ministry has been the principal source of politically motivated aid to Africa.

The CFD, usually headed by a civil servant, regards itself as a professional development organization rather than a political one. According to one former senior official, it has sought successfully to protect its autonomy through its complicated programming process (much as USAID has done) and through playing off other agencies (especially the Treasury and the Ministry of Cooperation) against one another.[30]

A multitude of other agencies of the French government provide aid to Africa. The Treasury (part of the Ministry of Finance) provides balance-of-payments support, the Ministry of Research is active in African countries, the Ministry of Education provides support to education, and other ministries—Agriculture, Interior, Defense—all fund activities. As noted earlier, in the mid-1980s an expert on French aid added up the amount of that aid for sub-Saharan Africa and showed that the Ministry of Cooperation provided just over half of it with the Caisse providing another quarter.[31] The rest was provided by eight other ministries.

The fragmentation in the organization of aid has led to a certain incoherence and duplication within the program. And the distribution of responsibilities for development among a variety of agencies weakens support for a strong development program within the government. No single agency can speak for France's development policies, and no single agency is responsible for them. The government has long been aware of the fragmentation of its aid organization. The problem was pointed out in the Jenneneay Report of 1963 and the Gorse Report of 1971, both recommending that aid be centralized in a single institution. A later effort to reform the organization and functioning of French aid by Jean-Pierre Cot, the first minister of cooperation under the Mitterand government in 1982, was only partially implemented and then reversed (in part due to the active and effective opposition to the reforms on the part of key African leaders).[32] Another report commissioned by the French government on its aid (the Hessel Report), completed in 1990, made the same recommendations for reform as have several after that. In 1993, the minister of cooperation supported the centralization of French aid in a single agency in a speech to the National Assembly.[33] Reforms under consideration in 1995 but later set aside by French leaders included a reorganization of France's aid system to ensure greater coherence. French political leaders have consistently ignored or rejected such recommendations. In 1996, the French government set up an interagency coordinating committee on development aid. And in 1998, as mentioned above, the new Socialist government announced a set of organizational changes in its aid program. A number of these changes were intended to address the problems of French aid, but it is too soon to say whether they will, in fact, do so or whether the new policies are really a case, as in the past, of *plus ça change*.

It must be asked why the French government tolerates such a fragmented aid system. Bureaucratic inertia based on support for the status quo by interests inside and outside government is undoubtedly part of the answer. But there is likely a further reason. The current arrangement fits the need of the French government to mobilize easily the concessional resources needed to back up its political and diplomatic goals. Funds have been in the past deployed for a variety of purposes that would be difficult to classify as developmental—providing last minute financing for a Franco-African summit, increasing the education budget of an African government so that it could persuade students to return to classes by paying their fees—in short, responding to a variety of pleas for help and favors from African leaders close to Paris, an arrangement one observer has termed *"cousinage et copainage"*—that is, helping friends and relatives. Thus, the strongly political nature of French aid in Africa may explain the continuing fragmentation in the organization of aid and the consequent weak voice for development goals within the councils of the French government.

As for other organizations or groups, the National Assembly plays almost no role in overseeing or influencing aid. It does, of course, appropriate the funding for aid programs. But it has rarely hosted active debates on aid and has had little impact on its allocation or use. Thus, the French government's accountability to the legislature and the public for the use and effectiveness of its development aid in Africa has been weak, another factor explaining its politicization and developmental ineffectiveness.

Supporting the use of French aid in Africa to further national political and commercial goals has been an informal network of current and former French government officials, members of political parties, and businessmen with an interest in Africa. This group is often referred to as the "Africa lobby" in France or the "Franco-African village."[34] There are said to be "clans" within this lobby, for instance, former *cooperants* who served in Madagascar with a particular interest in that country or individuals connected with Gabon who remain in close contact and collaborate on policy issues vis-à-vis Gabon.[35] The goals of the lobby typically include protecting the status quo in French relations with Africa (including close relationships with African leaders), a continuing preponderance of French influence in the region, and, at times, advancing particular business, political, or personal interests.

Also players in France's Africa policies are African leaders themselves, whose personal relationships with an array of French public figures, including most senior members of the French political class (from all parties), give them exceptional access and an opportunity to lobby at the highest levels on issues of importance to them. Some of this access likely derives from the contributions a number of African heads of state are believed to have made to French political parties. Professor Stefan Brune, a German scholar of French aid, has observed that "apart from the newly-founded ecological parties, all the French parties have had access to quite considerable funds from Africa to finance election campaigns. Le Pen's journeys to Gabon, more or less discrete donations by Gnassingbe Eyadema (Togo) and Houphouët-Boigny's open support for Jacques Chirac should be mentioned in this context."[36] If France exerts considerable influence in African capitals, the Africans also wield significant influence in Paris, often through direct interventions with the French president.[37]

Turning specifically to French business interests in Francophone Africa, it must be recognized that these represent only a small proportion of French investment or trade abroad. But they do include some powerful firms which are accustomed to promoting their interests with the French government, for example, Elf Aquitaine (the large French oil company, formerly owned by the French government), Dassault,

Thompson, Alcatel, and others, as well as numerous smaller firms involved in activities aimed at local African markets. Many French firms protected from competition by trade restrictions and other regulations favoring them in African countries would, it is often said, be uncompetitive if their monopolies were lost. And it is widely believed that these firms have not been hesitant to call upon the French government (and French aid) for help on issues of importance to them.

All of these groups constitute a powerful constituency in favor of France's "traditional" role as the patron of Francophone regimes in Africa. On the other side, in favor of a normalization in France's diplomatic relations with Africa and a more development-oriented program is a group of technocrats in the French government, scholars of Africa, journalists, and a small group of NGOs. They are often referred to as the *modernistes*. The number of NGOs operating in the development field has grown over the past several years and exceeds several hundred. However, many of the NGOs remain small in size and very limited in their activities (for example, involving the provision of small grants to counterpart groups in Africa). But some are large and well known, including Secours Populaire Française, Secours Catholique, Solidarité Laique, Médicins and Vétérinaires sans Frontières and Comité Catholique contre la Faim et pour le Développement. Nearly all these NGOs are service deliverers, still new to political advocacy and often reliant on the French government for funding. There are a few NGO umbrella organizations that have begun to get involved in advocacy, for example, Coordination Sud. But their influence has thus far been small.

The Ministry of Cooperation began to work with NGOs only in 1982 with the reforms of Jean-Pierre Cot. It has continued to strengthen the NGOs and to work more closely with them, reflecting the recognition of senior career officials that they represent a potentially important constituency for development in France and can also implement community-oriented projects often more effectively than a larger government agency. The government has also created a Commission pour le Cooperation et Développement with equal representation from government and NGO representatives to discuss development issues. But the influence of French NGOs on French aid policies remains weak. Decision making in government still lacks transparency, with information not always available to the public. Points of access to government for NGOs are limited, and the NGOs themselves are not yet experienced or powerful enough to challenge the strongly political orientation of French policy and French aid in Africa.

Public opinion in France has been generally supportive of French aid, with nearly 60 percent favoring its increase.[38] The French government has been able to justify its aid to Africa not only on the basis of the moral duty of France to assist the needy but also on the basis of historic and, above all, linguistic and cultural ties. However, aid and development issues have not been very salient in French politics. The frequent criticisms by journalists and academics (and occasional officials) of aid and Africa policies in the press have thus far apparently had little effect on public opinion. But, with the repetition of those criticisms over time, if combined with the eruption of major scandals around France's Africa policies (as occurred when it was revealed that former president Valéry Giscard d'Estaing received diamonds and other gifts from the odious "Emperor" Bokassa of the Central African Republic and in 1998, with scandals involving France's role in Rwanda and shady deals involving high French officials and the French oil company, Elf Aquitaine, active in Africa), public demands could be mobilized for reform or even for a decrease in French aid to Africa.

In sum, the emphasis in French aid on promoting diplomatic and political goals in Africa has come from the highest ranks of the government—the presidency—and has been supported by an informal but influential Africa lobby. On the other hand, the voices inside and outside the government in favor of development have remained weak. This configuration of influential interests, leading to a politicized aid program, explains part of the ineffectiveness of French aid as well as the limited autonomy of the Ministry of Cooperation in particular.

Capacity

In contrast to the aid of other donors, the French program has never had a development doctrine to guide it. There is no general framework to provide a strategic focus for French aid, no means of prioritizing the activities funded in the name of development, and no basis for holding aid agencies broadly accountable for their activities. The French government has ascribed to a general view of economic management that state planning and modern technology are keys to successful development and has over the past decade or so affirmed the importance of a supportive policy environment if development is to occur.[39] These views provide a broad policy context for aiding development abroad. But beyond these points, French aid has been extraordinarily unconstrained doctrinally, and so is able easily to accommodate a highly political program.

Convenience and flexibility are not the only reasons there is no development doctrine to guide French aid. Another reason is the fragmentation in the management of that aid. One analyst of French aid commented that "no one inside the government ever formulates such a comprehensive view [of French aid], since it is no one's responsibility to do so."[40] Strategic thinking about aid overall and about its allocation and use in individual countries is difficult when policy and implementation responsibilities are dispersed among numerous agencies.

Nevertheless, France's two principal aid agencies in Africa—the Ministry of Cooperation and the Caisse Française de Développement—have a set of programming procedures not dissimilar to those of other donors. (However, the procedures of the Ministry of Cooperation have been widely criticized within the French government as being too limited and too loose.) Each year, the Ministry of Cooperation and CFD field missions jointly draft a Country Assistance Strategy to cover their country for three years, with the coming year as the key one programmatically. These strategies, not available to the public, are reportedly more descriptions of the state of political, economic, and aid relations between France and the country in question than overall assessments of the development needs. They are reviewed and approved by a committee in Paris chaired by the minister of cooperation. The heads of the two separate field missions then draft an overall plan for their countries (again, on a three-year rolling basis) for approval by Paris and an authorization to initiate programs and projects. With that authorization (which is usually pro forma), French aid missions in the field are then empowered to decide when and how those programs are designed and implemented and are free to call on their headquarters agencies for technical help or to seek such help from outside consultants.

In regard to the staffing of France's aid agencies, according to studies comparing the amount of aid programmed per year with the staff of aid agencies, France has among the best-staffed agencies, with each employee responsible for roughly $1.8 million of bilateral aid, well below the DAC average of $3.1 million. In terms of the quality of French aid staff, it appears to be high especially in terms of knowledge and experience of Africa. French aid officials typically have extensive experience in the region, serving four to five years in their assigned country and repeating assignments in that country during their careers. And in Francophone Africa, they have the enormous advantage of a common language and even, to an extent, a shared culture with most educated Africans. However, the staffing of French aid agencies appears to be weak in the

area of economic analysis. There are reportedly relatively few economists, and this contributes to the limited abilities of these agencies to
program their aid strategically for economic development as well as to
undertake macroeconomic analysis that would support and inform
economic-policy dialogues.

The field missions of both the Ministry of Cooperation and the Caisse
Française are staffed with a dozen or so senior managers and technical
staff plus as many as fifty local staff in the larger countries. Next to the
United States, France has the largest number of staff in the field. Where
the size and use of French aid is not dictated by political concerns in
Paris, the heads of these missions in the field have considerable authority
over what kinds of projects and programs they finance with their aid.
This has the advantage, according to French aid officials, of enabling the
field mission directors to shape their programs to local conditions. It has
the disadvantage of lacking a strategic framework and leaving mission
directors quite vulnerable to pressures from African officials to fund their
pet projects, which may not be of high developmental priority. The process of systematically evaluating French aid is a relatively new one, being
set up in the late 1980s. It has the apparent advantage of examining with
considerable frankness the overall impact of French aid in recipient countries. (The frankness of these evaluations undoubtedly explains why few
of them are available to the public.)

Conclusion

Based on available studies and evaluations, it appears that French aid
is one of the least effective in promoting development in Africa. French
aid has often been used to support the political status quo; its projects
appear to have encountered problems similar to those of other donors;
and the French government has played a limited role at best in discussions on overall development issues in Africa. The reasons for these
limitations are clear: much of French aid has been provided for political
and diplomatic rather than development objectives and often to governments with a limited commitment to development. The capacity of
the French aid system, with its fragmented organizational arrangements, has also been weak—reflecting the strongly political thrust of the
overall program. These limitations are unlikely to change as long as the
French government, supported by the Africa lobby, views its relationships with Africans as a key element in its foreign policy and as long as
the voices within government and outside it in favor of a greater development focus in that aid remain weak. As a result, the great potential for

France to promote effective development in Africa will continue to be unrealized.

The United Kingdom

At midnight on March 6, 1957, the British government lowered the Union Jack over the Polo Field in Accra and raised the red, green, yellow, and black of the new government of Ghana, marking the beginning of the move to independence of British territories in Africa. Most other British colonies there had gained their independence by 1965.

Although the British government had since the interwar years provided aid to its African territories to promote development there,[41] it was not originally the intention of the British government to continue such transfers after independence. A government white paper published in 1957 declared that "the special responsibility which Her Majesty's Government has for Colonial dependencies ceases when they achieve independence. The Government therefore does not envisage Government to Government loans as a normal means of assisting such countries."[42] London assumed that newly independent African governments would be able to borrow from international capital markets the funds they needed for development financing.

But the British policy of "no aid after independence" quickly proved untenable. First, the American government was already beginning to press its allies to create or expand their own foreign-aid programs. Britain did not escape this pressure. Second, the Canadians, at the Commonwealth Trade and Economic Conference in Montreal in 1958, added to the pressures on Her Majesty's government to extend its aid to African countries into the independence period by proposing that a Special Commonwealth African Assistance Program be established. The Canadian idea, not surprisingly, was enthusiastically supported by the Africans present at the conference. (Ghana was represented, as well as soon-to-be independent Nigeria, Kenya, Tanganyika, Uganda, and Sierra Leone.) The British government, at the very least to avoid embarrassing itself and the Canadians hosting the conference, could not oppose the Canadian proposal and so opened the door to aiding its former African colonies.

Which Countries to Aid?

Britain began its aid programs in Africa as a means of disengaging smoothly from the responsibilities of empire while maintaining British prestige, influence, and economic interests in the region. Some countries, including Malawi, Botswana, and Lesotho, whose independence approached far more rapidly than the United Kingdom had originally envisaged, were in no position to finance even their own modest government budgets at independence. Aid was necessary just to keep their governments from collapsing. For others, like Kenya, aid proved essential to finance the large land transfer program from British settlers to Africans to ensure that the settlers got a fair price for their land and, more broadly, to encourage political stability after independence. Another postcolonial "clean-up" program was the payment of pensions of former British colonial officers. At independence, the British persuaded the governments of Kenya, Uganda, and Tanganyika (soon to become Tanzania) to accept responsibility for payment of these pensions. But the notion that the newly independent African governments should use their scarce resources to pay the pensions of their former colonial masters soon became a serious political irritant. The British had begun to pay some of these pensions during the 1960s and agreed in 1971 to allocate part of their aid to East African countries for that purpose.[43]

Not surprisingly, in the early years of African independence, British aid to the region was provided almost entirely to seventeen countries that had at one time been British colonies (or some part of which had, as in the case of Somalia and Cameroon).[44] During the 1970s, this picture changed little, as small aid programs were initiated in Ethiopia and Mozambique. By 1994, however, British aid looked much like the aid of many other donors: much of it remained concentrated in favored countries (mostly, its former colonies) while small aid programs existed in almost every other African country. By 1994, Britain provided at least a million pounds in aid to twenty-eight African countries and smaller amounts to the nineteen others.[45] The spread of British aid reflected the pressures from British ambassadors in Africa wanting an entrée to the governments to which they were accredited that we have observed with American ambassadors.

Even with the end of the 1960s and the immediate postcolonial period in Africa, the British continued to try to concentrate their aid in their former colonies, particularly in southern Africa, in support of their efforts to bring about a settlement of the rebellion in white-ruled Southern Rhodesia (for which they needed the diplomatic support of neighboring black regimes). In the former case, a settlement was attained in 1980 and the new state of Zimbabwe became independent. In 1964, just before Rhodesia declared its independence, British aid to its six former colonies in southern Africa (Tanzania, Malawi, Zambia, Botswana, Lesotho, and Swaziland) amounted to 31 percent of its total aid to Africa. By 1979, just before the end of the rebellion in Rhodesia, it had risen to 46 percent. By 1986, the proportion of British aid provided southern African countries had dropped back to 30 percent.[46]

One country that was not a former British colony came to receive substantial amounts of British aid. Mozambique, neighboring on South Africa, had gained its independence in 1975, with the sudden withdrawal of the Portuguese. While the country was extremely poor, it did have several ports on the Indian Ocean that offered potential alternatives to ports in white-ruled South Africa for exports from the landlocked countries of southern Africa. African members of the Commonwealth were pressing Britain to impose sanctions on South Africa as a means of pressing for an end to white rule. Britain, with substantial economic interests in the country and a million South Africans with the right to relocate in the United Kingdom, refused to impose sanctions. But as part of a diplomacy of balancing its interests in the region, British aid to Mozambique began at three million pounds in 1977 and rose to over seven million pounds ten years later, making it a medium-sized aid program and the only one of significant size not in a former British colony.

How Much Aid to Provide?

The answer to this question was in the first decades after independence driven by British diplomatic goals and, increasingly in recent years, by developmental considerations, tempered by domestic budgetary stringencies. British aid to Africa peaked at £82 million (in current pounds) per year in 1964–66 and then remained below this level until 1976. That year, U.K. aid to Africa reached £107 million and continued to rise thereafter. The increase in aid to Africa was a result not only of pressing British interests in ensuring cordial relationships with countries in southern Africa but also the changes in its own aid policies. As other major donors—the United States and the World Bank in particular—began to reorient their aid programs toward poverty alleviation, the British government published a white paper, entitled *Overseas Development: The Changing Emphasis in British Aid Policies—More Help for the Poorest*.[47] This document stated the government's intention to reallocate its aid to the poorest countries, many of which were in Africa, providing the basis for an increasing flow of aid to that region.

Shortly after the 1975 white paper, British aid to Africa rose rapidly, reaching a new high in 1981 of £266 million, shortly after independence for Zimbabwe. That aid then fell, only to rise once more in the latter half of the 1980s when, along with other aid donors, Britain began to shift its aid to African countries to help meet their economic crisis and finance their economic reforms. That aid peaked again in 1991 and has drifted downward since that time.

The Use of British Aid

When it first began aiding Africa, the British government had no development doctrine or strategy to guide its aid. Its official statements said that "aid should help to buttress stability in the developing countries" and lead to a general expansion in world trade.[48] This formulation left the British government with a great deal of flexibility but little focus in its aid program. During the early 1960s, the British financed a broad range of projects and programs: the Volta Hydro-electric Scheme in Ghana, credits for two ships for the Ghanaian merchant marine, the construction of buildings for Ahmadu Bello University in Nigeria, general assistance to the development programs of Nigeria, Tanganyika (as Tanzania was then called), Uganda, and Sierra Leone. Technical assistance and scholarships for study in the United Kingdom were also part of British aid at this time. In many cases, Britain was the "donor of last resort" to which governments would turn for financing of projects they wanted that other donors were unwilling to fund.

In 1964, the government decided to establish an Overseas Development Ministry to manage the British aid program. The ODM began to publish a series of white papers on aid policy.[49] But they still lacked a development doctrine or strategy, provoking the Overseas Development Institute, a London-based think tank, to describe Britain's aid and development policies in 1969 thus: "Decision on the actual use of aid funds within the country allocations is still dominated by an *ad hoc* response to individual recipient requests. Guidelines are either vague and general—e.g. to fit in with the recipients' development plan proposals—or too narrow and of dubious development relevance."[50]

With the 1975 white paper, *More Help for the Poorest*, mentioned above, the British government had a broad development strategy. Its aid began to reflect that strategy with a growing focus on rural development, much like other donors. Also like other donors, Britain gave priority in its aid to Africa in the 1980s to promoting economic-policy reforms. By the 1990s, British aid funded a broad and varied portfolio of activities, grouped into four general categories: promoting efficient markets and good government; helping improve health and education, particularly for women; enhancing productive capacity and protecting the environment; and supporting multilateral development institutions and international activities for sustainable development. In 1997, the newly elected Labour government issued a new white paper on British aid, *Eliminating World Poverty*, which again emphasized the importance of poverty reduction as a goal of British aid.[51] In both its rhetoric and in its widening portfolio of activities, the British aid program resembled those of most of the other donors examined here.

The Effectiveness of British Aid

British aid, by reputation, is among the more effective aid programs in Africa.[52] It has avoided the major scandals and disasters that have plagued a number of other programs. It has also, for the most part, avoided providing significant amounts of aid to governments that were highly repressive, incompetent, or corrupt. And where governments have become repressive or irresponsible in their economic management (for example, Ghana during the late 1960s and much of the 1970s, or Uganda during the 1970s), Britain has tended to reduce (though not eliminate altogether) its aid program, signaling that it did not approve of their behavior.

Turning to the experience of British aid projects and programs, several synthesis reports provide insights. A report on projects completed between 1991 and 1993 found that in Africa, only two-thirds of its projects performed satisfactorily. Further, projects in central and southern Africa were substantially worse in achieving their objectives than in any other world region. There were also problems in timeliness, efficiency of procurement, and delivery of inputs. Projects and programs also carry conditions—in the latter case, these usually include the implementation of economic reforms. The record on the implementation of conditions was varied: just over half of the agreed-to reforms were fully implemented; reforms were partially implemented in another 39 percent of the programs in central and southern Africa; but in East Africa, only 20 percent of the conditions were implemented. Sixty percent of the projects in East and West Africa were judged to be sustainable, and three-quarters of the projects in Central and southern Africa were foreseen as sustainable. (To compare, projects in East Asia and the Pacific were judged likely to be 100 percent sustainable, but only 64 percent of those in South Asia were foreseen as sustainable.) The reasons for problems with effectiveness involved, first and foremost, deficiencies in the design and appraisal of projects (including taking into account the broader political and economic environment in which the project was to operate). The weakness of African partner institutions was another significant explanatory factor.

A second report based on project completion reports from 1993 and 1994 found a slight improvement in performance (though performance in Africa remained below that of other regions), with 69 percent of the projects there rated as satisfactory. The estimates of sustainability did not, however, change. The major problems continued to be in the design and implementation areas.

It is difficult to assess the role of Britain in development discourse in Africa. Its aid agencies produced few reports that changed thinking about development problems and their solution and did not fund major efforts to gather data on particular development problems. (However, some of the best work on development in Africa produced by the scholarly community comes from Britain, some with public support.) British aid officers have participated actively in development dialogues in specific countries and in the shaping of British aid programs to support economic reforms and in other initiatives vis-à-vis African development. And British aid officials pride themselves in having been particularly active in the discussions organized by the World Bank in the Special Program of Assistance for Africa (a vehicle for donor discussions and collaboration, particularly on economic-reform programs in Africa, described in more detail in chapter 8 in the case study on the World Bank). Thus, while Britain has not been one of the most influential leaders in development discourse in Africa, it has been an active participant.

The Future of British Aid

As with other aid donors, in the 1990s the British government began to grapple with the impact of the changes in the world and Britain's membership in the European Union. In 1992, the British government agreed at a summit meeting of the European Commission in Edinburgh to a formula by which it would contribute to the European Union aid program an amount linked to its GNP. Since Britain's contribution to that program had thus far been relatively small, it would have to raise that amount significantly—by 60 percent in real terms between 1992 and 1999. In addition, British aid for the countries of Eastern Europe and the former Soviet Union was rising, as was aid to address the increasing number of emergencies in the world. These changes were taking place within an overall aid budget that was projected to be relatively stagnant during the remainder of the 1990s. That meant that bilateral aid for development would decline, as indeed it was projected to do by nearly 20 percent between 1993–94 and 1998–99.[53] These trends provoked the following concern, expressed in a House of Commons report: "The effect of trends in expenditure on overseas aid is to change significantly the whole pattern of British overseas aid effort, with serious policy implications, particularly for the bilateral aid programme and for the amount of UK aid going to the poorest countries."[54] The United Kingdom was later able to adjust its planned contribution to European aid downward modestly; but the major problem of a trade-off between multilateral commitments and bilateral program levels remained.

The British aid program had also come to resemble the U.S. program in that it had broadened its portfolio of activities as well as the number of recipients of its aid. These trends, at a time of budgetary stringencies, provoked expressions of concern within the government itself. In 1995, a Fundamental Expenditure Review of the Overseas Development Administration (as the British aid agency was then called), warned that "ODA is working in more countries and undertaking more complex activities, while the resources available for bilateral programmes have been shrinking and are expected to continue to decline."[55] The new white paper on development, cited above, signaled no change from the breadth of activities and countries funded with British aid.

Finally, the United Kingdom decided to reorganize its aid program with the election of a Labour government in 1997. The Overseas Development Administration was taken out of the Foreign Office (FO) and made a new ministry, the Department for International Development (DfID). The new minister, Clare Short, declared that British aid would henceforth focus far more on poverty reduction, and the new ministry claimed considerable new authorities over coordinating government policies in developing countries. It remained to be seen what differences these changes actually made in British aid programs in Africa and elsewhere.

Analysis

Autonomy

No government has changed the organizational location of its aid program as often as have the British. The Department of International Development was the last in a line of shifts of the British aid program into and out of the Foreign Office (without, however, perceptible change in the actual aid programs). The first aid agency was created in 1964 as an the independent Overseas Development Ministry. It was then merged into the Foreign Office in 1968 under a Conservative government and then made independent again when Labour gained power in 1972. In 1978, with the return of the Conservatives, it was again merged into the Foreign Office.

In fact, it had been the intention of those who planned Britain's first aid agency (Professor Thomas Balogh and other Fabian socialists) to create an agency with a considerable measure of autonomy from the Foreign Office and other government agencies, giving it a significant voice for development by placing responsibilities in it for all British aid (both bilateral and multilateral), providing it with a professional staff, and giving it a measure of status and independence as a separate ministry. While the ministerial status was soon lost, the agency remained professionally strong and organizationally intact regardless of whether it was part of the Foreign Office or independent of it. As a result, while British aid has been spread widely throughout Africa (reflecting the influence of British ambassadors) and, during the 1970s, concentrated in southern Africa, where British diplomacy was active in trying to bring about peace in Rhodesia, it has rarely been provided in significant amounts over extended periods to grossly incompetent or corrupt regimes. This may be partly luck in that Britain's important African partners have not numbered among the worst-governed countries there. But it is also likely a reflection of the influence of the aid agency as well.

Other factors reinforcing the relative autonomy and influence of the DfID over the allocation and use of aid in Africa is that the Diplomatic Wing of the Foreign Office appears to have accepted the legitimacy of the development mission. And the professionalism of DfID's staff is widely respected within the British government.

There are other players within the British government that have sought to influence British aid. One is the Department of Trade and Industry (DTI), the principal voice for British business interests. In 1977, the Labour government, in response to lobbying from British businesses for more aid to support British bids for contracts abroad and in an effort to garner their support for substantially increased levels of overall aid, established the Aid and Trade Provision (ATP). Five percent of overall aid monies would be set aside to promote British business abroad, largely in better-off developing countries of Asia, and to finance developmentally sound projects. After the election of the Thatcher government in 1979, these terms were further eased with a larger proportion of development aid set aside for ATP and more liberal criteria for its use.

Pressures to expand the ATP at the cost of development aid have receded somewhat, helped by a scandal involving ATP funding of the Pergau Hydroelectric Dam in Malaysia. The proposal to fund the construction of this dam was opposed by the permanent secretary of ODA (DfID's predecessor) on the grounds that it was contrary to the development interests of Malaysia. The permanent secretary was overruled in this case by the foreign secretary (apparently because the prime minister had made a personal commitment to Malaysian officials to fund the dam). The World Development Movement—a prodevelopment NGO— then took the case to court and won a decision that the foreign secretary had acted illegally, in contravention of the Overseas Cooperation and Development Act, by using ODA funds to finance the dam. This public embarrassment to the government served to bolster further the autonomy of ODA vis-à-vis those inside and outside government wishing to use aid funds for commercial purposes, according to the then–minister for development.[56]

In fact, British commercial interests in Africa declined with the deepening economic crisis there, reflected in the declining amount of ATP funds allocated to the region. In 1977, nearly half of the ATP credits went to the better-off countries of Africa, including Cameroon and Botswana. By the mid-1980s, only a quarter went to Africa with 70 percent allocated to Asian countries, in response to a more attractive business climate. By 1994, the proportion of ATP funds allocated to African countries was under 10 percent of the total.

Traditionally, Parliament has exerted relatively little influence over the aid program. The Foreign Affairs Committee of Parliament has held numerous hearings on foreign aid. But since the committee is controlled by the majority party, it has not played the intrusive role Congress has in U.S. aid. Moreover, Parliament invariably passes the government's annual Estimates Bill (which contains the budget for foreign aid) without amendment or restriction.

It is worth mentioning here, in contrast to the situation with France, that Africans have played almost no role in London in influencing the organization, size, or composition of British aid. They do, of course, make their views known to British officials in their home countries when aid issues are discussed. But they do not normally lobby British officials or politicians on aid issues.

However, one group that attempts to influence government decisions on foreign aid is the development lobby. This is a relatively small but articulate and active group of NGOs, made up of churches and organizations engaged in development work (roughly one hundred in 1994), research institutes (for example, the Overseas Development Institute), and prominent scholars working on development issues. (The participation of scholars in a prodevelopment lobby is unusual and does not exist at present in any other aid-giving country to the extent it does in the United Kingdom, though Sweden comes close. It has allowed the proaid lobby to reach British intellectuals as well as grassroots humanitarian organizations with a message favorable to development.) Several prominent scholars and NGO leaders in the development field formed a group in the 1980s known as the Independent Group on British Aid and published a series of monographs that were well-informed critiques of that aid, emphasizing the need to do more to help the poorest.[57] These publications received wide circulation and considerable attention by the foreign-policy elite and government officials. In the mid-1990s, EUROSTEP and other umbrella organizations representing development NGOs began to publish in London an annual report on the aid programs of all major donors, entitled *The Reality of Aid*. This analysis, written from the point of view of development-oriented NGOs, provides not just information but critiques of the programs of major aid donors and is beginning to become the focus of an informal collaborative network of NGOs from donor and recipient countries involved in development.

The prodevelopment NGOs have been allies of DfID and its predecessors since it was created in 1964. They have lobbied against cuts in British aid and lobbied in favor of a development program oriented toward poverty alleviation. They have criticized the merger of ODA into the FO when it has been an issue, fearing an increase in diplomatic influences over British aid, and have supported its creation as an independent ministry. And they have lobbied hard against the influence of commercial interests (including the ATP) on British aid. More than one expert on British foreign policy has commented on the collaboration between the DfID and development-oriented NGOs.[58] The prodevelopment NGOs have helped bolster the autonomy of DfID by in effect taking its side on issues in public fora.

But the lobby has its limitations as well. Its potential influence has been greater when the British public was concerned with humanitarian or development problems abroad, as during the Ethiopian famine in 1984. But when the government has been intent on implementing a policy the NGOs have opposed (such as a merger of the aid agency in the Foreign Office or the creation of the ATP), the NGOs have seldom been able to block that policy.

In the 1990s, DfID made an effort to expand its collaboration with NGOs. A Joint Funding Scheme in which DfID provides 50 percent of the financing of NGO projects in certain sectors abroad quadrupled between 1990 and 1994, reaching roughly $45 million, reflecting the rapidly expanding collaboration between DfID and NGOs. In 1994, there were fifteen hundred NGO projects with ODA funding. However, this collaboration and the financial dependence it implies may begin to circumscribe the independence of many of the NGOs, a situation already remarked upon by government officials and NGO staff themselves.

A word needs to be said about British public opinion vis-à-vis development aid. The British public has long been relatively supportive of foreign aid, with about three-quarters of the public favoring an increase in aid to developing countries throughout the 1980s and 1990s.[59] However, polls taken in the late 1960s and late 1970s show an even higher level of support for British aid to poor countries.[60] What may be reflected in this decline is a diminution in the interest of the British public in aid and development issues. As in other countries, that interest has tended to rise in times of crisis—for example, the droughts in the Sahel in the early 1970s or the droughts in Ethiopia in 1974 and 1984—and then fall off.

The government has typically appealed to the British public to support their country's doing its part to help others abroad and to ensure a peaceful and prosperous world. The business community and trade unions have been generally favorable toward foreign aid. And there have been few significant groups challenging these positions. Foreign aid has rarely been the source of contentious debate in Parliament or an issue there for one party to attack another. Nor have criticisms of foreign aid become an election issue in the United Kingdom. In short, the political context within Britain for foreign aid has been generally friendly.

Capacity

A number of indicators suggest that the British aid program is among those with the strongest capacity. A fundamental advantage of British aid is that nearly all of it—both bilateral and multilateral—is managed by one agency.[61] The planners of British aid rightly foresaw that consolidating all aid into one agency would make that agency stronger and likely more effective in promoting development. The experience of Britain and other aid-giving countries bears that assumption out. A single agency carries more influence within government circles, ensures greater policy and program coherence in its area of responsibility, and can usually call on a broader range of talent to implement its responsibilities effectively than a diverse range of agencies working in the same area.

The white paper of 1975 mentioned earlier—*More Help for the Poorest*—offered for the first time a development doctrine to guide its aid, albeit quite a broad one. It strengthened the importance of need for the country allocation of British aid and bolstered the focus on poverty alleviation, leading to a growing proportion of projects in the social sectors. While British officials have amended this doctrine in past speeches and put an emphasis during the 1980s on aid in support of macroeconomic-policy reforms, the core focus on poverty alleviation was never entirely jettisoned and has been reaffirmed in the most recent white paper, *Eliminating World Poverty*, mentioned earlier.[62]

However, the goal of poverty alleviation leaves considerable room for diverse activities, allowing the British government to augment the types of projects and programs it finances to reflect changes in mainstream development thinking. For example, in the late 1970s, it initiated projects in rural development along with other major aid donors. Again, along with other donors in the 1980s, it added policy reform to the scope if its aid-financed activities in Africa and elsewhere, and by 1990, nearly a third of British aid in Africa financed policy reform programs. It has since added work in the area of environmental conservation, democracy and governance, and women in development to its portfolio. In fact, the British bilateral aid program, albeit relatively small in worldwide terms, covers a range of activities in twenty major sectors that are broader than those covered by larger aid programs. The geographic and sectoral scope of British aid have raised questions about the ability of DfID's staff to manage such a diverse portfolio of activities.[63]

In addition to a broad development doctrine, DfID has for several decades had a well-developed set of programming procedures. Each year, overall spending proposals for foreign aid are developed. To decide how that spending will be divided among programs, the government adopts an "Aid Framework" document that sets out the government's broad plans for the coming three years with a particular emphasis on the coming fiscal year. For all major recipients of British aid, a Country Strategy Paper is also produced every two years to cover a four-year period. ("Country Objectives Papers" are prepared for smaller recipients.) With the approval of that paper, which contains both the strategy and spending plans of the government, specific projects and programs are developed, approved, and implemented. These programming documents have not been available publicly, though some are now being published. They are taken quite seriously within the government and both guide and constrain the British aid program in individual countries and bolster DfID's autonomy in managing the program.

DfID has a sizable staff relative to its annual level of programming. Its personnel numbered 1,590 in 1994, to manage a portfolio of $3 billion, or roughly $2 million per person per year. (This overestimates the average amount per person year since multilateral aid, which requires relatively little management, is included in the $3 billion.) These figures are among the higher staff-to-portfolio ratios among major aid agencies.[64] However, the number of staff is projected to fall in coming years, raising further questions about the long-run capacity of the agency to manage such a diverse and dispersed portfolio.

The staff itself is largely career civil service who typically spend their entire careers in DfID. It includes engineers, economists, agronomists, and others technically trained in development-related fields. It also includes experienced generalists who manage country programs. The quality of the British civil service is widely recognized as high, and this view is shared by many who have worked with DfID personnel.

DfID is partially represented in the field. It has three "development divisions" in Africa: one in Nairobi, one in Harare, and one in Pretoria. These divisions cover not only their own countries but several neighboring ones. They are staffed by technical specialists and program managers. These divisions have delegated authority to commit up to $3 million to a project without having to get London's approval. It is estimated that roughly half the decisions on programming bilateral aid are made in the field.[65] Britain, it can be said, has one of the stronger regional field presences of any aid donor in terms of its capabilities and particularly its authorities. But the ability to develop the familiarity with country conditions and to follow events on a regular basis necessary to support effective complex interventions in Africa is limited by the regional nature of these missions.

Britain also appears to suffer from the bureaucratic imperative present in most aid programs: the pressure to spend monies, a problem noted by several experts on British aid.[66] These pressures are, however, less than those in other governments—for example, in the United States— where an often hostile legislature will cut budgets if monies are not fully committed within their allotted period or where compelling political objectives require that monies be spent no matter how poor the economic performance of the government receiving them. (It is also the case that DfID, responsible both for bilateral and multilateral aid programs, can shift funding between the two when planned levels are not committed for one of them.)[67]

Conclusion

The British have avoided the major aid disasters experienced by others in Africa arising from providing large amounts of funding over extended periods to incompetent, repressive, or corrupt regimes. This is a result of a less politically motivated aid program and a relatively autonomous aid agency. The relative autonomy of DfID derives from the goals and organizational decisions of its original planners—to create a capable, independent aid agency that would be a strong and credible voice for development within government councils and among the public. The autonomy of DfID is bolstered by an active and vocal development lobby, which is able to mobilize public support behind aid when a major issue— like a famine—arises and is able at times to embarrass the government when it seeks to divert significant amounts of aid for nondevelopmental purposes. The relative autonomy of DfID over policies and programs in Africa is also enhanced by the low and declining diplomatic priority that region has had for Her Majesty's government.

Despite its relative autonomy and its considerable capacity, DfID experienced problems with the developmental effectiveness of its aid in Africa similar to those of other donors—deficiencies in design and implementation and limits on sustainability. The source of these problems is much the same as those that have affected the U.S. aid program—the limited technologies and local knowledge necessary to design and implement socially complex interventions. These problems may play an even greater role in the British aid program in the future, given its broadening sectoral scope, declining workforce, and limited presence in the field.

Chapter Seven

Sweden, Italy, Japan

Most Western European governments provide development aid to the countries of sub-Saharan Africa, and many concentrate a large proportion of their aid there. This chapter examines the aid programs of three of the more interesting ones—Sweden, Italy, and Japan. Sweden is often classified as a "humane internationalist"[1] in discussions of aid donors—a government whose foreign policies reflect a moral obligation to promote the well-being of people beyond its borders. The motivations of its aid are similar to those of other Nordic countries and the Netherlands, making many of the insights of Sweden's experience in Africa applicable to other donors as well. Italy's aid program in Africa has followed one of the most unusual trajectories of rise and collapse of any donor and is worth examining for the lessons it provides. Japan, with few economic or political interests in Africa and relatively little past experience in the region, has nevertheless become one of the larger donor governments there over the past two and a half decades, and its performance in promoting development is important to consider in a study of aid effectiveness in the region.

Sweden

Although one of the smaller countries examined in this book, Sweden has consistently had one of the highest ratios of aid to its GNP of any government worldwide. Half of that aid has gone to countries in Africa, making Sweden one of the medium-sized donors there, providing between $350 and $500 million per year during the 1990s. Swedish aid has not been the tool of Cold War or postcolonial diplomacy, as it had been for the United States, France, and Britain. Rather, Swedish aid has been an expression of Swedish values as well as Sweden's ambition to be the "conscience of the world"[2]—in particular, to demonstrate "a feeling of solidarity with the poor people of low-income countries . . . [to] in some measure counterbalance the capitalist and neocolonialist forces that threatened equitable development in poor countries."[3] This ambition was reflected in the aspiration of the Swedish party leader Olaf Palme, to build a "third road"—that is, a political and ideological path between the capitalist West and the socialist East.

Which Countries to Aid?

From the early days of its aid program, the Swedish government, recognizing that it would never be among the largest aid donors worldwide, decided to concentrate its aid in a limited number of major recipients, termed "program countries." Reflecting the humanitarian thrust in Swedish aid and a large domestic NGO constituency that supported it, these countries were chosen from the poorest in the world. Of the first six program countries, three were African: Ethiopia (where Sweden had a history of missionary activity), Kenya, and Tanzania.

In the late 1960s, coincident with the intensification of the war in Indochina and the outbreak of antiwar protests in a number of Western countries, there was a "youth revolution" in Sweden, adding a radical tone to Swedish aid and Swedish foreign policies. The "radical" tone influenced the country allocation of Swedish aid, now including as recipients countries of southern Africa neighboring the white regimes of Rhodesia and South Africa (to bolster their independence) and to national liberation movements, including those of South Africa, Mozambique, Angola, Zimbabwe, and Namibia. The help given the liberation movements became aid to newly independent governments, once those movements gained power.

In addition, political party preferences played a role in Sweden's choice of aid recipients, with the Social Democratic Party (in power until the mid-1970s), favoring developing country governments—for example, Tanzania—with similar ideological or policy orientations. The Conservative Party (gaining power in 1976) favored aid to Ethiopia (before the coup by left-wing military officers). And the Liberal Party had ties with the governments of Zambia and Botswana.[4] In contrast to the United States and United Kingdom, it was not only Swedish ambassadors de-

Table 7. Top Five Recipients of Swedish Aid to Africa

1970–71	1980–81	1994–95
Tanzania	Tanzania	Mozambique
Ethiopia	Mozambique	Tanzania
Kenya	Zambia	Zambia
Zambia	Ethiopia	Ethiopia
Sudan	Kenya	Zimbabwe

Source: Development Assistance Committee, *Development Cooperation* (Paris: Organization for Economic Cooperation and Development, 1997), p. A80.

manding an aid program that led to the increase in the number of those programs (although there were these pressures too) but rather the pressures of political parties. As a result, the list of program countries has tended to grow over time, reaching twenty-one by 1996, including thirteen countries in sub-Saharan Africa (see table 7).[5] It is also important to note that Sweden, much like a number of other donor governments considered here, has provided small amounts of aid to a large number of countries, totaling 120 by the mid-1990s.[6] And like other governments, the concentration of its aid in its major recipients has been falling since the 1970s.

How Much Aid to Provide?

An important determinant of the size of Swedish aid to individual recipients has been the overall level of Swedish aid worldwide. During the period of political radicalism in the late 1960s, support for solidarity with the poor and oppressed abroad was at its height and provided the impetus for the Swedish government to commit itself to providing 1 percent of Swedish GNP in foreign aid and to increasing the aid budget by one-quarter in 1968 to begin to reach that percentage by 1975.[7] Aid as a proportion of GNP reached the international target of 0.7 percent of GNP in 1975 and finally reached a target of aid as 1 percent of GNP in 1992, leading to a steady increase in the absolute amount of Sweden's aid for the countries in Africa.[8] However, continually rising aid levels were not to last.

In the early 1990s, the Swedish government, like many other governments, began to cut its aid program and reorganize its aid agencies. Overall aid commenced a decline after reaching an all-time high in 1992. While the decline was the result of the government's effort to reduce its overall budget deficit, it did demonstrate that development work abroad was far from sacrosanct. In 1995, aid dropped by 8 percent, bringing the overall aid budget down to a "floor" of 0.7 percent of GNP. In 1997, the Swedish parliament abandoned its commitment to the 1 percent of GNP level for aid, dropping back to a commitment of 0.7 percent. This was described by the parliament as a "temporary" reduction, with the 1 percent to be reinstated when financial pressures on government eased.

Reflecting the decline in overall Swedish aid, that country's aid to Africa also began to fall. From a peak of $604 million in 1993 (in 1995 prices), aid to Africa declined by over $200 million, to $388 million in 1995.[9] More telling perhaps was the decrease in the proportion of aid to Africa—from over 50 percent in 1986 to just under one-third in 1996, reflecting the priority now accorded to helping the states of the former Yugoslavia and a greater caution and selectivity in Swedish programs in Africa.

Data on Swedish aid in 1996 shows an increase in its overall level (by nearly 8 percent in real terms from 1995) and in the level of aid to Africa, which rose to $433 million. It remained to be seen whether these increases marked a reversal of the trend of previous years.

What Does Swedish Aid Finance?

Long before the United States, United Kingdom, and other aid agencies oriented their aid toward alleviating poverty, the Swedes had already done so. The basic legislation underpinning the Swedish aid program was contained in Bill 100, passed in 1962. It reflected the general support of the Swedish population and its large and active NGO community for helping the poor abroad. The bill formally established an aid program whose major thrust was poverty alleviation. This objective would be achieved through the pursuit of four important goals: promoting economic growth, supporting economic and social equality, supporting economic and political independence of recipient countries, and supporting the development of democratic societies. Bill 100 also specified that Swedish aid should be free from the influence of Swedish commercial interests abroad.

Finally, Swedish aid should be "recipient oriented," meaning that to the maximum extent possible, the recipients of that aid—which were independent, sovereign countries—should be able to decide on how it would be used. This led the Swedes frequently to take a much more hands-off approach than most other donors to determine which projects would be supported and in designing and managing the implementation of those projects. In the early 1970s, the government initiated a "country programming" approach to aid in which priority countries would receive Swedish aid over a multiple-year period, facilitating long-term planning on the part of the recipient government.[10] (Other donors, for the most part, were unwilling to commit themselves to provide given levels of aid for more than a year at a time.)

However, the Swedish experience of ineffective aid in Tanzania, as we shall see, combined with a more conservative political environment within Sweden and greater pragmatism in Swedish aid in the 1980s, led that country to alter its "recipient orientation" to one of "concerned participation" and to take into account the overall economic-policy environment of the country in decisions on the allocation and use of aid. In the mid-1980s, for example, Sweden began to back the World Bank and IMF in their pressures on the government of Tanzania for policy reform and tied their own import support to the adoption of appropriate policies.

The Effectiveness of Swedish Aid

Since the early 1970s, the Swedish government has undertaken evaluations of projects and sector programming. In the 1980s, it introduced country evaluations of its aid. A number of these evaluations, covering three of the principal African countries receiving the aid are available in English.[11] An evaluation of Swedish aid in Botswana between 1966 and 1993 is generally positive, although it does not analyze the performance of specific Swedish projects and programs in that country. It highlights in particular Sweden's contribution to capacity building, for example, in education, and concludes that "Swedish assistance to Botswana has been quite successful in comparison to aid efforts in other African countries."[12]

An assessment of Swedish aid to Zambia describes the findings of a variety of project and program evaluations in agriculture, health, and education—areas where Sweden typically focuses its assistance. The performance of the projects was mixed, with specific tasks usually being completed but often with a disappointing result. A project supporting a technical and vocational teachers college in Luanshya, for example, was generally successful in constructing the planned buildings. But the new facilities were only partially used for want of Zambian staff.[13] A common problem identified in these project evaluations has been poor specification of goals and an inadequate involvement of Sweden in their planning.

A particularly well-done evaluation of Swedish aid to Tanzania, described by the DAC as "a significant work for all interested in development cooperation" (especially for its willingness to examine macroeconomic and other side effects of that aid) turned out to be highly critical. Sweden has long been among the principal donors to Tanzania and often the largest one. Its "recipient-driven" aid in Tanzania has provided highly flexible funding for the Tanzanian government, whose emphasis on development with equity the Swedes strongly supported. The evaluation found that assistance to education and health had helped expand these sectors, but the expanded services proved unsustainable. The relatively large amount of Swedish assistance to the government-owned industrial sector was described as a failure, primarily due to the faulty policies and poor management of that sector by the Tanzanian government. The evaluation further suggests that the indirect effects of Swedish assistance to Tanzania were pernicious, encouraging the government to maintain faulty economic policies and delay necessary reforms. The report concludes that more attention should be paid by the Swedish government to careful project preparation and evaluation, and that an effort should be made to begin reducing Tanzania's high dependence on aid by preparing the government to take more responsibility for its own development.

The experience of Swedish aid is in some ways rather similar to that of other donors in Africa—more effective in the simpler types of projects and less so if institutional change was required for success. Yet in one way, Swedish aid has been quite different: Sweden's "recipient-oriented" approach to aid, particularity in Tanzania but also in Zambia, left those governments with much more responsibility for identifying projects and managing the aid. This approach, according to the evaluations, led to a serious waste of Swedish resources in those countries.

In terms of Sweden's contribution to development discourse in Africa, it can be said that the consistent focus on poverty alleviation by Sweden and its work in preparing country strategies drawn from poverty analyses of each of its major recipients have helped maintain and sharpen the focus of other donors and of Africans on this issue. The Swedes continued this focus even during the 1980s, when the primary emphasis in discussions of international development was on economic-policy reforms to promote growth. With many aid agencies emphasizing again the importance of reducing poverty and working through NGOs, the experience of Sweden may well be seen as broadly relevant and provide that country with a leadership role in development discourse it has not previously enjoyed.

Swedish Aid in the 1990s and Beyond

"Sweden's development co-operation programme is at a critical turning point," observed the most recent DAC review of Swedish aid.[14] A number of currents suggested that Sweden had entered a period of transition in its aid. The earliest emphasis on poverty alleviation has been renewed and extended. In 1996, parliament adopted a set of goals for Swedish aid that reiterated earlier ones but added several new ones: growth of resources (in recipient countries), economic and social equality, economic and political autonomy, democratic development, sustainable use of resources and concern for the environment, and gender equality.[15] Furthermore, Sida, the principal Swedish aid agency, has been strengthened by the merger into it of several smaller agencies (providing aid for research, training, and technical assistance to better-off developing countries).

These changes may suggest a return to earlier policies. However, other changes point to a more fundamental redirection of Swedish aid. The Swedish aid budget rose somewhat in 1996 but remained at roughly the same real level as in 1988. And responsibility for evolving overall aid policies and country aid strategies—formerly lodged in the Department of International Development Cooperation of the Ministry of Foreign Affairs—is to be decentralized to regional bureaus of the ministry to ensure that "a more cohesive approach to political and development cooperation relations between Sweden and recipient countries can be attained."[16] These changes could lead to greater diplomatic and commercial influences on Swedish aid budgets in the future.[17]

Analysis

Autonomy

The key organization within the Swedish government responsible for managing development aid is the Swedish International Development Agency, or Sida. (Before the recent reorganization, it was called the Swedish International Development Authority, or SIDA. It will be referred to here henceforth as Sida.) Sida was set up in 1965. Its origins give important insights into the orientation and evolution of Swedish foreign aid.

Sweden was one of the first countries in the postwar period to create a program of foreign economic assistance. In 1952, following the example of Norway, Swedish officials urged their extensive NGO community to form a committee to consider what aid and development policies Sweden should pursue and to undertake programs of development education aimed at the Swedish public.[18] Forty-five NGOs (trade unions, employers' confederations, cooperatives, missionary groups, adult education societies, teachers' and journalists' organizations, youth groups, and others) formed a Central Committee for Swedish Technical Assistance to Less Developed Areas, known as CK. The CK identified several countries in which to begin Swedish aid and undertook several successful national campaigns to raise funds for development. It also began an extensive public-education campaign, targeting key groups and individuals who were "opinion makers" to explain the importance of "solidarity" with the disadvantaged abroad and solicit support for the country's development efforts. Finally, CK was so successful in generating requests from foreign governments for assistance from Sweden that the Swedish government decided to establish its own aid agency. The origins of Swedish aid thus owe much to the support and involvement of Swedish NGOs. Those NGOs, like many NGOs working in relief and development in other parts of the world, put a priority on people-to-people work at the grassroots level aiming at reducing the poverty of the least advantaged. These factors help explain the orientation of Swedish aid, evident from its commencement, toward alleviating poverty.

Sida is semi-independent from the Ministry of Foreign Affairs (MFA). The MFA sets broad development policy guidelines, reviews Sida's budget, defends it before the Ministry of Finance, and coordinates the activities of Sida and the several other government agencies with spending programs in developing countries. Sida itself is headed by a director general and has the unusual arrangement of being governed by a board of directors. Sida's board includes representatives from the four main political parties, the NGO community, trade unions, employers' associations, and senior members of the Sida staff. Its governance by a developmentally oriented board, and the fact that Sweden has had few compelling foreign-policy objectives in Africa, has provided Sida with a considerable measure of autonomy in managing aid there—its relationship with the Ministry of Foreign Affairs notwithstanding.

However, Swedish aid has not been entirely free from diplomatic influences. Sweden long supported the independence of African governments neighboring on the white-ruled redoubts of Rhodesia and South Africa. This policy affected the selection of countries receiving Swedish aid—increasing the priority of Zambia, Botswana, and Mozambique.

(These countries would have likely been recipients of Swedish aid based on that country's development priorities and political party preferences. However, the diplomatic importance of these countries to Stockholm likely served to boost their overall aid.) The other indication of the diplomatic influence on aid is its distribution, albeit in small amounts, to a large number of countries, reflecting (as in other aid-giving countries) the wishes of Swedish ambassadors for an aid program of their own.

The Swedes, more than other aid donors, have sought to exclude national commercial interests from influencing their foreign aid. As we have seen, the original legislation establishing an aid program specifically isolated it from commercial influences; it was intended to remain a "pure," development-oriented program. However, in the 1970s, with the doubling in oil prices and the ensuing economic recession in Sweden, the Social Democrats lost power and were replaced by a Conservative coalition government. Not only did the concerns of Swedish industry have a greater voice in that government (and a concomitant lessening in the influence of the churches and cooperatives), but the economic recession risked eroding support for Swedish aid generally, enhancing the importance of creating as broad a coalition supporting aid as possible—including Swedish business. Thus, in 1978, the government decided to accommodate these pressures by creating a new program, called the Swedish Fund for Industrial Cooperation with Developing Countries (SWEDEFUND), organizationally separate from Sida but to be financed out of aid monies. SWEDEFUND was to encourage Swedish firms to invest in joint ventures in developing countries. Earlier, in 1975, the Swedish Agency for International Technical and Economic Cooperation (BITS), had already been set up on an experimental basis, financed out of bilateral aid monies, to fund technical cooperation in better-off developing countries where Swedish business might have an interest. In 1981, BITS was charged with managing Sweden's new mixed export credit scheme in developing countries. Funding for this scheme, also drawn from the aid budget, grew rapidly and soon provoked a lively debate between those who supported a "pure" aid program (without commercial purposes) and those who supported the use of aid to promote Swedish business interests abroad.[19] This debate may have been resolved—at least for the moment—with the merger of BITS into Sida.

The Swedish parliament actively debates foreign aid and development issues, including the selection of "program countries" and policies governing the aid. But the parliament is controlled by the same party or coalition controlling the government and normally supports government finance bills (including aid funding) as presented. Swedish political parties have all supported a sizable aid program. The Social Democratic Party has for the most part favored more purely "developmental" aid, as has the Liberal Party. The Conservative Party, with its ties to Swedish industry, has supported a stronger commercial orientation in the aid, and this was reflected in its creating SWEDEFUND when the Conservatives were part of the governing coalition in the late 1970s. As we have noted, political parties have also wanted certain countries to receive aid and may have played a role in the choice of recipients in Africa. The impact of party preferences on the selection of "program countries" appears to have contributed to the ever growing number of those countries, despite Sweden's goal of keeping the number of program countries limited.

NGOs have played a more prominent role in Swedish aid from its inception than in any other aid program considered in this study, bolstering the autonomy of Sida, in particular vis-à-vis commercial pressures on the program, influencing the overall policy orientation of Swedish aid and helping to implement the aid program.[20] At government urging in the 1950s, they established their own program of aid for development abroad and have helped implement government aid programs since the 1960s. NGOs have also served on the board of Sida and have worked to inform the Swedish public of the importance of helping the disadvantaged abroad. Their approach to development—like NGOs elsewhere in the world—has emphasized the human element, focusing on work in the social sectors or activities directly benefiting the poor. These preferences have been reflected in the general orientation of Swedish aid toward poverty alleviation since the 1960s (before other donors adopted similar approaches in the 1970s).

Interestingly, the Swedish NGOs have not had the impact on Swedish aid that American NGOs have had on U.S. aid—increasing legislatively mandated program directives that have constrained the autonomy of USAID. There are two reasons for this difference. First, political institutions in the two countries are different. The Swedish parliamentary system is less fragmented than the U.S. system and legislators act less independently than members of the U.S. Congress. Second, the NGO community is also less fragmented into groups with distinct program emphases and is more accustomed to working together, with the government, on development issues. There has been far less distrust between NGOs and the government on aid issues and less suspicion of government intentions on those issues than has been evident in the United States.

While NGOs have been the principal constituency for Swedish aid and have had a major influence over its policy orientation, their views have not always prevailed in decisions on the size and direction of that aid. Despite their support for a purely development-oriented aid program, funds have been used over their objections to finance the commercially oriented BITS and SWEDEFUND, albeit as agencies separate from Sida. And the recent decisions by the government to reorganize the aid program and to reduce aid to 0.7 percent of GNP have been implemented despite NGO resistance. As in other countries, when a policy or budgetary change is of broad national priority, pressures from NGOs are rarely sufficient to block it.

A characteristic that has differentiated Sweden and other Nordic countries from donors elsewhere has been the national consensus on the size and policy directions of their aid. Sida pays for an annual opinion poll on the Swedish population's views of foreign aid. For much of the last several decades, public support for maintaining or even increasing aid remained at 85 percent—an exceptionally high level among donor governments.[21] Such a strong national consensus in Sweden has undoubtedly been a reflection of broader values shared by much of the populace: an acceptance on the part of the Swedish public of a major role of government in their own economy and generous state programs to help the least advantaged. These values have created a prism through which foreign aid for development could be presented and supported. The extensive and continuous efforts of NGOs and the government to inform the public about the needs for help abroad have also been very important and effective in gaining support for foreign aid. But these efforts have no doubt also benefited from a predisposition on the part of the populace toward supporting the goals of social justice and a strong and legitimate role for government in achieving those goals.

However, beginning in 1989, public support for aid began to fall, dropping to 52 percent in 1992 and rising somewhat to 59 percent in 1995.[22] A 1996 survey showed that this percentage had sunk even further—to 44 percent.[23] The drop in public support can be attributed primarily to economic stresses in Sweden that have contributed to a demand even at home for lower taxes and less government regulation. News reports in the early 1990s of ineffective and wasteful Swedish foreign aid have also likely contributed to a decrease in public support. The decline in support may thus be transient. But it may also reflect a more fundamental change in the attitudes of the Swedish populace toward the role of government in their society. If this proves to be the case, there may well be a permanent

decrease in support for high levels of aid abroad and a continuing downward trend in Swedish aid in the future.

Capacity

The Swedish government has had one of the clearer development doc-
trines of any significant aid donor. The primary objective—stated in legislation, in official statements, and in many speeches—has been the alleviation of poverty. In pursuing this objective, Swedish aid, as of the
mid-1990s, was guided by six goals: the four included in Bill 100 in 1962
(to contribute to growth, to economic and social equality, to economic
and political autonomy, and to democracy) plus two added since: protecting the environment and promoting gender equality. The addition
of the latter two goals reflects a broader trend evident among aid donors—the expansion in the number of sectors in which the agencies fund
projects and programs.

In the early 1970s, Sweden introduced the concept of "country programming" and began to evaluate its aid. Country programming was a
process rather different from that of most other doors—though, as we
shall see, not unlike the approach followed by the European Commission. It involved creating a multiyear programmatic and financial framework for aid to individual countries, based on joint planning with recipient governments. This approach was a logical outgrowth of Sweden's
recipient-oriented aid. However, Stockholm's disappointing experience
with recipient-driven aid has led it to tighten its programming procedures
in recent years. In 1993, a new programming system was introduced,
including country strategy documents for each of its "program countries"
and a greater conditioning of Swedish aid on the performance of the
recipient government in the areas of economic-policy reform, human
rights, and democratization. There is also a heightened concern for the
effectiveness of Swedish aid and a greater emphasis on assessing its results.

Sida has a staff-to-aid ratio in the midrange of DAC donor agencies,
with just under $2 million per employee, roughly on the order of the
United States.[24] It cannot, therefore, be said that the Swedish aid program is understaffed relative to the programs of other donors. However,
Sweden has a very limited field presence, with only about 15 percent of
its staff posted in program countries. (The United States has about half
of its staff in the field.) This staff, formerly in separate Development
Cooperation Offices with considerable decision-making authority over

aid programs and now part of Swedish embassies, is responsible largely for gathering information on the country and advising on program strategies and for monitoring the implementation of aid activities. Sweden's limited field staff is related to its past approach to programming: leaving much of the initiative to recipient governments. As Sweden moves toward a more active engagement in the identification, design, and management of its aid programs and projects, and as it broadens the functional scope of its portfolio, it may confront a challenge in managing that aid effectively with a staff located primarily in Stockholm.

Conclusion

The performance of Swedish aid in Africa has been mixed, with problems of design, implementation, and sustainability similar to those of other donors. However, Swedish aid has experienced an additional problem rather distinct from those of other donors. Its recipient-oriented approach has resulted not in more effective aid, but—in Tanzania and perhaps elsewhere—in less effective aid that may well have hindered rather than helped development. This problem was not a result of a lack of autonomy on the part of Sida. The limitations on the effectiveness of Swedish aid derive from the capacity of Sida and of the approach of the Swedish government as a whole in addressing development problems abroad. Swedish aid policies have been strongly shaped by the values of Swedish society, the projection abroad of the "Swedish model" of government-led development and social justice, Sweden's image of itself as a voice in the world for a morally based foreign policy, and by the main constituents of its foreign aid—the NGOs. With little knowledge of the African countries where it decided to undertake aid programs and lacking staff in the field to inform it, the Swedish government accepted the political rhetoric of a Julius Nyerere of Tanzania at face value, assuming that his government had the commitment and capacity to realize the ideals it espoused of development and social justice in its own society.[25] This proved to be a mistaken judgment in Tanzania and elsewhere and led to much wastage in Swedish aid to that country and possibly others.

Not only did ideology influence Swedish aid programs in particular countries; it also influenced the way the Swedes managed their aid. By relying heavily on recipients to shape and manage aid programs, Sida did not until recently develop the systems of programming and evaluation that would permit it to manage and monitor aid closely. The lesson from the Swedish experience in Africa is that if "donor-driven" aid is often ineffective, "recipient-driven" aid can be equally ineffective. What is needed are systems that combine both the broad development expertise and technical knowledge of donors with the sense of priorities and local needs and conditions that often come only from recipients.

Italy

"The recent history of Italy's aid programme demonstrates that money does not buy success," observed the DAC in a recent review of Italian aid.[26] Italian aid in Africa is the most unusual story of any examined in this study and will therefore be recounted chronologically (rather than within the structure of three questions used in the other case studies).

Italian aid to Africa was at one point among the largest programs in Africa and also the least effective of any considered here. (One must infer the quality of Italian aid from sources other than evaluations since there were none for much of the period covered by this study.) The quantity of Italian aid surged during the 1980s, making Italy the second largest source of bilateral aid to Africa after France by 1986 and creating what the Italians themselves recognized as a "crisis of increase." Much of the aid was concentrated in the Horn of Africa, where Italy had historical ties, having had as colonies Italian Somaliland, Eritrea, and, briefly, Ethiopia. Much of it was used for large construction projects that proved to be poorly planned, politically driven, and riven with waste and corruption involving Italian businessmen and political party officials.

The scandals involving Italian aid broke during the early 1990s, although the ineffectiveness of aid had been the object of criticisms in the Italian parliament and from the DAC during the 1980s. Audit Office reports on Italian aid after 1987 were highly critical. In 1995, the parliament set up an inquiry commission to investigate aid policy. The extensive media reporting of waste and corruption has turned Italian political elites and public opinion against aid and led to a collapse in the aid effort.[27] In 1996, Italy provided roughly one-quarter of the amount of aid it had allocated to Africa in 1988. The rise and fall of Italian aid is the most dramatic demonstration of the importance of both the autonomy and capacity of aid agencies in the effective use of development aid.

A History of Italian Aid

In 1979, Italian aid worldwide was the smallest as a proportion of the country's GNP of any Western industrialized country. Most was multilateral, with bilateral aid amounting to just over $30 million. The country had no aid agency either independent of or within the Ministry of External Affairs. Unique among Western governments, Italy's aid had actually declined in absolute terms during the latter part of the 1970s. Sergio Alessandrini summed up Italian aid at the end of the 1970s in these words: "Italian aid policy was almost non-existent, diffuse, unregulated and insufficiently well defined in aims and purposes."[28]

Since the mid-1970s, Italy's foreign aid had been an issue of debate in parliament. Italian aid levels had sunk by 25 percent between 1970 and 1980. Annual reports by the DAC showed Italy as the country with by far the lowest ratio of aid to GNP of all its member states. Meanwhile, stories of hunger and starvation in Ethiopia and Somalia during the mid-1970s were widely reported in the Italian press. In 1979, Marco Pannella, the charismatic leader of the Radical Party, began periodic hunger strikes to call attention to "the holocaust of 40 million hunger-related deaths"[29] and to press government to increase aid. In 1979, the Italian parliament voted to double aid between 1980 and 1983, bringing the aid-to-GNP ratio up to the average for DAC countries, to raise that ratio by the middle of the 1980s to the average of other EC countries, and to reach the UN's target of 0.7 percent of GNP by the end of the decade. In the same year, the parliament also voted to create within the Ministry of External Affairs (MEA) a Department of Cooperation for Development (DCD). In 1985, the government decided to double its aid again, to spend the new monies within an eighteen-month period, and to set up a new agency within the MEA—the Italian Aid Fund (FAI)—to disburse the aid. The idea behind these initiatives was rather simple: there was hunger in the world—especially in Africa—and Italy was not doing its share to alleviate it.

The Italian government had to decide where and how to spend the aid windfall. It had few diplomatic or significant commercial interests in Africa to support. As with other donors, the Italians looked first to historical ties with developing countries to guide their decisions. It is not always remembered that Italy was once a colonial power in Africa. The Italian government got into the scramble for Africa late and ended up with only two colonies: Italian Somaliland and Eritrea. The Italians had attempted to establish a colony in Ethiopia but had been defeated by the army of Emperor Menelik II at Aduwa in 1896. Under Mussolini, Italy again invaded Ethiopia in 1935 but was expelled in 1943 by the British. Italy was expelled from Somaliland and Eritrea at that time as well. After the Second World War, the United Nations needed to make a decision on the disposition of Italy's former colonies. The Italian government lobbied hard for them to be returned to Italian control. There were still Italians living in Italian Somaliland, some Italian economic investments remained there, and a great deal of national pride was associated with regaining control of at least one of its former colonies. Moreover, Italian was still the second language of many educated Somalis, a further source of pride for Italy.

In 1950, the United Nations decided to grant Italy a limited trusteeship over Italian Somaliland. The Italian government would administer the territory for ten years while preparing it for independence. The Italians would finance an expansion in health services, education, and infrastructure. The Italian government maintained its aid to Somaliland after the country became independent in 1960, marking the beginning of Italian assistance to independent African countries. Thus, the decision to concentrate the dramatically increased level of Italian aid in the Horn of Africa, where there was a recurring problem of hunger and where Italy had historical ties, was logical. And within the Horn, Italy decided to practice a policy of "equal distance" between Ethiopia and Somalia (often providing them with roughly the same amount of aid annually) to avoid becoming enmeshed in the tensions that periodically erupted between those two countries. In the late 1980s and early 1990s, Italy attempted to broker a domestic reconciliation in Somalia between the government of Siad Barre and the opposition forces, largely in the north. This diplomatic effort resulted in failure and embarrassment for the Italian government.

But there was more aid than could feasibly be spent in the Horn of Africa. The Italian government decided to allocate a proportion of its aid to countries of southern Africa, in particular to Mozambique. That country was extremely poor, did not have a major Western European patron, and was thus one where a smaller power like Italy could be visible and make a difference. One of the foremost experts on Italian aid, Maria Cristina Ercolessi, cites "the importance in some cases (the area of the Horn) of historical ties and the presence of a significant community of Italians and the existence of [political] spaces in areas of recent decolonization, as in Southern Africa after the independence of Angola and Mozambique."[30] A smaller portion of Italian aid was provided the Sahelian countries, which were particularly vulnerable to drought and problems of food security. These three regions received nearly 90 percent of Italian aid to Africa, with half allocated to Somalia and Ethiopia alone.

Another important element in the choice of countries to receive aid was the preferences of political parties. The leftist parties (including the Italian Communist Party) felt ties of common ideological orientation with socialist governments in Africa. The Communist Party took a particular interest in Mozambique and Angola (both led by Marxist-oriented governments in the 1970s and 1980s), while the Italian Socialists had ties with the socialist-oriented government of Siad Barre in Somalia. (The leader of the Italian Socialist Party, Bettino Craxi, was said to have been close to Siad. And there were ties between the Somali Socialist Revolutionary Party and the Italian Socialist Party.)[31] The socialist orientation of Tanzania also made that government attractive to leftist parties in Italy, and it became an important recipient of Italian aid.

Reflecting these choices, Somalia and Ethiopia were among the top three recipients of Italian aid during the 1980s; Italy soon became the largest single source of aid to Ethiopia and Somalia. By 1988, Italy was providing Somalia with aid equivalent to nearly half of its gross national product. In the 1980s, Mozambique also became one of the top five recipients of Italian aid.

With little expertise in development in the Italian government, uses of aid were strongly influenced by Italy's economic interests and, it has been alleged, by personal and political interests of Italy's political class.[32] A large proportion of the aid was spent on infrastructure projects with procurement tied to Italian construction and engineering firms. A portion of the aid was channeled through Italian NGOs for small-scale development work. In contrast to other donors, very little of Italian aid (around 10 percent) was allocated to technical assistance.

Criticisms of the management of Italian aid began to surface in the 1980s. In several of its press releases describing its reviews of Italian aid, the DAC urged the government "to accelerate measures to strengthen aid administration so as to ensure speedy and effective implementation" of the assistance.[33] By the beginning of the 1990s, parliamentarians were beginning to criticize aid in Africa, particularly in Somalia. Feeding this criticism initially was the absence of economic growth despite very high levels of assistance. And Italian diplomacy in the region had proven a failure. But more telling was evidence of extraordinary cost overruns on projects, which were themselves proving unsustainable. And there were signs of potential abuse: the firms designing the projects were frequently the firms awarded the construction contracts (often without competitive bidding).[34] In 1992, stories of pervasive corruption in the Italian government, involving illicit payments from Italian business firms to political parties and government officials, broke in the press. Some of these scandals involved Italian aid—again in particular to Somalia. Particularly cited were several projects: the construction of a road from Garoe to Bosaso (across barren desert but in the region of Somali president Siad Barre's clan); the establishment of the University of Somalia (where the teaching initially was in Italian by Italian instructors) even though few Somalis had access to primary education; and the inevitable modern hospital that the Somalis were not yet prepared to operate. One newspaper report declared that "Italy sponsored 114 projects in Somalia between 1981 and 1990, spending more than a billion dollars. With few exceptions (such as a vaccination program carried out by non-governmental organizations), the Italian ventures were absurd and wasteful."[35]

Criticisms were not directed only at aid in Somalia. The Italians built the Bakolori dam and irrigation complex in Sokoto, Nigeria, the home state of President Shehu Shagari. The Nigerians never repaid the loans for this project, as had been predicted by some critics.

The ineffectiveness and corruption associated with Italian aid to Africa, combined with pressures to reduce the budget deficit, led to a decline in Italian aid worldwide and a free fall in its aid to Africa, decreasing from over $1 billion per year between 1987 and 1990 to $322 million in 1996. It also led to a reform involving a reorganization in the Directorate-General for Development Cooperation (formerly the DCD, still part of the Ministry of External Affairs), the adoption of programming systems for project appraisal, implementation, and evaluation, and a competitive procurement process. These reforms are still in process of implementation, and further reforms—including the establishment of an independent aid agency—are being debated. These changes promise more effective Italian aid in Africa but not higher levels of aid.

Analysis

Autonomy

This analysis will focus on the characteristics of the Italian aid system at the beginning of the 1980s, when the level of that aid began its rapid rise. During the 1960s and 1970s, Italian aid was distributed by various bureaus of the Ministry of External Affairs, the Treasury (allocating contributions to multilateral institutions), and seven other government ministries without any apparent policy or coordinating mechanism. With the increase in aid in 1979, a new Department of Cooperation for Development was set up within the Ministry of External Affairs; and the Interministerial Committee for Foreign Policy was charged with shaping aid policies. The size and administrative experience of the DCD were limited at the time of the first surge in aid in 1980, and as a result, the aid was obligated only slowly.

With the second jump in aid levels in 1986, an additional organization was created—the FAI, mentioned above—charged with obligating that aid within the eighteen months allotted by the parliament. The FAI was widely regarded as under the control of the Socialist Party. It is not surprising that much of the aid managed by the FAI went to Somalia, where the Socialists had ties with the Somali political leadership.

Both of these aid organizations were small, weak, and inexperienced. They proved to have little real autonomy vis-à-vis powerful commercial interests. Nor were they able to resist pressures from powerful politicians to program the aid according to their personal or ideological preferences. Indeed, a party leader was put in charge of the FAI. The alliance between party officials and commercial interests was clearly more than the new aid agencies could deal with. The voice for development within the government was almost nonexistent, and formal systems of accountability— for example, oversight by the parliament—were extremely weak.

The diplomatic goals of the Ministry of External Affairs played a relatively small role in the allocation and use of the aid. Italy, in reality, had few diplomatic goals in Africa at this time except enhancing its presence in the region and doing what it could in Somalia and later in Mozambique to bring about peace between warring political factions. The large amounts of Italian aid to Ethiopia and Somalia provided the Italian government with an opportunity to take a forceful lead in shaping events in the Horn of Africa. It used the opening to raise issues with governments it aided. But it proved unwilling to deploy that aid as leverage in support of its preferences. This might have been a laudable approach if the governments it was aiding had a commitment to developing their countries, and if the aid itself had been used to promote priority development goals. But the commitment of governments receiving the aid was weak in both cases. And the aid, it appears, was already associated with Italian commercial and domestic political purposes.

The relationship of NGOs to the Italian aid program involved mainly the implementation of projects abroad. Italian NGOs lacked the capacity during the 1980s to monitor the use of aid or to play the role that British and Swedish NGOs have in resisting commercial purposes. Italian NGOs remain weak today, struggling with the impact of a sudden decrease in aid previously channeled through them (and on which they had become highly dependent).

Capacity

The entities responsible for Italian aid during the 1980s lacked all the requisites for capable management. Their mission was vague and included an emphasis on the use of aid for commercial penetration of foreign markets. There were no country strategies and no overall plans for aid interventions in particular countries. Projects were vetted for technical quality but not for long-term sustainability. Nor were they adequately monitored or evaluated. The development staff were officers of the Ministry of External Affairs, on loan from other ministries, or fixed-term contract employees. There was no permanent staff with an expertise in development or the management of aid resources. There was, needless to say, no field presence.

Conclusion

The Italian government has learned the hard way what it takes to manage an effective aid program—by making all the mistakes that lead to an ineffective one. It undertook a rapidly increasing development assistance program for domestic political reasons without either the policies or organizational capacity to implement it and without an influential constituency inside and outside government not only to protect the developmental goals of the aid but to hold it accountable as well. As a result, the aid was captured by political parties and commercial interests and allocated for questionable and, at times, corrupt purposes. Once the mismanagement of aid was publicized, the public turned against it, and the aid declined as rapidly as it had risen. Italy is implementing reforms intended to strengthen the effectiveness of its aid. However, it seems unlikely that Italy will ever play a major role as a donor of foreign aid in Africa again.

Japan

Japan emerged from the Second World War defeated, occupied by the U.S. military, in many ways a developing country and a recipient of aid from the United States and the World Bank. In 1954, it recovered enough to begin paying war reparations to countries of Asia it had occupied during the war. Japan also joined the Colombo Plan and began to contribute technical assistance to India and other, poorer countries of Asia.[36] In the early 1960s, Japan established several government agencies to implement its growing program of assistance, largely in Asia.

In the early 1960s, Japan had little in the way of economic or political interests in Africa and provided almost no aid to the region. However, the Nigerians inadvertently forced Japan to begin an aid program in 1966.[37] In the wake of Nigerian independence in 1960, Japanese exports (particularly textiles) to Nigeria increased rapidly while its imports from Nigeria remained small. Soon, Nigerian officials attempted to persuade Japan to increase its imports from Nigeria, with little success. The Nigerians then began to threaten the Japanese. Chief Obafemi Awolowo, one of the most prominent Nigerian politicians, warned in 1963:

> Unless the Asiatic countries undertake right now to buy from us equivalent value of goods in return for what we buy from them, our national interest dictates that we should stop forthwith buying from them. . . . Of all the Asiatic countries, Japan is the chief culprit in this matter. We cannot afford to go on year in year out to lose money to a very rich—almost over-rich country like Japan. We must insist on equitable trade with all our overseas customers.[38]

In 1963, the Nigerian government put limits on imports of certain Japanese goods. Nevertheless, the deficit with Japan continued to widen until 1966, when Prime Minister Tafawa Balewa imposed a total embargo on Japanese imports, except textiles. The Japanese, apparently surprised by this move, responded with an offer of a £10 million concessional loan to Nigeria to offset the trade deficit. The Nigerians, equally surprised, decided to accept it, declaring, however, that it was inadequate to deal with the trade imbalance. The threat of sanctions was apparently so effective in producing an offer of concessional credits that Kenya, Uganda, and Tanzania quickly followed Nigeria's example, provoking similar offers of aid from Tokyo.[39] Japanese aid to Africa had begun. By 1995, Japan was the fourth largest aid donor in Africa, providing over $1 billion to the region per year.

Which Countries to Aid?

The Japanese government allocated its aid in Africa on the basis of several criteria. In the early years, interest in protecting expanding markets for exports played a role. In the 1970s, another commercial concern— securing needed imports of raw materials—affected the selection of countries. In 1970, after a visit to Africa, Fumihiko Kono, chairman of Mitsubishi, articulated the role of aid in maintaining access to Africa's minerals:

If Japan really wants to approach Africa with the consideration to [sic] the importance of underground resources of Africa, Japan must extend fairly substantial economic aid to these countries. At present the African nations are friendly towards Japan. However, this can well change if Japan fails to show its sincere attitude concerning its economic aid to them because other advanced countries of the world have been giving assistance on a large scale.[40]

Nigeria, Zaire, and Zambia—all mineral producers—were among the early recipients of Japanese aid. Niger—a source of uranium—was one of the few Francophone countries in Africa to receive significant amounts of Japanese aid.

Second, the Japanese provided aid to "regional influentials," in economic or political terms, including Kenya and Tanzania. Kenya was long among the more promising economies in Africa. It was an obvious country to aid in that it might one day become an attractive market for trade and investment. Tanzania under President Nyerere had significant regional influence, and Japan wanted to establish a close relationship with influential African governments. Tanzania's role in pressing for change in white-ruled South Africa was also a consideration. The Japanese government had an active trading relationship with the South Africans and wished to mitigate criticisms of that relationship from other Africans. Providing generous aid to Tanzania was one way to achieve that goal.[41] A similar policy also explains in part the relatively large amount of Japanese aid to Zambia.

Sudan was the recipient of significant amounts of Japanese aid during the 1980s, illustrating yet another influence over allocation. Aid to Sudan was almost certainly the result of encouragement (or pressure) from the United States, which wished to reward Sudan for its support for the Camp David Accords. Indeed, it appears likely that a number of Japan's choices of aid recipients in Africa were influenced by the United States. U.S.-Japanese consultations on policies toward Africa began in the early 1970s and often included references to African countries in which the United States had an interest.[42]

By the end of the 1970s, the United States was much more direct in its approaches to the Japanese government for aid to priority countries. In the case of Sudan, when pressures from midlevel U.S. officials failed to produce an increase in Japanese aid to Sudan, Secretary of State Alexander Haig wrote directly to Foreign Minister Sakurauchi, urging more Japanese aid. Japan soon agreed.[43] Japanese aid to Liberia and particu-

Table 8. Major Recipients of Japanese Aid to Africa (Cumulative Millions of Dollars, 1990–94 Disbursed)

Kenya	1,359
Zambia	896
Tanzania	864
Nigeria	783
Ghana	767
Sudan	521
Senegal	505
Zaire	397
Malawi	391
Madagascar	365
Total	6,848
Total Japanese Aid to Africa	9,271

Source: Ministry of Foreign Affairs, *Japan's Official Development Assistance: Annual Report, 1995* (Tokyo: Ministry of Foreign Affairs, 1995), pp. 373–433.

larly to Somalia during the 1980s (albeit relatively small) likely also emerged largely from a U.S. concern to bolster friendly but troubled governments.

Aid to Nigeria and Zaire was tied to the minerals those countries produced plus their size and potential political influence in the region. Aid to both Sudan and Nigeria was cut back sharply during the 1990s as political conditions deteriorated. See table 8 for details.

During the 1970s and 1980s, Japan's choice of African aid recipients was influenced by its commercial and political goals as well as its relationships with the United States—providing financial support for U.S. diplomatic priorities there. In the 1990s, Japan began to allocate aid to promote its own diplomatic objectives—specifically, to gain a seat as a permanent representative on the UN Security Council. Japan was now one of the most developed countries in the world, and Tokyo felt that its economic and political position justified a permanent seat. But such a seat required that the membership of the Security Council be expanded. There needed to be enough votes of all UN members to support such an expansion as well as enough votes for Japan as one of the new members. The Africans had the largest bloc of votes in the organization, and their support would be crucial. Japan's aid—by 1996 at least a small amount to nearly all African countries, even including the better-off ones like Gabon and Mauritius—was important in its search for support. Another element in Japan's strategy to gain a Security Council seat was to host a series of international conferences in Tokyo, one of which was the 1993 Tokyo International Conference on African Development

(TICAD), attended by a number of African heads of state plus high-level representatives from donor countries. TICAD focused on a wide range of African development issues, including what lessons the experience of Asia had for Africa. Following the 1993 conference, in 1996, a Conference on Development Strategy and a high-level Seminar on African Development were held. Japan soon announced a second TICAD in 1998. Such conferences permitted Japan to showcase its own approach to successful development, as well as to provide Japanese officials opportunities privately to lobby Africans for their support for a Security Council seat.[44]

Finally, Japanese aid in Africa has not been without its own special—even emotional—ties. Japanese aid to Ghana was in part based on the work of a well-known Japanese medical scientist who had undertaken research on yellow fever and eventually died of the disease in Ghana. A proportion of Japanese aid to Ghana has funded a research center in Accra in memory of the scientist.[45]

How Much Aid to Provide?

The size of Japanese aid to African countries has been primarily a result of the overall size of its aid program worldwide and the percentage of that program assigned to Africa. With the growing strength of the Japanese economy evident in the 1970s, the United States urged Japan to assume a greater share of the burden of world security through enlarged aid programs and to allocate more aid to regions other than Asia, where Japanese aid had thus far been concentrated.[46]

At a UN Trade and Development Conference in 1972, the Japanese government committed itself to raising its aid to 0.7 percent of GNP. The prime minister announced at the Bonn Summit in 1978 the first of a series of "medium-term plans" to double Japanese aid, in this case in three years. They met this target in 1980. In 1981, the Japanese government set another doubling target to be reached by 1985, followed by a third, fourth, and fifth plan for substantial aid increases. By 1995, Japan had become the world's leading aid donor, providing $14.5 billion in foreign aid annually. (The next largest donor was France at $8.4 billion annually.)

From the 1970s, Japan began "globalizing" its assistance, much as the United States had urged. The Japanese adopted a policy of allocating roughly 70 percent of their aid to Asia and another 10 percent each to Africa, Latin America, and the Middle East. With the trend in the rest of the world during the 1980s and early 1990s to increase the proportion of aid to Africa, the Japanese raised their aid to the region to 13 percent by 1996.

Thus, with the increase in overall aid and the rise in the proportion going to Africa, Japanese aid there began to increase rapidly during the 1970s and later, expanding from $18.5 million in 1973 to $233 million in 1980—a jump of over twelvefold in seven years. It then doubled in size from 1980 to 1995. However, with the announcement by the government of Japan in 1997 that it would be decreasing its aid worldwide, its aid to African seemed likely to drop.

What Should the Aid Finance?

The rhetoric of Japanese aid suggests that it finances many of the same types of social-sector interventions that typify the aid of the United States, United Kingdom, and other major donors. Statements by Japanese officials in the mid-1990s emphasized providing for basic needs of the poor, promoting democracy, helping to protect the environment, and supporting gender equality and girls' education. But the reality of Japanese aid, as evinced by project descriptions in its annual reports and evaluations (and consistent with my own experience), is that it has primarily funded physical infrastructure in various sectors, provided equipment and training, and offered food aid to African recipients. Japanese aid in Africa has also included nonproject assistance in support of policy reform.

During the 1980s, the increases in Japanese aid to Africa began to outrun the abilities of the government to program the aid, a problem recognized by the Japanese themselves. In theory, their system was "request based," rather like the Swedish system, in which recipient governments came to the Japanese government with a request for funding and the Japanese responded. In practice, however, the Japanese system was very different from that of Sweden. Recipient government requests for assistance were often generated by Japanese trading houses or business enterprises abroad, working through recipient governments. This system permitted the Japanese government to operate a large aid program with a minimum of staff, relying to a considerable extent on its private sector to help identify, design, and execute projects. And it resulted in aid projects that also frequently coincided with the interests of Japanese business. However, there were few such businesses represented in Africa, and the region itself was generally too poor for the large, loan-financed infrastructure projects that the Japanese were used to funding elsewhere. Not surprisingly, much of the increase in Japanese aid, particularly after the mid-1980s, was for nonproject assistance in support of economic reform, provided as cofinancing of the World Bank reform programs.[47] The Japanese also hired British Crown Agents to manage procurement of their nonproject economic assistance. Some of the aid was channeled through the United Nations Development Program and other international agencies.

Effectiveness of Japanese Aid

There are no overall assessments of the effectiveness of Japanese aid in Africa known to this author. Should such an assessment be written, it would have to include an estimate of the amount of Japanese aid to Africa's failed states. Japan, at times under pressure from the United States, provided aid to Liberia, Somalia, Sudan, and Zaire. The aid to Somalia, Liberia, and Zaire, totaling $1.1 billion over the period of this study, likely qualifies as largely lost with the collapse in these economies. This amounts to just over 10 percent of Japan's total aid to Africa—considerably less than the proportion of U.S. aid to these countries.

Turning to the effectiveness of Japanese projects and programs in Africa, it was only in 1981 that the Japanese government began a program of systematic evaluations of its aid projects abroad.[48] These evaluations do not include Japanese nonproject assistance for economic reform. (That assistance was normally coordinated with the World Bank; and thus, Japan's experience would be little different from that of the Bank, i.e., only partially successful economic-reform programs.) The evaluations point to many of the same problems of effectiveness experienced by other donors in Africa, particularly the institutional weakness of local government agencies (which at times failed to fulfill their obligations within the projects) and the financial sustainability of the projects themselves. At times, it also appears that the Japanese equipment provided African organizations was too sophisticated for local needs and capabilities.

One of the more detailed summary evaluations of Japanese aid involves Kenya, where Japan has become the largest donor.[49] This evaluation observes that "Kenya has demonstrated a great deal of success in implementing aid projects. . . . Nevertheless, judging from our past experience with foreign aid, it still seems that there is much to be done in the Kenyan situation."[50] The reasons for the report's doubts about Kenya and the effectiveness of Japanese aid were three: Kenya's development planning and economic reforms were inadequate and created uncertainties about future government policies; the capacity of the Kenyan government was weak; and the sustainability of projects was uncertain. The report also worried about Japan's performance as a donor in Kenya as it suffered from "a shortage of local staff and a lack of understanding about Kenyan development problems."[51] The report went on to find a number of Japanese infrastructure projects in Kenya successful, for example, several bridges in Mombasa that relieved traffic congestion, in an important area for tourism. The report also highlights major problems: on the Kenyan side, the government at times did not meet its local cost obligations; and there were problems with local counterparts in technical cooperation. On the Japanese side, there was an absence of policy to determine when project and nonproject aid should be provided; a lack of information on Kenyan government capacity; and a shortage of Japanese aid staff in Kenya. The report remarks that these problems are "more or less common in all the African countries."[52]

The evaluations reviewed for this study indicate several things about the effectiveness of Japanese aid in Africa. First, there have been few if any major disasters, either in terms of a significant proportion of aid wasted in highly corrupt or collapsed states or on large projects or classes of projects (for example, involving integrated rural development) that have failed. The more complex and risky interventions undertaken by other donors, involving efforts to bring about social, economic, and political change, have played a very limited role in Japanese aid in Africa. However, Japan—even with the limited focus of its aid—has not escaped a number of the problems of design, implementation, and sustainability that other donors have experienced.

Finally, the aspect of Japanese aid most commented upon by other aid agencies is the absence of the Japanese from development discussions in the region. The intellectual impact of the Japanese on development discourse in Africa appears to have been very little over most of the period of this study. In the 1990s, however, the Japanese have tried, in the TICAD, mentioned above, to demonstrate the efficacy of their approach and that of other Asian nations to development—state-guided, export-led growth—and its applicability to Africa. This remains a controversial view.[53]

The Future of Japanese Aid

Like so many of the donors in this study, the Japanese appear to be in a period of transition, involving the size, organization, and orientation of their aid. In 1996, after years of increases in overall aid, including aid to Africa, the Japanese reduced aid, including aid to Africa, which fell from $1.4 billion to $1.1 billion. Further, the government announced the intention of decreasing its aid in 1997 by 10 percent per year, to be followed by further decreases in subsequent years. This decrease almost certainly portends a continued decline in the amount provided Africa. The decrease has arisen from efforts on the part of the Japanese government to decrease its budget deficits at home. But it is also almost certainly an indirect result of the major decreases in U.S. aid that took place several years earlier. The Japanese have tended to follow the lead of other major aid donors in much of their aid program. Once the United States began to decrease its aid, it is likely that budget cutters in Japan's government were able to argue that it was unnecessary for Japan to continue to increase its aid.[54] And since Japanese aid had expanded well beyond the level of aid from any other donor, it had no need to increase further or even maintain that level to remain the world's largest donor.

Like other donor governments, the Japanese have also begun to reorganize their aid program. It was decided that the Overseas Economic Cooperation Fund (OECF), responsible for implementing loan-based aid, was to be merged with the Japanese Export-Import Bank (JEXIM) by the end of the decade. This was an effort to streamline government and reduce the number of agencies engaged in development activities abroad. Although OECF had in earlier decades been part of the Export-Import Bank, the merger raised questions about whether the influence of Japanese commercial interests over the concessional loan program would not increase once the merger had been accomplished. A private panel advising the Japanese government recommended further organizational changes in the country's aid. One involved putting more power in the hands of the Ministry of Foreign Affairs to determine country aid programs and coordinate the country's fragmented aid system. Another involved enhancing the role of Japanese NGOs in the implementation of the country's aid abroad.

Analysis

Autonomy

Japanese aid has suffered from a number of the same problems of effectiveness experienced by other aid donors in Africa. But the strengths and weaknesses of Japanese aid are peculiar to Japan. The Japanese aid program is among the most fragmented organizationally of all the aid programs examined in this book—even more so than the French aid program. There is no single government agency responsible for managing it, no formal locus of control, oversight, political responsibility, or accountability. Policy and implementation are separated organizationally, and a number of separate ministries and agencies participate in policy decisions and in supervising the organizations implementing the aid. A total of eighteen ministries run their own aid programs, albeit most are quite small.

Over half of Japan's bilateral aid worldwide is provided as loans, often for infrastructure projects. The Overseas Economic Cooperation Fund is responsible for implementing such projects. But decisions on whether to approve major loans are taken by four ministries: the Ministry of International Trade and Industry (MITI), the Ministry of Finance, the Ministry of Foreign Affairs, and the Economic Planning Agency (which is also responsible for supervising OECF).

Japanese technical assistance and other grant programs are implemented by the Japanese International Cooperation Agency (JICA). Policy decisions on grants and technical assistance executed by JICA are made primarily by the Ministry of Foreign Affairs but usually after informal consultations with the Ministry of Finance and other ministries as relevant. In addition, most other ministries have their own small aid programs abroad. OECF and JICA—where Japan's development expertise would logically be located—are themselves largely led by officials cross-posted from a variety of other government agencies. For example, in 1990, eleven of JICA's eighteen departments were headed by officials from other agencies.[55] All of these arrangements produced an organizational environment in which the autonomy, accountability, and influence of individual aid organizations are weak and dispersed.

Since the 1950s, there have been calls from inside and outside the Japanese government for a reform of its aid machinery that would include the creation of a single aid agency.[56] The government has resisted taking such a decision, mainly because of internal bureaucratic opposition. The Ministry of Foreign Affairs has resisted the idea, fearing it would lose control over foreign aid. Other ministries, deeply entrenched in shaping decisions on foreign aid, hold similar fears (and not without reason). Thus, the organizational environment has remained little changed (with the exception of the decision to merge OECF into JEXIM, mentioned earlier.)

Turning to other potential players in policy choices on Japan's aid, the prime minister rarely gets involved in aid policy or program decisions. One expert on Japanese politics argues that because the prime minister was in the past elected by the Liberal Democratic Party (LDP) in the Diet, he had to balance key factions in the LDP through his appointments to powerful ministries, including MITI, the Ministry of Finance, and the Ministry of Foreign Affairs. He then found it difficult to take policy positions opposed to those ministries, including policy positions involving foreign aid.[57] This is even more the case with a coalition government in power as of this writing.

The Japanese parliament—or Diet—plays a very minor role in foreign-aid issues. It can question officials, conduct debates, and pass resolutions regarding foreign aid, but it is not organized, nor does it have the capacity to provide oversight. Political parties also play a minor role in aid decisions in Japan. All Japanese political parties have been supportive of foreign aid, though opposition parties have occasionally criticized the aid program for being too commercially oriented and for mismanagement. There has been some speculation that LDP politicians have favored certain countries over others as recipients and that some well-placed politicians are able to influence the ministries in their decisions on the allocation and use of aid. Political parties do not, however, appear to have the degree of influence over country allocations of aid that they have enjoyed in other countries—for example, Sweden.

The main influence on Japanese aid outside government has been the Japanese business community, both as implementers of Japanese aid programs and as supporters of the size and orientation of the aid. They maintain close ties with government bureaucracy through a practice known as *amakudari,* in which senior officials retiring from key government ministries are hired by commercial enterprises. Sometimes those enterprises also second their own employees to government ministries, all creating strong and widespread informal networks that influence aid decisions, particularly the type of aid projects undertaken.[58]

Japanese enterprises are organized into a number of umbrella groups, the Japanese Federation of Economic Organizations (Keidanran) being among the largest and most powerful. Keidanran has close ties to the LDP, acting as an important funding source for the party.[59] Keidanran and other quasi-public organizations (many of which were actually set up by MITI) maintain close contacts with MITI and other government agencies and also can influence foreign-aid decisions.[60] Additionally, they act as a constituency for Japanese aid within the country. And while Keidanran's interests and those of Japanese business are not always exactly the same, there has been a strong commonality of objectives among them over a period of decades.

However, an important change may be taking place in the support provided by these organizations for Japanese aid. Under pressure from the United States and other DAC members, the Japanese government has untied a considerable proportion of its aid, with the result that fewer Japanese firms are benefiting from government aid contracts.[61] Officials from Keidanran as well as Japanese journalists have reported that with the untying of Japanese aid, the large trading houses have begun to complain loudly about the changes and show signs of losing interest in foreign assistance.[62]

In contrast to many of the countries examined here, NGOs play a minor role in influencing or implementing Japanese aid. There are approximately four hundred Japanese NGOs engaged in development activities. However, most of these have been established in the past twenty years and remain financially and administratively weak. Nearly 90 percent of NGOs lack legal and tax-exempt status. To obtain legal status, an NGO must be registered with one or more government ministries (and in effect, be "overseen" by those ministries). The requirements for registration are stringent and imply that the NGO must have substantial financial reserves, excluding the many smaller NGOs that cannot meet these standards. Once an NGO is registered, it is eligible to receive 50 percent matching grants from the Japanese government for activities it implements abroad.

One of the main sources of aid funding for NGOs is the Ministry of Foreign Affairs. Another important source derives from the Postal Savings System's Voluntary Deposits for International Assistance Fund, established in 1990. Depositors can donate 20 percent of the interest on their savings to NGO development activities abroad. The Ministry of Posts and Telecommunications decides on the allocation to NGOs of the sizable quantity of funds produced by this arrangement. Government funding for NGO activities abroad reached $364 million in 1994, up from $290 million a year earlier.[63] Although increasing, the total amount of NGO funding remains very small (2.6 percent of Japan's aid budget) compared to ratios in the Nordic countries and the United States of around 20 percent to one-quarter of bilateral aid. The small amount reflects the limited number and capacity of Japanese NGOs. But it also reflects a history of hostility and distrust between NGOs, a number of which had attacked government policies in the past, and government officials. One NGO official described the relationships this way: "The typical perception of NGOs held not only by bureaucrats but by the public in general was non-conformists or deviants, if not antagonists. That was because the Japanese society had traditionally placed heavy emphasis on harmony and conformity instead of diversity. Those who raised an objection (even if it was a legitimate one), or 'rocked the boat,' had typically been marginalized or even ostracized."[64]

Japanese NGOs, like their counterparts elsewhere, favor a greater focus on grassroots development in their government's aid program, more collaboration between NGOs and government on aid policy and broad programmatic decisions, and a greater reliance on NGOs to implement aid programs. Japanese NGOs also favor an easing in the restrictions governing their registration with government and their legal and tax status. NGOs active in particular sectors, for example, environmental NGOs, have had some success as advocates on particular issues, forcing the government for example to cancel a project involving the distribution of toxic pesticides to Cambodian farmers. But for the most part, Japanese NGOs have little experience and limited influence as advocates for development with their government.

While the Japanese government has begun to utilize NGOs in its work abroad, there are serious obstacles to a substantial NGO role in Japanese aid. On the government side, the aid program itself, as described above, has long been strongly oriented toward commercial goals and influenced by a powerful and entrenched constituency inside and outside government committed to those goals. Working with NGOs in a significant way would involve a shift in direction of Japanese aid away from commercial objectives and a reliance on Japanese enterprises to implement aid projects toward an emphasis on a more participatory, social-sector-oriented program, relying on NGOs to implement it. A significantly greater reliance on working with NGOs might also require a change in views on the part of many bureaucrats who in the past have regarded NGOs with some disdain and distrust. While the government professes a growing commitment to such an orientation, it is unclear that without major changes in policy and organization, the Japanese aid program could accommodate such a shift. And while there are signs that the government is willing to expand its collaboration with NGOs, there is also evidence of resistance to a greater reliance on NGOs within the Japanese bureaucracy and LDP. In 1996, a law easing the restrictions on NGO registration with government was discussed by a committee of the Diet but never passed, primarily due to the opposition of LDP members (thought to be acting in part at the behest of government officials wary of encouraging greater independence by NGOs and so, losing authority over them).

On the part of the NGOs, there are also inhibitions to working more closely with the Japanese government on development. The basic one is common to most NGOs working with governments worldwide: how does an organization that is heavily dependent on government for funding maintain its independence from government? This is a particular problem for Japanese NGOs facing a government accustomed to exercising considerable control over its programs when the NGOs have few natural allies and little political leverage.

Japanese NGOs, mindful of their weak position vis-à-vis government, have created an umbrella organization—JANIC—that plays much the same role as similar organizations in other countries. They have enjoyed a boost in their visibility and access from the UN summits on population, the social summit, and the conference on women, where the Japanese government, like other governments, included them in the official delegations. And they have also attempted to utilize their contacts with foreign NGOs to strengthen their position vis-à-vis the Japanese government. In 1993, for example, JANIC organized a two-year research project on government support of NGOs elsewhere in the world and on the impact of NGO development work in poor countries. Northern and southern NGOs were involved in both elements of this project and participated in the symposia on the findings. A final International Symposium on NGO Support Schemes was held in Tokyo in 1995 with Japanese NGOs and U.S. and other Northern NGOs lobbying the Japanese government to demonstrate the importance of working with nongovernmental organizations.[65]

The effort to encourage foreign NGOs to lobby the Japanese government was a reflection of the growing political sophistication of the NGO movement—echoing the role of *gaiatsu* ("foreign pressure") in policy choices of the Japanese government. *Gaiatsu* most often comes from the United States and is most effective when there is support for U.S. policy preferences within the Japanese government. On aid issues, this has frequently involved an informal alliance between the U.S. government (the Department of State and occasionally USAID) and the Ministry of Foreign Affairs. Officials from MOFA have, in fact, at times solicited U.S. pressures on issues they favor to strengthen their bargaining power with other ministries.[66] In 1993, a more formal channel for U.S.-Japanese consultations (and *gaiatsu*) was established—the creation of a "Common Agenda" in which officials from both governments would meet biannually and agree on joint activities. The United States has used these meetings to persuade (or pressure) the Japanese government to expand its funding of projects in the area of family planning, environment, women

in development, and a host of other areas where Japan has not traditionally been active. Whether as a result of *gaiatsu* through the Common
Agenda or not, policy statements from Tokyo have incorporated these
activities more and more into the rhetoric of Japanese aid.

The Japanese public is one of the most supportive of its government's
aid program of any among major donor countries. As of 1994, polls on
the public's view of foreign aid showed that 46 percent supported existing
levels, with another 33 percent favoring increased aid.[67] However, those
"actively in support of ODA" have been declining over time, and those
in favor of decreasing or terminating it have been increasing.[68] But even
with a modest increase in the number of Japanese skeptical of foreign aid,
the public remains extraordinarily favorable to the program, minimizing
controversy and leaving government with considerable freedom of action. The interesting question is why public support for aid has remained
so high in Japan.

Experts often refer to the trust Japanese citizens put in their government and their disinclination to question government policies. This may
be cultural, but it may also be a result of the way the Japanese government
has functioned vis-à-vis its aid program. There has been little public controversy over aid policies emanating from the Diet, and the Japanese bureaucracy has effectively limited information on its program that might
prove controversial. At the same time, the Japanese government has
funded an extensive public-education campaign on the importance of
foreign aid, with conferences, numerous publications, and an annual "International Cooperation Festival" explaining the needs of developing
countries and Japan's programs there. There is even an International
Cooperation Plaza in Tokyo where interested Japanese can learn about
aid and development. Finally, there is relatively little media reporting
that deals with controversies. There have been criticisms of corruption
and mismanagement associated with Japanese aid in the past, but these
stories have been short lived, as the government has effectively controlled
the availability of information and debates in the Diet that might give
such stories credence and duration.

Capacity

Three criticisms have been directed at the Japanese aid program consistently over time: the lack of a single aid organization, the absence of
an aid philosophy or development doctrine, and the weak capacity of
government to execute aid programs. The Japanese government has re-

sponded to the latter two problems by publishing an ODA charter in 1992 and making an effort to expand the staffing of its aid agencies over recent years. Most recently, as mentioned above, a private panel advising the government on its aid program has raised the issue of the fragmentation in Japanese aid programs and the need for their reorganization.

For years, the Japanese government had resisted promulgating a formal statement of the philosophy guiding its aid program or the passage of legislation with similar intent. Such a statement, if meaningful, would inevitably constrain that aid; and it would be difficult to gain internal consensus on such a document, given the multiple ministerial interests involved in the program. But with the ascension of Japan to the world's largest donor, with the resulting increased worldwide scrutiny and criticisms of Japanese aid (particularly its strongly commercial orientation), and with voices in favor of reform increasing inside and outside the Japanese government (including by the influential Keidanran), the government decided to issue a statement of principles governing its aid, published in the ODA charter.

In fact, the charter has little to say about aid philosophy or development strategy. It opens by citing famine and poverty in developing countries and the need for Japan to play a role "commensurate with its position in the world to maintain world peace and ensure global prosperity." It refers to the importance of supporting self-help efforts of developing countries and mentions a variety of potential activities that might be included in Japan's aid: tackling global problems (especially environment and population), addressing basic human needs, supporting human-resource development, and promoting infrastructure improvement and structural adjustment. Considerations influencing the allocation of Japanese aid include the use of aid for military purposes, the level of recipient countries' military expenditures, and the promotion of basic human rights, democratization, and market-oriented economies.[69]

The ODA charter covers virtually the entire gamut of possible aid-financed activities, giving little indication of the priorities that Japan assigns to any one in particular. Nor does it spell out the way Japan views development occurring or the government's strategy for promoting it. However, the language of the charter is similar to the language used by other aid donors, bringing Japanese development policies rhetorically in line with those of other governments.

As noted above, Japanese aid programming has long been based on a "request" system in which (in theory) the recipient government brings a request for assistance and the Japanese government responds. The request-based system obviated the need for country programming. It would make little sense for the Japanese government to undertake comprehensive country analyses and develop country strategies to determine what its aid program should look like if that program is essentially decided in response to requests from recipient governments. (OECF and JICA have produced their own individual country studies, but these have not served as overall aid planning documents.)

However, recently Japan has begun to move away from the request-based system, recognizing that it has become a major donor in many countries and cannot, if its aid is to be effective, continue to ignore the state of the recipient's economy, the policy environment, needs and opportunities, what other donors are doing, and other relevant local conditions. In a move toward country programming, in 1993, MOFA began to publish an annual "State of Implementation" report for the cabinet that contains policy statements for selected countries. The government is beginning to downplay the request-based approach, presaging perhaps a more extensive shift to approaches to aid programming common among other donors.

The government of Japan's aid agencies does not have field missions. There are regional offices of the OECF and JICA field offices, but decision-making authorities and the vast bulk of the staff remain in Tokyo. The ratio of professional staff to aid program has been among the lowest of any donor worldwide and a source of continued criticism inside and outside Japan. Full-time staff in Japan's aid agencies totaled 1,842 in 1995, compared with 3,742 in the United States, giving Japan roughly half the staff of the United States to manage a bilateral program 15 percent larger. One of the implications of the staffing levels of Japan's aid agencies is limited in-house expertise in the many types of projects the Japanese government is committed to financing. Some of the needed expertise can be hired through consultancies, but when key managers do not also have technical or geographical expertise, they can have difficulties making informed implementation decisions. The problem of limited geographical expertise is acute when it comes to Africa, where Japanese expertise is exceptionally constrained.[70] And the organization of JICA along functional lines inhibits the acquisition of geographical expertise.

But there are several other elements in the staffing of Japan's aid organizations that are worthy of note. One has already been mentioned: the hiring of retired officials from key ministries as senior officials in these agencies. The head of JICA, for example, is often a retired MOFA official. But more extensive is the seconding of personnel to JICA and OECF from other government agencies, often taking up the bulk of the senior positions. These retired and seconded officials bring little development expertise to their postings and block the advancement of JICA or OECF career staff to senior positions. Finally, those in the MOFA and other agencies making policy decisions on foreign aid also bring at best limited development experience to their jobs. The key officials in MOFA involved in aid matters, for example, are often drawn from deputy chief of mission positions in key Japanese embassies abroad (frequently from the Japanese embassy in Washington). They serve two or three years and then move to another diplomatic posting. It is hardly surprising that the Japanese government has found it challenging to provide leadership in development policies to other aid-giving governments when its senior policy and implementation officials are relatively limited in development expertise themselves.

Conclusion

Based on the weak autonomy and capacity of Japan's aid agencies, one would have thought that Japan's aid would be among the least effective of any aid donor in Africa. It appears that this has not been the case, though neither can Japanese aid be classified as one of the stronger aid programs in Africa. Japan has lost approximately 10 percent of its aid to collapsed states, the largest amount in Zaire. (Its aid to Somalia and Liberia was always relatively small.) Its projects have apparently experienced problems similar to those faced by other aid donors, though if Japanese evaluations were more detailed, rigorous, and comparable, they would provide a surer basis for judgment on the performance of aid-funded activities in Africa. Japan has contributed little to discussions of African development issues. In short, Japan has not made major mistakes in its allocation and use of aid in Africa, nor has it achieved marked successes or had a significant impact on development in the region.

The lack of capacity of Japan's aid agencies, especially in the area of programming and staffing, helps explain the country's low impact aid in Africa. The limited number of staff and the limited experience in Africa not only among its aid officials but in its intellectual community generally have kept Japan from having the impact on African development discourse its relatively large aid program would seem to invite. But the caution that has kept it from being a leader in African development has also kept it from major aid disasters in Africa as well—at least as far as can be ascertained from available materials.

Chapter Eight

The Multilaterals

The focus of this study thus far has been on the effectiveness of bilateral aid programs. We now turn to the two most prominent multilateral agencies: the World Bank and the European Commission. (The Commission's aid in Africa is financed through the European Development Fund, managed by Directorate General VIII of the Commission.) But first, how shall we conceive of these international, nonstate entities? They were created and are governed by member states. Can they rightly be thought of as distinct organizations with a measure of autonomy over their policies and programs—as "actors" much like states in the international arena? Or should they be regarded simply as extensions of the most powerful member state?[1]

These two international entities clearly qualify as international actors in their own right. As we shall see in the case studies in this chapter, they are not simply "captured" or controlled by their most powerful member states—though those states do at times exert considerable influence over the allocative decisions of these institutions. Their management is large and professional and enjoys a considerable degree of policy and managerial autonomy over most aspects of the organizations' activities. Indeed, these multilateral agencies have much in common with bilateral aid agencies, including the problems of the effectiveness of their aid in Africa.

The World Bank

The proposal to create an International Bank for Reconstruction and Development (IBRD)—which soon came to be called the "World

Bank"—emerged from Allied planning for the postwar international economy. At the Bretton Woods conference in 1944, it was agreed that the World Bank should be set up to help fund the reconstruction of war-damaged economies and to encourage, primarily through its guarantees but also through direct loans, a flow of private investment to developing countries to help promote their economic growth. The new bank was financed with contributions and callable capital from member governments and from borrowing on international capital markets. The World Bank opened its doors in June 1946. A decade later, the International Finance Corporation was set up as part of the World Bank Group to lend to private borrowers investing in developing countries. And in 1959, the International Development Association (IDA) was created to provide soft loans to poorer borrowers. These institutions remain the three major components of World Bank Group.[2]

To Which Countries to Lend?

The World Bank made its first loan to an African government in 1950 when it financed a road rehabilitation project in Ethiopia. As the independence period commenced in Africa, more countries joined the World Bank and began to receive loans. By 1970, there were thirty-six African members of the Bank, and each had received at least one loan. By 1996, all African countries save one (Namibia) had received loans from the institution, though not all received new credits each year.

The World Bank, as a multilateral agency, has attempted to provide at least a minimal level of lending to all its eligible borrowers. (In countries where states have collapsed, where governments have had such poor records of economic management that development was unlikely, or where governments have refused to service their debts to the Bank, the Bank has ceased to lend.)

In addition to a minimum level of lending for its eligible borrowers, the Bank has had internal lending targets for each borrowing country, covering three-to-five-year periods. For IDA credits (the principal type of lending in Africa), these country "targets" have been based on the size of a country's population, its degree of poverty, and its economic performance. Lending levels are supposed to be set according to a country's rating: a high level for "good performers," which almost always includes loans in support of structural- or sectoral-adjustment programs (usually implying an adjustment program in place), an intermediate level of lending for moderate performers, and a base level, involving only proj-

Table 9. Top Ten Recipients of World Bank Lending to Africa (Cumulative Millions of Dollars)

Nigeria	7,151
Ivory Coast	4,177
Kenya	3,781
Ghana	3,277
Tanzania	3,138
Zambia	2,281
Ethiopia	2,267
Uganda	2,249
Cameroon	2,063
Sudan	1,519

Source: World Bank, *Annual Report* (Washington, D.C.: World Bank, 1997), pp. 245–47.
Note: These figures include both IBRD and IDA lending.

ect financing for those governments whose performance on reform was poor or nonexistent (see table 9). The numbers in table 9 suggest that, for the most part, the Bank has followed its reported lending criteria. Nigeria, with a population estimated to be around 100 million, is by far Africa's largest country. Ivory Coast, Ghana, Zambia, Uganda, and Cameroon are all among Africa's medium-sized countries (all having populations of less than 20 million) but have at one period or another in the past several decades been viewed as "good performers." However, in a number of cases, the Bank has been reluctant to end adjustment lending even where a government has proven to be a poor performer. Rather, it has tended to cancel adjustment programs and promptly negotiate new ones—as in the case of Democratic Republic of the Congo (DRC, formerly Zaire), the twelfth largest recipient of Bank lending, during the 1980s or in the case of Senegal (the thirteenth largest recipient) even though that government implemented few agreed reforms and reversed some that it had put in place. (We shall explore the reasons for this reluctance below.)

How Much to Lend?

How much is lent to individual African countries is determined largely by two factors: the informal targets mentioned above and the overall amount of funding available for lending in Africa. Overall lending to Africa rose rapidly during the late 1970s with the expansion of IDA (which permitted the Bank to offer highly concessional terms to its poorer African borrowers). Bank loans in Africa soared again during the latter half of the 1980s as worldwide attention to the deepening economic problems in the region grew, as the level of IDA replenishments rose, and as an increasing proportion of those replenishments was committed to assisting Africa. (In the 1980s, it was agreed as part of replenishing IDA that at least 40 percent of its loans would go to countries of Africa. By 1990–91, that percentage reached 46 percent.)[3]

From a peak of just under $4 billion in 1992, World Bank lending to sub-Saharan Africa in 1996 declined to $2.7 billion,[4] reflecting the overall drop in IDA replenishments as the United States reduced its contributions, with other member states following suit. This decline also reflected a drop in the proportion of IDA lending to Africa to 40 percent, as lending increased to some of the former socialist states of central Europe and the former USSR.

What Activities to Finance?

The types of activities financed by Bank lending in Africa have reflected mainstream thinking on how economic development occurs and the role of foreign assistance in promoting it. In the 1960s in Africa, the Bank provided annually nearly two-thirds of its loans for power, transport, and mining. While continuing its lending for infrastructure, during the 1970s, with its new commitment to poverty alleviation, the Bank increased its lending in Africa for agriculture and rural development projects to between one-quarter and one-third of its total loans there.

At the beginning of the 1980s, the Bank began to expand rapidly its lending for structural adjustment. Adjustment lending came to average nearly a third of total Bank operations in Africa in the years between 1985 and 1995. However, in 1996 another change in lending policies appeared in the offing as the new World Bank president, James Wolfensohn, promised that the institution would refocus its efforts on poverty alleviation, implying a greater emphasis on funding social services (including presumably both economic reforms in these sectors as well as investments in social-sector projects).

The Effectiveness of World Bank Aid

One of the characteristics of a number of bilateral aid programs examined here is their allocation of sizable amounts of funds to governments with diplomatic priority but with little competence or commitment to development. In theory, a multilateral development agency should not be subject to pressures to allocate its funding for nondevelopmental purposes to poor performers. Has this been the case with the World Bank? To a considerable extent, this Bank has not been compelled to lend to poor performers in pursuit of nondevelopmental goals. And yet, at the same time the Bank has often proved reluctant to discontinue its lending to those poor performers. We have already mentioned Bank lending to Zaire despite Mobutu's government's well-known incompetence and corruption.[5] The Bank continued lending to Francophone African states in the late 1980s and early 1990s, despite their overvalued exchange rates, which clearly blocked economic growth as well as the success of aid programs and projects.

In these and other cases, the Bank was urged by several of its major member states to continue operations in these countries. Mobutu had the support at various times of the United States, France, and Belgium. France energetically pressed the Bank to continue lending to the CFA states, despite its wish to discontinue adjustment loans. Internal memos and documents clearly show that Bank officials were reluctant to continue lending to the Ivory Coast, Cameroon, and others but did so in large measure because of French pressure.[6] In both of these cases, the Bank eventually reduced or terminated its lending but not before considerable sums had been provided to governments whose policies constrained rather than supported economic progress. In the end, the Bank discontinued its lending to these countries, but the pressures of its member states likely prolonged that lending and contributed to what must be seen as largely wasted resources.

Another factor in the Bank's reluctance to diminish or discontinue lending has been two of its own bureaucratic imperatives—internal pressures to spend available funds and pressures to be the lead development agency in Africa. (We shall discuss these pressures in more detail in the section below on the capacity of the Bank.) These pressures contributed to a reluctance to reduce or terminate lending operations, particularly in Africa's larger countries, which usually also have the region's most influential governments and which can absorb large amounts of funds. These are, not surprisingly, countries where the World Bank wishes to do business.

The continuation of Bank lending to nonperforming governments likely also contributed to the prolongation of their faulty policies, for projects and programs funded by the Bank, like those of the major bilateral aid donors, also carry not only large amounts of resources but a measure of approbation of the economic policies. As the premier aid agency, the Bank's programs are often seen as bestowing a "Good Housekeeping Seal of Approval" on recipient governments, and World Bank adjustment loans are at times a precondition for balance-of-payments support from bilateral aid agencies and for debt rescheduling.

To sum up, the World Bank has not escaped entirely from political influences on decisions on the allocation of its aid—political pressures that at times were from member states and at times from the organization's own imperatives. However, these pressures did not play the role in World Bank aid in Africa that they did in the aid of several of the bilateral aid agencies examined in this book. The effectiveness of World Bank aid in Africa has depended more on the nature of the aid projects and programs themselves and the organization's intellectual leadership in the region.

The World Bank has the most comprehensive and accessible evaluation studies and summaries of evaluations of its aid of any of the aid agencies examined in this book. It publishes an annual summary of the results of its evaluations, which include completion reports, audits, and impact studies of a selection of projects and adjustment operations throughout the world. Since many of the projects are assessed on the basis of their economic rates of return, they can be compared across sectors and countries and over time. The Bank also produces studies of the effectiveness of its interventions in particular countries and in particular sectors. These various studies are among the most forthright of those of any donor in their descriptions both of successes and failures of Bank-financed projects and programs throughout the world and allow us to gain insights into the causes of the problems of effectiveness of Bank aid in Africa that are not usually available in the often less rigorous or less informative evaluations of other aid agencies.

The findings of these evaluations vis-à-vis the effectiveness of World Bank assistance in Africa are similar over the twenty years during which they have been undertaken (and not significantly different from the findings of several other aid agencies considered here). Evaluations of Bank operations by region between 1974 and 1994 show that from an overall satisfactory rating of 81 percent in 1974, the outcomes of Bank operations in Africa fell to 76 percent in 1980, to 57 percent in 1990 and to 51 percent in 1994. (The comparable figures for Bank operations worldwide were 86 percent, 82 percent, 69 percent, and 67 percent, respectively.)[7] By 1995, less than one-quarter of the projects were judged likely to be sustainable. This figure was well below the overall average for the Bank of 46 percent and was on a downward trend.[8] The Bank, like other donors, encountered particular problems in aid for agriculture and institutional development—two key areas for sub-Saharan African development and two typically involving complex aid interventions. Of those Bank operations involving institutional change, terminating in 1995 and evaluated in that year, for example, only 12 percent were judged to have had a "substantial" positive impact (compared to 27 percent for the Bank as a whole). Forty-three percent were judged as having a "negligible" impact in Africa and the remaining 45 percent as having a "modest" impact. These figures were significantly worse than those found for Bank operations ending in the years 1990 to 1994 and evaluated in 1995, indicating a further downward trend in the effectiveness of Bank operations in Africa. Both of these trends ran counter to positive outcomes for Bank projects and programs elsewhere in the world.[9]

In the 1980s, the focus of World Bank lending in Africa turned to financing structural- and sectoral-adjustment programs. We have already reviewed in chapter 3 the experience of aid-funded economic-reform programs in Africa. These reform programs were often joint efforts on the part of donors, and so, it is difficult to disentangle the impact of any single one. However, the programs were often designed and negotiated by World Bank staff, and the Bank played a major role in coordinating donors in their economic-reform programs in the region. Thus, to a considerable extent the performance of these programs reflects on the performance of the Bank. It will be remembered from chapter 3 that while reforms in the area of exchange rate adjustments and (to a more limited extent) in reducing fiscal deficits and barriers to trade were implemented, there is still much to be done in these latter two areas. Progress has been made in removing domestic price controls, particularly in agriculture. But rather less progress has been achieved in civil-service reform, privatization, and financial-sector reform.[10]

The relatively limited achievements in economic reform in Africa (compared to other regions of the world) are disappointing, given the nearly fifteen years of effort and the large number of structural- and sectoral-adjustment programs financed by the Bank in the region. There has been a pattern on the part of African governments of agreeing to extensive reform programs and then only partially implementing those agreements. The Bank has nevertheless continued to lend for reforms and has been reluctant to terminate reform programs because of a failure to perform on the part of borrowing governments.

The Bank's approach to technical assistance (TA), particularly for purposes of institutional development in Africa, has come in for special scrutiny. As we have seen in chapter 3, not only has technical assistance often been found ineffective in strengthening capacity in Africa, but it may actually have inhibited the development of that capacity. Roughly 10 percent of Bank lending there finances technical assistance for training and expert advice to government agencies with the ultimate aim of strengthening those agencies. An internal Bank review of the impact of its assistance for institutional development (ID) during the period 1981 through 1985 found "serious weaknesses in the way in which TA and particularly ID-related TA, is managed by the Bank. The frequently hasty and poor design of TA projects, in part attributable to inadequate diagnosis of TA needs, tends to be compounded by defects in implementation such as recruitment delays and difficulties in finding suitable consultants (particularly for training), problems associated with the employment of long-term expatriate advisers, lack of adequate counterparts, lax supervision by the Bank, poor coordination with other donors and the inadequate administrative capacity of the borrower. These are especially serious problems in Africa."[11]

The problems of effectiveness are echoed in assessments of the impact of Bank activities in specific countries. For example, in an evaluation of projects and programs in Senegal from 1960 to 1987, the Bank's Operations Evaluation Division found that while Bank activities made significant contributions in a number of areas, including the extension of transportation infrastructure, "many Bank-supported projects were beset with major problems that compromised the overall effectiveness of the interventions."[12] The data on the effectiveness of World Bank projects and programs in Africa has thus far highlighted problems in its operations. The relatively high-quality and quantitative nature of World Bank evaluation studies (in contrast, unfortunately, to the evaluation materials of most other aid agencies) make detailed assessments such as these possible. It does not imply that World Bank activities in Africa were less successful than those of other donors. Others appear to have shared many of the same problems. Moreover, it is clear that much of what the Bank has funded has contributed to African development, particularly in the area of infrastructure. Moreover, there is one other important aspect of the impact of the World Bank in Africa that is not picked up in evaluations of its projects and programs. The World Bank has come to play a leadership role both in development discourse in Africa and in certain areas of donor coordination. Since the 1970s, it has been the intellectual leader among development aid agencies operating in the region and the most active coordinator of the efforts of those agencies, at least in the field of financing economic-policy reform.[13]

An important element in Bank leadership in development in Africa is its economic memoranda on each borrowing country as well as data and analyses of a wide range of development issues. These documents are widely used by other aid agencies as well as private banks and commercial enterprises operating in Africa. But most influential of its public documents have been its reports and analyses of African economic problems, beginning with its 1981 report, *Accelerated Development in Sub-Saharan Africa*, also known as the Berg Report from its principal author, Elliot Berg. This report was the first study published by a major aid agency that pointed to the adverse impact of African economic policies on development in the region and urged extensive policy reforms. The report's findings were welcomed by many aid donors. But, not surprisingly, it turned out to be quite controversial with Africans. While Africans agreed that they faced a deepening economic crisis, many objected to the substance of the report's recommendations—in effect, reducing the role of the state in the economy and relying on free markets—and the fact that an international aid agency was criticizing their economic policies, which was viewed by many Africans as an infringement of their sovereignty. During the 1980s, the Economic Commission for Africa (ECA) sought to produce an alternative to the Bank's analyses by publishing its own, somewhat different interpretation of the economic situation in the region, emphasizing structural impediments to growth.[14] But the ECA's own analysis was weak and unconvincing, making its challenge to the preeminence of the Bank in Africa both brief and unsuccessful. It is a measure of the Bank's influence in Africa that the analysis and recommendations for policy reform in its 1981 report were, by the mid-1990s, widely accepted throughout the region even if governments had been reluctant for political reasons to implement many of the recommended reforms.

In its efforts to bring about economic reform in Africa, the Bank quickly recognized the importance of coordination among donors to ensure a coherent approach and to reduce the opportunities for African governments to play one aid agency off against another. The Bank employed two types of coordinating mechanisms. The first was the consultative groups (CGs) for individual countries. This was not a new device; consultative groups had existed before the era of economic reform in Africa. But many more were created during the 1980s in Africa because they proved useful in promoting and coordinating reform programs for individual African countries. CGs, established for most African countries by the end of the 1980s, are made up of major aid donors and representatives from an African government. They meet periodically and review the economic-reform program of that government and the plans of aid donors to finance it. The CGs are not usually venues for negotiations on reform programs or on the financing of those programs by donors (both of which have typically been finalized in advance of a CG meeting) but, rather, are rituals of presentation and approval. However, the calling of a CG by the World Bank implies Bank approval of a reform program and typically triggers increased aid from aid agencies in support of reform programs and so is an incentive for African governments to agree to such programs. (The World Bank also frequently uses the prospect of a CG informally to lobby donor governments to increase their assistance for the government whose CG is planned.) The ability of the World Bank to call a CG further adds to its leverage with its African borrowers and its ability to coordinate aid donors.

To bring aid donors together to coordinate their overall policies and reform financing for Africa, the Bank created in 1987 a second grouping called the Special Program of Assistance (SPA) made up of donors only. The SPA was organized to function over three years. It has thus far been renewed after each three-year period. The renewal of the SPA has become the occasion at which donor agencies make commitments of the amounts of assistance they plan to provide over the coming three years to support reform in Africa. The SPA has become a significant forum for donor coordination on policies involving economic reforms and, increasingly, donor activities in particular sectors. It has also become something of a pressure group of donors on donors to set generous financing targets for Africa and to avoid practices that would disrupt adjustment operations.

Another Bank-led effort at coordination (and consensus building) on development in Africa was the Global Coalition on Africa, set up in 1991. This organization, cochaired by several African leaders and leaders and prominent persons from donor countries[15] and made up of representatives from all African governments, international and regional organizations operating in Africa, and representatives of donor governments and NGOs, was intended to help broaden support for economic reforms in Africa, for generous financing for those reforms from aid donors, and general agreement on other salient economic and social issues involving the region.[16] Its modus operandi is to hold periodic meetings of its "Policy Forum," made up of officials representing its various participating states, international organizations, and NGOs to discuss important issues and to produce an annual report with information on economic and political developments in Africa.

Another significant Bank initiative—launched jointly with the IMF in 1996—involved coordinated efforts to reduce the debt of highly indebted, low-income countries, most of which were in Africa. Endorsed at the annual meetings of the World Bank and IMF in 1996, the plan would provide up to 80 percent debt relief on all types of debt (including for the first time multilateral debt) for countries sustaining a stabilization program over six years. The initiative was criticized as too long in coming and limited in immediate impact, but it represented a beginning in dealing with the particularly difficult issue of large debts held by many African states and others to the Bank and the IMF. (These two organizations were "preferred lenders" and, so, did not reschedule their debts. But that position was proving untenable, as the debts owed to them by many of the poorest countries had become so large as to be unserviceable and a potential block to investment and future growth.)

It has been argued, with some merit, that the Bank has at times been slow to recognize and address development problems and shortcomings in its own analysis and approach.[17] But without its leadership, it seems likely that considerably less would be known about development in Africa, and coordination among donors in addressing development problems would likely be far weaker.

Analysis

Autonomy

The potential limits on the autonomy of the World Bank or other multilateral organizations are quite different from those of bilateral aid agencies. They may derive from a larger multilateral body that the organization may be associated with. They may derive from member states of the organization and the institutional arrangements that govern the influence of individual member states and how that influence is exerted. They do not, in theory, derive from the legislatures, private interest groups and NGOs, or the public opinion in member states. What are the sources and degrees of constraint on the autonomy of the World Bank?

The World Bank, in the words of Moises Naim, one of its more astute observers, is "large, complex, relatively autonomous, and with a significant capacity to influence its environment."[18] The World Bank is an agency of the United Nations, linked to the UN through the charter and by a formal agreement. The UN charter specifies that the Economic and Social Council of the UN "may coordinate the activities of the specialized agencies through consultation with and recommendations to such agencies and through recommendations to the General Assembly and to Members of the United Nations."[19] ECOSOC can also require periodic reports from specialized agencies, of which the World Bank is one.[20] To give greater specificity to the relationship between the Bretton Woods institutions and the UN, each institution signed an agreement with the UN. These agreements made explicit the independence of the Bank and Fund from the UN. Actions by other UN bodies were not to constrain that independence. And in the case of the Bank, the UN would "refrain from making recommendations to the Bank with respect to particular loans or with respect to the terms or conditions of financing by the Bank."[21] The relationship that has evolved between the UN and the Bank over the past five decades has preserved the independence and autonomy of the Bank from the United Nations, including the General Assembly, the various committees of the UN, and other specialized agencies.[22]

More pertinent to the question of the autonomy of the Bank to make allocative decisions is the role of the member states of the World Bank (i.e., the governors) and their representatives on the Board of Executive Directors—the key formal mechanism of governance of the organization. Each of the 188 member states of the World Bank has a representative on the Board of Governors with voting power weighted according to the relative size of its contribution to Bank resources. This body meets once a year to review the activities of the Bank and set future directions. The authorities of the governors are delegated to the Board of Executive Directors, made up of twenty-four individuals located on a full-time basis at the headquarters of the Bank in Washington. Some of these individuals represent only one state—a large contributor to Bank capital such as the United States, United Kingdom, France, Japan, or Germany—while others represent groupings of member states (for example, Francophone African states or members from Central America) that are smaller contributors to the Bank's capital. Decisions by the board are usually taken on the basis of consensus. (Voting strength depends on the contributions of members, and when voting is required, it is usually based on a simple majority of votes cast.)

During most of the period of this study, the board occupied itself with deciding on overall Bank policies and on reviewing individual project and program loans. In most cases, policy changes as well as projects and programs were initiated and developed by the management of the Bank and presented to the board for discussion and approval. Policy proposals were usually eventually approved (albeit sometimes amended by the board), and project or program loans were rarely rejected. This was in part a result of informal logrolling in which directors from borrowing governments avoided criticizing project or program proposals for other countries, hoping that projects proposed for their country would be similarly treated. But also important were efforts by management to avoid presenting projects that would provoke strong opposition by board members, particularly from the larger shareholders. (At times, Bank staff did propose lending operations known to be opposed by influential member states but with the knowledge that most other members would support them. For example, the Bank proceeded with renewed lending to China despite the opposition of the U.S. administration and Congress.[23] In Africa, the Bank continued to lend during the regime of Col. Mengistu in Ethiopia, despite U.S. opposition.) And when an influential member of the board has strongly favored lending to a particular country or the adoption of a particular policy, Bank staff have often tried to accommodate that member, particularly when there is support among Bank staff for the policy or lending operation advocated by the member state.

In 1993, the board decided to change its approach to governance of the Bank. It would review overall policies and country assistance strategies. It would also review structural-adjustment programs, but it would no longer review individual projects unless a board member requested such a review. And it would create a Committee on Development Effectiveness of board members to examine in greater detail problems of effectiveness of Bank operations worldwide. These decisions were intended to remove the board from the details of lending operations while concentrating its attention on the overall strategies that guided lending to individual countries. These reforms may, in fact, enhance the influence of the board over the broad thrust of Bank activities. On the other hand, they could further limit the influence of the board over what the Bank actually finances in its borrowing countries. In the end, its lending operations remain the key instrument of Bank influence on development in borrowing countries.

The foregoing discussion suggests that the Bank has enjoyed a considerable degree of autonomy from its board, based in part on the nature of the board and in part on the strength of the management of the Bank. Moises Naim echoed this observation, commenting that "a divided board of overwhelmed directors, many of whom cannot afford to irritate the

Bank's management, and usually leave by the time they begin to be more effective, is no match for a usually brilliant group of professionals with decades of experience at the Bank."[24] A number of factors have contributed to the relative autonomy of Bank management from the board. One is the size of the board and the distribution of power within it. With voting power based on the amount a member state contributes to the Bank's capital, no single member has a majority of votes. (The United States has the largest single proportion of votes—20 percent.) Thus, no single state can dominate board decisions.

Another factor is the duration of membership on the board, which tends to be for relatively short periods (around three years) so that executive directors often do not have the time to become familiar with Bank processes and operations. A further factor is the lack of technical expertise on the part of most executive directors and their staffs to evaluate in detail proposed lending operations or country strategies. For these reasons, constraints on the Bank's autonomy emanating from its Board of Executive Directors have been limited, albeit punctuated from time to time by strong pressures from individual board members in favor of or opposed to lending to particular countries or to particular policies, on a very few occasions with the board refusing to adopt the Bank's administrative budget until certain changes were adopted.

However, member states constrain the Bank through several avenues outside the board. One involves periodic replenishment negotiations of IDA. As with government agencies, periodic decisions on funding provide those making the decisions with an opportunity to press for their favored policies. Member states have sought to condition their contributions on a variety of policy changes. The Japanese have demanded a larger share of voting rights to accompany their increased contributions. The French have, it has been said, demanded special arrangements for their clients in Africa. The United States has pressed for greater attention to the environment, closer collaboration with the IMF, and controls on administrative expenditures by the Bank.

Another little-recognized vehicle for shaping the operations of the organization (and, in effect, constraining its autonomy over what it funds) are the hundreds of trust funds (worth $552 million in 1997) members have set up within the Bank, usually for particular purposes or operations and which the Bank manages. These include funding for feasibility studies, regional programs, training, and research.

Offsetting somewhat these constraints are the Bank's increasing profits, running at over $1 billion per year, from past lending operations.

In the mid-1990s, the Bank was able with board approval to supplement its IDA funding with its own resources. Should this source of finance increase in the future, it will likely strengthen the organization's autonomy. (The financial crisis in Asia in 1997–98 has forced an allocation of funds—including a portion of the organization's profits—to that region, at least temporarily. It remains to be seen whether the increased demands from Asian countries for Bank loans will serve to tighten Bank resources on a more permanent basis.)

Like other aid agencies examined in this study, the Bank itself has not remained passive during negotiations involving its funding. It has lobbied for higher levels for IDA by pressing heads of state (usually from influential borrowing governments) to urge the heads of reluctant contributor governments to support large levels of funding. For example, the Bank reportedly persuaded President Julius Nyerere of Tanzania to approach Swedish prime minister Olaf Palme to lobby other leaders of developed countries on behalf of IDA in 1975. It was successful in getting Indian prime minister Indira Gandhi to urge British prime minister Thatcher to support a generous IDA replenishment in 1982. Mrs. Gandhi was so effective that Mrs. Thatcher subsequently lobbied other G-7 heads of government also to support a high IDA replenishment.[25]

NGOs

We said earlier that in theory multilateral organizations were accountable to their member states but not to the legislatures, interest groups, or publics of those states. While this may have been the case with the World Bank in the past, it has become less so with the increase in the number and influence of development-oriented NGOs worldwide and their growing abilities to collaborate in worldwide networks.

While it might be expected that development-oriented NGOs would be a natural constituency for the Bank in member countries, the opposite has often been the case: a number of NGOs have been vocal and effective critics of the Bank. Two sets of issues have fired NGO criticisms: the impact of its projects on the environment and on human rights, and the impact of structural-adjustment programs on the poor. The former set of issues has focused primarily on the Bank's activities in Asia and Latin America; the latter has also focused on the impact of the Bank in Africa. The environmental and human-rights issues have been by far the more prominent of the two and are well illustrated by the infamous Sardar Sarovar dam and resettlement project in India.[26]

This project, involving a number of dams on the Narmada River in northwest India costing as much as $12 billion, would displace or adversely affect as many as a quarter of a million people. The government of India wanted the dams and irrigation to expand agricultural production. The Bank agreed to help finance the project, beginning with a loan in 1979 to start preparation of plans. The project itself was approved in 1985 (with a loan of $450 million and others to follow).

A number of NGOs objected vigorously to the project on several grounds: despite the regulations of the Bank itself, the project violated the rights of those who would lose their land (and there was little sign that the Indian government intended adequately to compensate those displaced.) And, contrary to its own rules and assurances, the Bank paid little attention to the environmental impact of the project, which, it was argued, could be substantial and negative. Confronted by these criticisms, the Bank was generally unresponsive. And, after having asked Bradford Morse (a respected international civil servant) to review the project, the Bank ignored Morse's recommendations to discontinue it.

In response to these and other environmentally controversial projects, a coalition of NGOs began a campaign to force the Bank to adopt and implement environmentally responsible policies and—equally importantly—to be far more transparent in its deliberations. For example, in the mid-1980s, NGOs began to organize their own meetings on World Bank and IMF policies at the same time and place as the annual meetings of those two organizations. These parallel forums were platforms for criticizing the Bank and IMF and attracted considerable media coverage. The NGOs also criticized Bank policies in the media and before the Canadian parliament and the U.S. Congress, even urging the latter not to appropriate funds for IDA. For example, the Environmental Defense Fund stated in a hearing before Congress in 1993 that "it would be environmentally, socially and economically irresponsible to appropriate any funds for either the IBRD or IDA, given the alarming evidence of the World Bank's lack of the most basic accountability and sense of responsibility for the environmental and social impacts of its projects."[27] Several U.S. NGOs used the fiftieth anniversary of the Bank in 1995 to launch an attack on the Bank with the slogan "Fifty Years is Enough," urging termination of funding for the institution.[28] And in 1996, when the new, Australian-born Bank president visited Australia, a group of NGOs there organized public demonstrations, particularly focused on problems of resettling poor people displaced by Bank-supported adjustment programs in Papua New Guinea and other countries.

Many other NGOs, particularly southern NGOs whose countries relied on lending from the Bank, tended to be much milder in their criticisms or generally supportive of the Bank. But vocal criticisms of the
Bank by NGOs were increasing. And these criticisms took Bank staff by
surprise. Two staffers, writing about the organization in 1995, made the
following comment: "As the Bretton Woods institutions prepared last
year to celebrate their 50th anniversary, few could have anticipated the
orchestrated crescendo of criticisms against the two institutions and particularly the Bank, principally from Northern NGOs."[29]

The criticisms by NGOs in a number of the Bank's major member
states proved highly embarrassing. But what was most telling were statements by NGOs urging Congress to cut IDA funding. Support for such
funding was never strong, being limited to moderate Republicans and
liberal Democrats. Now NGOs that were one of the few sources of external support for the Bank were attacking the organization, raising a real
danger that the past congressional supporters of IDA would cease to support it. This tactic by NGOs provoked one former World Bank vice president to remark, "The Bank would have ignored the environmental
NGOs if not for IDA."[30]

The Bank began to respond to these and other criticisms. It increased
its staff working on the environment from 5 in 1985 to 162 in 1995. It
imposed a mandatory environmental review for all its projects. Under
threat of Congress's refusing to appropriate funds for IDA unless reforms
were adopted, the Bank opened several public information centers to
respond to requests for documents. And it created an "Inspection Panel"
to investigate complaints by the public and NGOs about World Bank
projects.

The Bank also set about trying to expand its relationships with NGOs.
In the 1980s, it had established an NGO-Bank Committee, made up of
representatives from twenty-six NGOs worldwide plus several senior
Bank officers, to meet periodically to discuss a variety of issues. The Bank
increased its consultations with NGOs in the planning and implementation of some of its projects, emphasizing a "participatory" approach to
project preparation through consulting NGOs in the countries where it
proposed to lend.[31] It appointed NGO liaison officers in many of its field
offices in Africa.

Finally, James Wolfensohn, who became president of the Bank in
1995, made a particular effort to improve relations with NGOs. He
promised greater collaboration with them, including joint studies with

NGOs of the impact of structural-adjustment lending. And in his public statements, he began to emphasize the importance of poverty reduction as the core mission of the World Bank—a focus strongly supported by NGOs. The NGOs have for the most part suspended their campaign of criticism to see what concrete changes in the Bank would follow these initiatives.

The NGOs had had an impact on the Bank, both directly and through their member states, leading it to cancel controversial projects, increase its attention to environmental issues, expand its collaboration with NGOs in the planning and implementation of its programs and projects, and promise a greater emphasis in its lending policies on addressing poverty. They had proven that they could influence and constrain the Bank. But the extent to which that influence leads to changes in the Bank's lending policies and practices and its impact on the effectiveness of the Bank in promoting development in borrowing countries is yet to be determined. There remains much skepticism among many World Bank staff about the abilities of NGOs to make significant contributions to development in poor countries.

Capacity

The overall mission of the Bank, captured in its title and Articles of Agreement, is a broad one: to promote reconstruction in war-torn countries and economic development in poor countries. The Articles do not specify the strategy the Bank should deploy to achieve its development goals, leaving the institution a broad field of action. Over the past several decades, Bank management has articulated its development goals much in line with mainstream development thinking: an early emphasis on growth; a shift to poverty alleviation during the 1970s; a renewed emphasis on growth in the 1980s and early 1990s; and, like most of the other aid donors examined here, a broadening focus during the 1990s on political and social issues, including governance, the environment, population and family planning, and in the mid-1990s as we have seen, a return to an emphasis on poverty alleviation.

Even though the Bank has claimed a broad field of action in its rhetoric, much of its lending in Africa has concentrated in a few areas—in particular, infrastructure (mainly rehabilitation of existing infrastructure) and economic-policy reform. There appear to be several reasons for this: these areas are where the Bank has a preponderance of technical staff, giving it not only expertise but an internal constituency in favor of such projects. These are also areas where an aid donor with a large amount of assistance can be relatively certain of being able to spend that assistance in a limited period of time.

Like many other aid agencies, the Bank relies on a country programming process to make its lending decisions.[32] This process involves the development of an overall framework for lending, called a Country Assistance Strategy. This document (which is drafted in consultation with the borrowing government but is not a joint document) includes priorities for Bank lending and the country's portfolio performance. The Bank's country economic and sector work (for example, its country economic memoranda, produced periodically for all borrowing countries) is also part of the documentation that provides the basis for lending decisions.

The next stage in a lending cycle involves the identification of projects—in theory, by the borrowing government, but in practice often (especially in Africa) by Bank staff. A project information document is drafted by the Bank, and once it is approved, the borrower is supposed to prepare the project. Again, this stage is usually undertaken by Bank staff themselves in the case of Africa. The Bank then appraises the project on a mission to the borrowing country. Once an appraisal report is agreed to by the Bank, negotiations begin with the borrowing government on the project or program. With an agreement on the details of the project or program, the lending operation is reviewed, and once it is through the board, implementation by the borrowing government begins.

The Bank supervises the implementation of its projects and programs through periodic visits to the country by staff. After the project is completed, an implementation completion report is prepared, rating the performance of the project. Ratings are often based on the estimated rate of return of the project when it was planned versus the actual rate of return after completion. Where a rate of return cannot be estimated, the performance of the project is evaluated against its planned goals.

While the evaluation service of the Bank is among the best of any donor, there have been criticisms within the Bank itself that the findings of the monitoring and evaluation process have not been incorporated into planning for other, similar projects. The limited impact of evaluations on an aid agency's planning is a common one, reflecting the emphasis on lending rather than the impact of that lending that has been apparent in most aid agencies and particularly in the Bank. It is undoubtedly part of the broader problems of aid effectiveness.

Pressures to Spend

Behind some of these problems of capacity is a bureaucratic imperative observable in most aid agencies but particularly evident in the World Bank: the pressures to spend available funds. Such pressures can reduce the flexibility of those agencies in designing and managing their activities consistent with conditions in the recipient country—especially including terminating activities where there is little likelihood of success. Pressures to lend gained prominence during the tenure of Robert McNamara as president of the World Bank (1968 to 1981). McNamara's goal was to expand the size and importance of the Bank as a development institution. He was extraordinarily successful, and the rate of lending to Africa and other parts of the world surged during the 1970s. The impact on Bank lending in Africa is described in an evaluation by the Bank, *The World Bank's Role in Human Resource Development in Sub-Saharan Africa:* "The rapid increase in lending authority, coming at a time when foreign aid from other sources was also expanding, set off a keen competition for investment projects and new initiatives that tended to overwhelm Bank as well as country absorptive capacity. There was little time for orderly investigation or pilot testing of new ideas, little patience for utilizing a participatory approach to project planning, a preference for an enclave approach to implementation . . . and a tendency to embrace and then drop, new initiatives too quickly."[33]

The pressures to lend and their impact on the quality of Bank operations were not confined to the McNamara era. They were identified as a major element in the deterioration in the overall performance of the Bank's portfolio much later in a report by the Portfolio Management Task Force (the "Wappenhans Report") in 1992. While a number of the problems underlying the Bank's declining performance had to do with global economic problems or development problems in borrowing countries beyond the Bank's control, several related directly to Bank practices, including "the Bank's pervasive preoccupation with new lending." The problem of a "culture of approval" cited in the Wappenhans Report continues. The pressures to lend have been formalized in the way Bank staff are evaluated by their superiors. Bank staff responsible for lending operations agree each year with their supervisors on annual performance contracts. Included in those contracts is often a commitment to accomplish an agreed number of lending operations. Staff are then evaluated according to whether they achieved the agreed target.

The pressures to lend have contributed to other bureaucratic patholo-gies, for example, a tendency toward excessive optimism on the part of Bank staff about conditions in the countries for which they are responsi-ble, the commitment of governments to economic reforms, and the likely impact of Bank-funded projects and programs. Stories of Bank staff over-estimating the likely increases (or underestimating the likely decreases) in commodity prices, the probable returns on their projects, or the likeli-hood that promised reforms would be implemented are legion and ac-knowledged privately by staff. Epitomizing the view that optimism is an indispensable quality for Bank staff was a dinner table remark I heard in 1996 from one Bank vice president for Africa, that it was his "moral duty not to be pessimistic."

Another problem deriving from pressures to spend involves game playing between the Bank and its borrowers, especially on structural-adjustment loans. African governments—aware of the pressures in the Bank to move available monies—have at times decided that they will not be seriously penalized by accepting proposed reform programs and then not implementing them fully. This has contributed to the disappointing effectiveness of such programs in Africa.

Behind the pressures to spend in the World Bank is the desire, evident in many bureaucratic organizations, to justify the same or an increased level of resources by spending all available funding. In the case of the World Bank, there is also another reason: the Bank's aspirations for worldwide development leadership. This was surely one of the major goals of McNamara, and it has undoubtedly been a motivation of Bank managers, particularly in Africa. But a sine qua non of international lead-ership on development must be the ability to provide significant, and preferably expanding, amounts of aid—and ideally, to become one of the largest sources of development finance in the world. Large and ex-panding aid levels can only be justified if available monies are all ex-pended. Pressures to lead thus fuel pressures to lend. And the pressures to lead have been among the strongest in Africa where, more than any other region, the Bank has successfully claimed a leadership role among aid agencies. (It must also be noted that not all the pressures to lend in the Bank have arisen from inside the institution. They have also come from many member states—both aid donors and Africans—which have pressed the Bank to increase lending in the region.)

There is one more factor we must mention that undoubtedly contrib-uted to the pressures on the Bank to lend in Africa in the 1980s—the danger that without an inflow of quick-disbursing loans, African governments would fail to service their debts to the Bank or its sister organization, the International Monetary Fund. The Fund had lent extensively in Africa during the first half of the 1980s in support of stabilization programs. Its loans were relatively hard—with short maturities (typically three to five years) and near market rates of interest. Fund programs had proven ineffective in bringing about a permanent resolution of the balance-of-payments problems of African borrowers. They restrained domestic demand but led to negligible increases in investment. And when they ended, governments proved unable to continue the demand restraint policies contained in the stabilization programs. Soon, Africans needed to begin repaying the Fund, with amortization charges rising from just over $2 billion in 1980–82 to $8 billion in 1985–87.[34]

Pressures on the Bank to step up quick-disbursing program loans in Africa (in support of economic reforms) rose as the danger of African defaults to the Fund grew. Once the Bank had increased its adjustment lending significantly in Africa, it also had a stake in ensuring timely servicing of that debt. A study by Paul Mosley, John Toye, and Jane Harrigan of World Bank–funded adjustment programs found that one of the reasons the Bank has hesitated to terminate adjustment lending to a number of African countries not fully implementing agreed reforms is that these countries are heavily indebted to the Bank, with repayments from earlier IBRD and IDA loans now due. Cutting them off would likely lead to a halt in repayments and a buildup of large arrears. Not only do arrears become an obstacle to future lending, but they will likely be seen as a failure of Bank programs. And if they are sizable enough, they can also have a deleterious impact on the Bank's own creditworthiness. More broadly, there was also a fear that in some countries, cancellation of a program could provoke a financial crisis on the part of the borrower or, in the more fragile states, even a political collapse. Bank lending in Africa— because of its large volume—had become hostage to economic conditions in its borrowing countries.

Turning to the staffing of the World Bank, the size, technical qualifications, and professionalism of its personnel are one of its most impressive strengths. The organization had an international staff of sixty-five hundred in 1996, including eight hundred economists, plus agronomists, civil engineers, lawyers, and a host of other professionals. (It is worth noting, however, that it has very few anthropologists, sociologists, or political scientists, despite the fact that much of its work has extensive social and political ramifications.) The Bank has the authority and autonomy to hire and promote its staff primarily on the basis of merit, often through a "Young Professionals" program that takes in recent graduates, trains them, and then retains them, often for their entire professional careers. The policies of promoting from within the Bank's career staff have produced a well-trained and highly socialized staff whose professional satisfaction often derives primarily from the organization itself. Although member governments lobby for larger numbers of their nationals to be hired by the Bank, they cannot themselves decide which individuals are hired and do not have a veto over those chosen. This has permitted the Bank to maintain a high-quality staff and avoid the problems of patronage-based appointments that have often plagued other international agencies.

But these same personnel policies have also contributed to a degree of insularity and inward orientation of its staff and perhaps a degree of arrogance and insensitivity, as African officials have often complained.[35] Responding to this latter criticism, on the walls of the building that houses the Africa Region of the Bank in the summer of 1996 large posters were mounted, entitled "New ways of working in the Africa Region," identifying barriers to the Bank's performance there: "Bank arrogance, lack of candor, neglecting beneficiaries/deferring to stakeholders, a control mentality and favoring lending over implementing." Bank staff were urged to avoid these habits and to practice other forms of desirable behavior toward their African borrowers and beneficiaries.[36]

Some of these complaints are probably inevitable since the Bank is in the position of persuading or pressuring Africans to agree to policy changes that are often costly and at times involve major shifts in attitude, creating tension and criticism. But the breadth and continuity of such complaints suggests that the problem is a real one.

The insularity of Bank staff may have been encouraged by the highly centralized nature of the organization. Most of the Bank's staff is located at the organization's headquarters in Washington and the identification, design, and implementation of most of the Bank's activities is handled there. There are seventy field representatives, but these offices have functioned mainly to facilitate communications between Washington and borrowing governments, to provide logistical support for missions of Bank staff to the field, and to represent the Bank in the borrowing country.

The question of whether the Bank should decentralize more of its authorities to the field has been raised periodically and rejected. It was raised again by the Wappenhans Report, but no action was taken. In 1995, a survey of its own staff on the issue of decentralization elicited this view: "The Bank's rigor, thoroughness, professional expertise and ability to bring to bear global experience are highly valued—but its willingness to adapt to the unique conditions, needs and requirements of individual countries is seen as inadequate."[37] After extensive discussions within the Bank and with its board, management proposed and the board approved a "strategic compact" that would reduce the overall number of staff, streamline programming procedures, give a greater emphasis on the results of its lending operations, and delegate greater authority to field representatives, the latter change suggesting that the Bank is moving in the direction of decentralization.

Conclusion

Several conclusions on the effectiveness of the World Bank's assistance in Africa emerge out of this analysis. The considerable autonomy of the Bank has helped it for the most part avoid concentrating its lending over an extended period of time on governments that were poor development partners. This was to be expected, given the multilateral nature of the organization.

The size and professionalism of the Bank has enabled it to claim a role as a leader in development, especially in Africa. Its data, analyses, initiatives, and efforts at coordination may be its most important contribution to development there. However, it appears from its evaluations that its projects and programs in Africa have suffered from many of the same problems that have confronted other aid agencies. These problems appear to derive primarily from two factors: the pressures to spend (which have been particularly prominent in influencing the Bank's lending) and the highly centralized nature of the institution, which has limited the local knowledge and experience of its staff (and perhaps their contacts with and accountability to the individuals and groups they propose to benefit) that can play an important role in ensuring that the design and implementation of projects and programs are both effective and sustainable.

The European Union

The European Commission (EC) is the bureaucratic arm of the European Union (EU). The EC is the third largest source of aid in Africa, providing just over $2 billion in 1996. The aid is contributed by member states primarily to the European Development Fund (EDF), which is managed by one of the directorates general (DG VIII) of the European Community. (The EC also distributes food aid and monies from a number of other Community funds to African countries. But the funding from the EDF is by far the largest single source of EC aid to the region.)

European aid to Africa emerged out of the Treaty of Rome, establishing the European Economic Community in 1957. At that time, France (which still had colonies in Africa) insisted that special arrangements, involving both trade and aid, be made for these colonies by the Community. Once France's and Belgium's colonies in Africa and elsewhere had attained their independence, the EC negotiated with them (the African, Caribbean, and Pacific--or ACP—states) a series of five-year conventions dealing with both grant aid and preferential trade arrangements. The first of these agreements was signed in 1963 in Yaounde, Cameroon, and came to be known as the Yaounde Convention.[38] The aid agreed to under this convention was financed with contributions to the EDF, already established in the Treaty of Rome.

The first Yaounde Convention was followed by a second one in 1968. With the accession of the United Kingdom to the European Union in 1973, the convention was expanded to include Britain's former colonies in Africa and the Caribbean and came to be known as the Lome Convention, signed in 1975. There have been four Lome conventions, the last one covering ten (rather than five) years. Since that time, nearly 90 percent of funding from the EDF has been provided to African countries.

Which Countries to Aid?

The European Community provides aid to all the African, Caribbean, and Pacific (ACP) countries that are members of the Lome Convention. By the mid-1990s, these countries numbered seventy, including most of the countries of sub-Saharan Africa.

To explain decisions by the Europeans on which countries to aid, it is necessary to understand the principles on which the Lome Convention was first based. Since its predecessor, the first Yaounde Convention, there has been an effort on the part of the Europeans to create a unique aid program, one that was based on a real "partnership," as distinct from the paternalistic relationships of the colonial period, and one that was free from the narrower concerns with national interests that so often influence bilateral aid programs. Reflecting this idealism, the three principles governing European aid to Africa have been equality among partners, respect for the sovereignty of the recipients, and security in the flow of resources.

Equality among partners is sought in an elaborate process of planning and administration of the aid involving both the EC and its ACP partners (described in greater detail in the section below on capacity). The emphasis on sovereignty is reflected in a requirement that proposals for aid projects come from recipient governments themselves and must be approved by a national authorization officer (usually the minister of finance) in each recipient country.

The principles of equality, sovereignty, and security have also been reflected in the "contractual" rather than "conditional" basis for EDF aid: once the level of aid for a country over the period of a Lome convention has been set by the EC, that level of aid has been assured the recipient government, regardless of its economic performance or other considerations. However, this particular arrangement has begun to change. The EC has included progress toward democratization as an additional criterion for its allocation of aid resources, and it has suspended aid to African countries with grossly incompetent, corrupt, or repressive regimes and to collapsed states. (As of the end of 1994, European aid to Nigeria, Gambia, Liberia, Somalia, Zaire, Sudan, Togo, and Equatorial Guinea was suspended.) Monies for structural adjustment have also been conditioned on the existence of an acceptable adjustment program, and adjustment funding is often provided as cofinancing for World Bank adjustment programs.

Finally, in the current Lome protocol (signed in 1995), it was agreed (reluctantly, on the part of the ACP countries) that henceforth, aid funds would be allocated in two tranches: only 70 percent of the aid levels for individual countries would be allocated at the beginning of the five-year programming period. The remaining 30 percent would be committed only after an assessment of the performance of the first tranche (which must be obligated within three years). This "phased programming" marks a reduction in the amount of contractually based aid and a further step toward performance-based aid.[39]

How Much Aid to Provide?

The amount of assistance to individual countries is based on a complicated formula that includes geographic, demographic, and macroeconomic factors—for example, total population, GNP per capita, external

Table 10. Top Five Recipients of European Development Fund Aid to Africa

1970–71	1980–81	1994–95
Cameroon	Sudan	Ethiopia
Zaire	Senegal	Ivory Coast
Senegal	Somalia	Mozambique
Madagascar	Ethiopia	Cameroon
Ivory Coast	Zaire	Zimbabwe

Source: Development Assistance Committee, *Development Cooperation* (Paris: Organization for Economic Cooperation and Development, 1996), p. A84.

debt, and the degree of a country's development. Studies have found that these variables have remained roughly the same in determining the aid levels of ACP states over much of the period of this study.[40] The use of such a formula is unusual among the aid agencies examined here. It reflects a desire on the part of the Europeans to limit national political influences on allocations and to provide the aid on criteria that are as objective and predictable as possible.

The recipients of EDF funding have changed over the past several decades as the number of ACP countries has increased, as phased programming has been implemented and as aid has been suspended to nonperforming countries (see table 10).

A second factor determining how much aid governments receive is the overall amount of funding agreed to in each Lome protocol. The protocol, enacting the first stage of the Lome IV convention, covers the period 1995–99 and includes a level of assistance from the EDF over that period of roughly $12 billion. This aid will fund projects and structural adjustment programs plus two compensatory financing schemes: Sysmin (a financing arrangement for ACP countries to offset declines in their earnings from mineral exports and to help upgrade mining companies in their countries) and Stabex (a financing scheme to compensate for declines in export earnings from a variety of primary products). Table 11 shows the breakdown of EDF funding among these programs for the remainder of the 1990s. In addition, the EC provides nonemergency food aid and NGO cofinancing in Africa.

How Is the Aid Used?

EDF funding has been used to finance a wide range of activities similar to those of other aid agencies. Yaounde I and II and Lome I emphasized economic and social infrastructure. Lome II and III still financed infra-

Table 11. European Community Aid to ACP Countries (ECU Millions)

	Lome I 1975–80	Lome II 1980–85	Lome III 1985–90	Lome IV 1990–95	Lome IV 1995–2000
EDF Total	3,072	5,409	8,500	12,000	12,967
Grants	2,150	2,999	4,860	7,995	9,592
Special loans	46	525	600		
Risk Capital	99	284	600	825	1,000
Stabex	377	634	925	1,500	1,800
Sysmin		282	415	480	575

Source: Antonique Koning, "Strengths and Weaknesses in the Management of the European Development Fund," Working Paper No. 8, European Centre for Development Policy Management, October 1995, p. 11.

structure and industry but also put a quarter of available funding into rural agriculture. Lome IV showed a greatly reduced funding level for rural development, infrastructure, and industry and an increase in structural adjustment, ongoing programs in water, health, and education (at relatively low levels), and a variety of special programs including emergency aid, environment, women in development, and democracy. A large proportion of EDF funds—one-third in 1992—were provided as transfers to governments through Stabex.[41] The EC, like donor agencies elsewhere, was broadening the types of activities it undertook.

The Effectiveness of EDF Aid

Assessments of the effectiveness of EDF aid show a mixed picture. A review by John Healey and J. Rand for the London-based Overseas Development Institute, *The Effectiveness of EDF Development Aid to ACP Countries in the 1980s,* reviewed forty-seven EDF evaluations (most of which involved projects in Africa), including overall EDF aid reviews, sectoral syntheses, country studies, and regional aid studies, covering more than two hundred projects. The review found a performance broadly similar to that of many other donors in Africa. Half of the projects were effective in planning and implementation, but only 40 percent were judged effective in terms of intended impact and sustainability.[42] The least effective projects—again, echoing the experience of other donors—were those that were more complex and involved institutional change. Transport projects, for example, were found to be relatively successful "because well tried methods have been used."[43] (Maintenance of these projects, as with those of other donors, was a problem.) Large-scale energy projects, including hydroelectric projects, were generally evaluated positively. (Here, too, however a familiar problem emerged: the projects were often larger and more costly than local needs required because of "designs which have suited the capacities and wishes of European contractors more than the needs of the local inhabitants.")[44]

Projects in the area of integrated rural development were among the least effective. (It is interesting to note that the EDF was still undertaking these types of projects in Africa during the late 1980s, well after other donors had stopped funding them because of their record of failure.) The quality of preparation of these projects was judged to be poor, based on flawed analyses and with too many objectives. Few were predicted to be sustainable. Studies of European aid in individual African countries showed modest success in Botswana and less in Niger and the Central African Republic. The ODI report summed up its findings in the following points:

> Road projects followed cost effective solutions, met cost limits but not timetables. Monitoring was effective, planned outputs were met and economic impact was positive for the majority of road projects. The weakness was sustainability. Large energy projects had effective monitoring but a half or more did not meet cost limits, timetables or planned outputs. They had positive economic impact and sustainability.
>
> Rural development programmes' cost effectiveness, cost and time limits were not met in the majority of cases, monitoring and outputs, economic and social impact were partially effective and projects were not very sustainable.
>
> Other agricultural projects were partially effective in impact and sustainability.
>
> Agro-industrial projects and fisheries (mainly artisanal) projects were generally weak in all aspects.[45]

The report went on to attribute the ineffectiveness of EDF aid to weak management: an absence of clear country strategies and objectives; lack of rigor in project selection and appraisal; and problems in the design and implementation of projects.

Interviews with African officials and aid officials from other governments familiar with EDF programs confirm many of these problems and point to one other shortcoming: the complicated and time-consuming process involved in the preparation and implementation of EDF projects. A large carryover of unspent monies from one five-year Lome protocol to another gives credence to this criticism. By 1994, for example, only 80 percent of the funds from the 1985–90 protocol, and only 30 percent of the current 1990–95 protocol had been spent.[46] The EC itself commented on problems of the Lome programming process when it remarked on its "ambitious but sometimes unrealistic framework" of operations but blamed the problems on its "assumptions about the ACP countries' institutional and political capacities that have not been fulfilled."[47]

The European Commission has not been one of the leaders in the development discourse in Africa, despite the large amount of aid it has provided. While it has been one of the few aid donors willing to support regional projects and organizations, even in this area it has not produced studies or reports that strengthen our understanding of regional cooperation and integration in Africa and the role of aid in promoting that integration. A major reason for the limited European impact in this area may be the absence of a significant research budget that would permit the Commission to develop the ideas that would have an impact on development discourse. The regular staff of Directorate General VIII (as with the staff of most of the aid agencies examined here) have little time (or incentive) to research and reflect on development problems in the region.

The Future of EC Aid

Like so many other aid programs, the EDF appears to be entering a period of change. The European commissioner for development, J. Deus de Pinhiero, remarked in 1995, "This is the last of the [Lome] Conventions as we have come to know them."[48] In 1996, the staff of Directorate General VIII began a "reflection" exercise on issues and options for the future of the Lome conventions. And in 1997, the EC circulated its *Green Paper on Relations between the European Union and the ACP Countries on the Eve of the 21st Century* as the basis of consultations on the future of Lome. After extensive consultations with ACP states on what arrangements should follow Lome IV, the EC published a further paper outlining its thinking for the negotiations on the future of Lome, to begin in late 1998.[49] In this paper, the EC agreed with the views of ACP countries, strongly expressed in the consultations, that it maintain its overall relationship with them in a broad framework agreement, to be worked out in upcoming negotiations. Within that agreement, however, the EC proposed to establish separate regional agreements with ACP states, reflecting the EC preference for "differentiation" among its developing country partners, including how its aid was managed. Implicit in the statement was the idea that the EC would take a more active role in managing its aid in African countries where domestic political institutions were weak. Notwithstanding the diplomatic language of the report, the EC also appeared to signal its intention to condition its aid on the implementation of market-oriented economic reforms and on good governance and democracy and begin to shift its compensatory aid (that is, Sysmin and Stabex) into more conventional aid programs, based less on offsetting foreign-exchange losses and more on need and merit. Additionally, the EC declared that it would focus its work within particular countries in fewer sectors and give greater emphasis to using its aid and advice to encourage regional economic integration among its partner countries. In many ways, the future directions of EC aid in Africa promised to resemble more closely those of other donors in coming years.

A related issue before the Europeans is the extent to which all aid from member states (bilateral programs as well as EC programs) is coordinated or even "communitized"—folded into one program. While EC aid as a proportion of all the aid of member countries is approximately 17 percent, that proportion has been growing, making the issue of coordination salient. In addition, the Maastricht Treaty included development cooperation as an objective of EC policies for the first time, creating the legal basis for a common European cooperation policy consistent with the goal of creating a common foreign policy. A number of member states—Germany and Belgium in particular—have emphasized the importance of better coordination and an allocation of specific development activities among the EC and its member states on the basis of the relative expertise of each member. A pilot project has been initiated in six countries.

Finally, there is the issue of future EC aid levels to Africa. The last Lome protocol had no increase in aid in real terms, a fact much lamented by ACP countries and NGOs. The stagnation in aid levels plus the uncertainty about the future of the Lome Convention itself raise a question about the size of EC assistance to the countries of sub-Saharan Africa during the next decade, putting the EC in that large group of aid donors that appear to be entering a new phase in funding development in Africa.

Analysis

Autonomy

The "contractual" approach to allocating EDF aid to the countries of Africa has already been described. It has imposed very tight constraints in the past on allocative decisions by the European officials managing that aid, though these constraints have now been eased somewhat. On the other hand, because of these and other organizational arrangements, EC aid officials have been relatively free from pressures of member states, legislative bodies, and private interests on their management of EDF funds.

The Council of Ministers of the fifteen member states is the principal governing body of the EDF. But, in fact, member states exert relatively little real influence over the country allocation of aid. Member states can exert some influence over the overall priorities and policies of the EDF and funding activities in individual ACP countries through their participation in the intergovernmental EDF committee that reviews planning and project documents.[50] Here, too, however, there are limits on the influence of member states based on the principal of partnership and sovereignty that assumes that ACP states will play a major role in how EDF funds will be spent in their countries. The permanent secretary of the United Kingdom's Overseas Development Administration (now called the Department of International Development) acknowledged the limits on his government's influence: "I do not pretend that the lever [over EC policies] is necessarily a very powerful one. We have a tight grip on a lever which is only one of 12 levers in Brussels."[51]

The European Parliament (EP) exerts little authority over the EDF since the level of EDF funding is set through negotiations between the EC and the ACP states. In contrast to other EC aid programs, the EDF is in effect an "off budget" item, requiring neither parliamentary approval nor oversight. A study by the Overseas Development Institute in London commented that "the European Parliament does not have a great impact and there is no dialogue between the Council and the Commission which the EP can effectively influence. EP institutional memory is small and reactions are too slow and therefore not effective. The EP does not undertake systematic reviews or any monitoring of Commission administered programs and members only occasionally visit developing countries."[52]

Two main groups outside the EC and its member states lobby the EC on its aid programs: business lobbies, whose numbers in Brussels are increasing, and nongovernmental organizations supportive of development activities. Business interests appear to have had relatively little influence on EDF activities in Africa—a region in any case of diminishing interest to traders and investors. The influence of NGOs, on the other hand, appears to be growing with the expansion in their numbers, their ties with NGOs in member states, and their political sophistication.

Their focus, as with NGOs elsewhere, has been on supporting high levels of aid directed at the alleviation of poverty.

NGOs in Brussels tend to be umbrella groups or networks, reflecting the multinational character of the EU. Two development-oriented umbrella NGOs stand out in particular. One is EUROSTEP, an independent, development advocacy organization with representatives of twenty-two NGOs from thirteen European countries. It was set up in 1991 by the heads of a number of European NGOs in the development field who recognized that the EC was a significant aid donor and that decisions on its policies would be made in Brussels, not in the capitals of member states; to remain informed and to influence those policies, a presence in Brussels was imperative.

Another NGO network active in Brussels is called the NGO Liaison Committee. This committee was set up in 1976 and is financed by the EC itself. It has as members "platforms" of NGOs in member states, usually with a small secretariat, who send representatives to serve on the committee in Brussels, who rely on the committee for information on EC activities, and to whom national platforms can communicate their views on issues of importance.

NGOs have even more limited scope for influencing EDF aid policies than do member states.[53] They often lack access to information on policy deliberations or decisions. However, they have at times attempted to influence decisions with which they strongly disagreed. NGOs have employed a number of tactics to make their influence felt. They have presented their views directly to European officials. They have urged their member organizations to lobby their governments and parliaments to put pressure on the Commission to support NGO positions on key issues. And EUROSTEP in particular has attempted to use the media in Brussels to influence EC policies.

EUROSTEP has had several successes with the media, though at times on issues only indirectly associated with aid and development. One well-known instance was a demonstration in front of the Council of Ministers' building in Brussels with Tuareg nomads and camels from West Africa against the Common Agricultural Policy, which subsidized frozen beef exports to Africa and undercut the abilities of Africans to sell their own meat products. This action (which gained considerable press attention) combined with careful research on subsidization (which was provided to the EC, the ministries of agriculture and development in member states, and the press) led to reductions in the rate of subsidization and a drop in EC frozen beef exports to Africa. The EC also reportedly imposed an internal policy on livestock intended to lead to a more coherent EC approach to supporting the West African livestock sector.[54]

In terms of the impact of these or other NGO organizations on EC policies in Africa, EUROSTEP has claimed some successes for its lobbying besides the reduction of beef subsidies. It has contributed to a decision by the EC to undertake a special initiative on economic recovery in countries of crisis, like Rwanda, and a budget line item for rehabilitation. Similarly, after EUROSTEP pressed for extra staff in Directorate General VIII with expertise in women in development and in external relations, the Commission agreed.

Despite these small victories, NGOs appear as yet to have had relatively limited influence on European Commission aid programs in general, including those involving African countries. They have yet to become a significant constituency for aid, as they have in Britain, or a significant constraint on the autonomy of the managers of that aid, as they have in the United States.

Capacity

The major problems of capacity influencing the effectiveness of EDF aid in Africa are similar to those of other agencies: despite field missions (called "delegations") in most recipient countries, local European Commission staff often lack local expertise and have relatively little authority to commit funds or change programs or projects. Nevertheless, they are often the designers and implementers of aid projects. In theory, at least, this should not be the case. According to the philosophy of the Lome Convention, recipient governments should take the initiative in designing and implementing aid projects. But this has proven difficult because, in the words of one observer, "African partners often lack the political will and the capacity to perform their roles."[55] And surely one reason they lack the political will to do so relates to another aspect of EC aid: the "contractual" nature of that aid that has guaranteed recipients a given amount of assistance regardless of their overall economic policies or performance in managing the aid.

There is another element of the capacity of the European Commission that relates to the effectiveness of its aid: a programming process that is centralized, complicated, and time consuming—so much so, that it has become a major focus of criticism, particularly by African recipients. That process works as follows: at the beginning of a protocol period, Directorate General VIII officials inform each ACP government of the size of its aid program for the coming five years based on the formula described above. EC delegations in the field then draft up a country strategy paper with their assessment of priorities for their aid in each recipient country. Together with the partner government, European field delegates also draft a National Indicative Program (NIP). This latter document includes the main development objectives and sectors in which it is proposed to fund projects or programs. The NIPs are discussed by EC staff in Brussels and passed on to the EDF Member States Committee for further discussion and approval. Once that approval is given, EC staff negotiate with the government a final framework document for developing projects and programs.

Once a framework of aid is established, recipient governments are supposed to come up with ideas for projects to fund. In many cases, they do not. But they must appear to do so, adding an additional challenge to EC officials responsible for managing the aid. The remainder of the programming process involves drawing up a project dossier; appraising it, submitting it to the EC; preparing the financing proposal, review and decision by the EDF committee; signing the financing agreement, preparing, evaluating, and approving tenders; signing of contracts; and commencement of implementation. These elements in the process may involve the EC delegate, the recipient government, or both jointly.[56]

Once aid projects are under way, the responsibility for supervising and monitoring them is in the hands of a national authorizing officer in the partner government and the EC delegate in the field. Monitoring of EDF aid has been identified in evaluations and by observers of EDF projects as weak due to the overburdened EC staff both in the field and in Brussels[57] who, like staffs of aid agencies elsewhere, have tended to put a higher priority on getting projects up and running than on monitoring their performance.

A final problem of capacity involves the goals and staffing of Directorate General VIII—the part of the European Commission responsible for managing aid to ACP countries. Title XVII of the Treaty of Maastricht, effective in 1993, commits the EC to three broad development objectives: promoting sustainable development, especially among the most disadvantaged countries; supporting a smooth integration of the developing countries into the world economy; and alleviating poverty. Another title commits the EC to supporting human rights, democracy, and the rule of law. Within the Lome Convention, the EC is committed to promoting the economic, social, and cultural development of ACP states. These objectives provide a broad framework in which EDF funds can be programmed. Within this framework the EC, like other aid agencies, has expanded the scope of its activities to include environmental conservation and women's and other issues. It is too soon to tie this broadening portfolio with the past effectiveness of its aid in Africa. But the expansion in its portfolio has raised concerns that the EC lacks the technical capacity in its staff to manage such a diverse set of activities.

Conclusion

The Lome agreement, with its funding through the European Development Fund, is an interesting and important experiment in managing aid programs in Africa. As with Swedish aid, its programming processes have been based on an ideology that has emphasized equality with the governments receiving aid and the assumption that those governments had the will and capacity to manage it effectively. Also like the Swedish program, these assumptions have often proven faulty. The "contractual" mechanism for allocating aid has reduced the discretion of EC officials in determining levels based on the performance of African governments while diminishing the incentives for those same governments to perform. The problems created by this approach have been recognized by the Europeans, and they have begun to move to a more performance-based system.

Also problematic is the capacity of the EC itself—particularly its cumbersome programming procedures for managing the aid, weaknesses in its field representation, limitations on the technical expertise of its staff in relationship to its expanding portfolio, and weaknesses in its evaluation system.[58] These problems remain a source of concern even as the EC considers the broader framework of its relationships with African countries and other ACP states.

Chapter Nine

Findings

It is now time to pull together the evidence and threads of argument in this study and suggest some directions for the future of aid in Africa. This chapter first addresses several sets of findings: broad conclusions regarding the effectiveness of aid in Africa, the performance of aid donors based on the case studies, and other findings, some of which are relevant to the fields of comparative politics and international relations. Based on these findings, a second section makes proposals—some of them significant departures from the status quo—on how the developmental effectiveness of aid in Africa can be enhanced.

Findings on the Effectiveness of Aid in Africa

We can now answer the question we began with: why, with so much aid, has there been so little development in Africa? Extraordinarily high levels of aid relative to the size of its economies have gone to the region over an extended period. At the same time, economic development has been disappointing by almost any standard. Foreign aid, which is supposed to promote development, has had some real successes in Africa, proving that it can be effective. But it has frequently proven unsatisfactory in impact and its positive results unsustainable over the long run. The more complex the aid-funded interventions (that is, the more they involved multiple activities and required social, political, and behavioral change), the less effective they have been.

A basic lesson is that while foreign aid can promote development, it does not guarantee development. And more aid does not necessarily buy more development. Indeed, unless it carefully avoids reinforcing flawed policies and poor governance, weakening African institutions and creating dependence, more aid can buy less development. This may seem an exceedingly obvious conclusion to many readers, but it has yet to become part of the public discourse on aid, judging from the continuing focus on the size, rather than the impact, of aid and the reluctance of many of the supporters of aid to recognize and address its failures and limitations.

On the other hand, large flows of aid do not automatically retard development, another basic lesson confirmed by this study. Data relating aid flows to growth show no strong correlation one way or the other. This may seem like another terribly obvious conclusion. But this is not apparent in many of the continuing criticisms of foreign aid. Behind both of these lessons is the point that factors other than the amount of aid—even when relatively large—often play a critical role in determining its effectiveness. This was noted early on in the literature on aid and development but has often been neglected in discussions of policy and even scholarly debate. The experience of aid in Africa cannot but remind us again of this important point.

What other factors explain aid's ineffectiveness in Africa? Much attention has been rightly paid to the responsibilities of Africans—in particular, a poor policy environment and weak institutions. The policy and institutional weaknesses reflect strong social forces and political tendencies within many African countries. But much of the responsibility for the ineffectiveness of aid must rest with the donors. They have always decided which countries to aid, and in Africa—more so than in other regions of the world—they have often had the predominant say about how their aid is used. Donors, usually for diplomatic purposes, often have chosen to provide large amounts of aid to governments with little commitment to development. While this aid may have attained its diplomatic goals, much has been wasted or even counterproductive from a developmental standpoint. But misallocation of aid from a developmental point of view is only a part of the problem. The other, more serious, problem involves the way the aid has been designed and managed by aid donors. There are three elements to this problem. First is the increasingly complex and experimental nature of aid interventions, often designed by foreigners with too little knowledge of local conditions (and frequently, without the engagement and assistance of Africans who have it), shaped by elaborate programming processes that are a poor fit for such experimental work.

Second are the constraints on aid programs deriving from domestic politics and bureaucratic imperatives within donor countries. These pressures, such as the imperative to spend available monies and the influence of political parties, private interests, and government agencies themselves, are described in the individual case studies. Third is the multiplicity of poorly coordinated aid agencies operating in individual African countries. By ceding such a large amount of discretion to aid agencies and failing to coordinate them effectively, African officials have deprived those agencies of what is in many other countries a form of mediation undertaken by recipient government officials by which they help shape the aid according to their local needs and capacities—and sometimes reject the aid when it appears inappropriate.

Aid Effectiveness and Donor Performance

Let us examine the specific findings of the case studies on the performance of aid donors in Africa that lie behind these more general conclusions. Many aid agencies exhibit similar patterns of performance, but nearly every one has a particular lesson to teach.

1. If an aid agency lacks both autonomy and capacity, significant and rapidly increasing amounts of aid are likely to end in programmatic and political disaster. At best, the aid is likely to be wasted. At worst, it may be captured by agencies and interests with no commitment to promoting development and, once it becomes known that the aid has been diverted to other uses, public support for aid is likely to plummet. Italian aid in Africa best exemplifies this finding.

2. The experience of Japan in Africa would seem to contradict this finding. Here is a case in which the autonomy of the two aid agencies active there—JICA and OECF—was weak vis-à-vis other government agencies and the capacity of both agencies was limited (though they were far larger and stronger technically than the Italian aid agencies). Yet, Japan seems to have suffered no major aid disasters in Africa. Several explanations of Japan's experience are plausible. One is that Japan has few high-priority diplomatic or economic interests in Africa and relatively little experience there, so the temptation to divert aid for nondevelopmental ends has been limited. Second, the Japanese have recognized the limitations on their capacity to program development aid in Africa and have sought to shift some of the responsibilities for designing and implementing programs to others—through cofinancing with the World Bank and procuring through British Crown Agents and by undertaking proj-

ects that emphasize infrastructure rather than the more complex and experimental interventions.

3. If the autonomy of an aid agency is limited and other government agencies are eager to deploy aid for nondevelopmental purposes, the aid allocated for those other purposes will tend to be sizable and less effective or even wasted from a development point of view. This is the case not only because the recipients may include incompetent or corrupt governments but also because deploying aid for one purpose usually constrains the ability to use it for other purposes and, in particular, the ability to withhold it if one of the other purposes cannot be met. The case studies best illustrating these findings are the United States and France. They had strongly diplomatic motives for aiding particular African regimes, and a number of those regimes turned out to be developmental disasters, leading to a waste of aid. However, with the end of the Cold War and with the economic stresses in the region during the 1980s and early 1990s, the diplomatic and commercial interests of most donor governments in Africa (the greatest exception being France) have diminished along with the pressures to divert aid for purposes other than development. This is a positive change from a developmental point of view.

4. However, an important finding of this study is that the diversion of aid for nondevelopmental purposes is only one explanation of the problems of aid in Africa and not the most important. The other major explanation involves the capacity of agencies to manage aid. For example, the World Bank is the most autonomous aid agency considered in this study, yet it has experienced considerable problems in Africa. These problems have involved the design and implementation of projects and programs on the part of Bank staff and are the result primarily of two factors: the absence of the extensive local knowledge and experience that can come from an informed and authoritative field presence, and the bureaucratic pressures to spend that have resulted in hasty project preparation and have limited the incentives for Bank staff to refuse to lend where conditions were unpropitious. This last point also applies to the European Development Fund, which has long had limited ability to refuse to provide agreed levels of aid to its African partners. Other donors have often been influenced by pressures to obligate available funds within given time periods, reducing their incentives to make prudent decisions.

5. There is an assumption—both intuitively persuasive and widely shared by development practitioners—that an extensive and authoritative field presence is important to the design and implementation of effec-

tive aid. This study does not prove or disprove definitively the validity of this assumption. It does, however, demonstrate that such a presence is no proof against problems of program and project design and implementation. USAID has the most extensive and authoritative field presence of any aid agency, and yet it has not avoided these problems, even in countries where it was the principal decision-maker on the size and use of the aid. USAID and the World Bank are interesting contrasts in this regard—one that has had an extensive field presence and one that has not. But the evaluations of project and program performance in Africa of the two aid agencies do not show substantial differences in the effectiveness of their aid. (It is possible that such differences exist, but they do not appear to be significant enough to be picked up in evaluations.) USAID's disappointing experience with its field missions appears to be a result of the bureaucratization of those missions—particularly because of the excessive demands put on mission personnel by Washington. It might be said that field missions have not produced the highly effective aid hoped for because they have never been fully free to do so.

6. One of the problems evident in many of the aid programs in Africa is that they have been "donor driven"—with projects identified, planned, and implemented with only a minimal input from African officials and private individuals. Not only do donor-driven projects risk being unworkable in the unfamiliar social and political environments of Africa, but as many have noted before they often lack "ownership" on the part of Africans—the sense of involvement and commitment by those affected and the generation of benefits that create a supportive constituency—so that when aid ends, the projects collapse. However, what is not so widely recognized in the development community is that "recipient driven" projects may fare no better, if the experience of Sweden in Tanzania is anything to go by. African leaders, like leaders of countries elsewhere, are highly political, and among their goals development may not rank high. African government agencies, too, tend to be greatly politicized and lacking in capacity. Aid monies left to them to allocate are likely to be used for purposes with a high political payoff. Donors concerned about the developmental effectiveness of their aid in Africa cannot take a hands-off posture on how it is used. The challenge confronting the donors is finding the right balance between control and diffidence.

7. The aid donor with seemingly a combination of the greatest autonomy and capacity is the United Kingdom. For much of the period of this study, DfID (formerly ODA) was formally part of the Foreign Office.

But it nevertheless functioned with a considerable degree of discretion in Africa. And its professionalism has also been highly regarded, though it has lacked an extensive field presence. Yet its own completion reports suggest a degree of effectiveness in Africa not significantly different from that of the World Bank. The performance of the more capable aid agencies suggests that in regard to effectiveness of aid in Africa, no agency has got it right yet.

To sum up, these findings suggest that an absence of autonomy and capacity in aid agencies can lead to disasters. Limitations on the autonomy of agencies can lead to a use of aid for nondevelopment purposes and to significant wastage from a development perspective. But even agencies with a considerable degree of autonomy and capacity have delivered ineffective aid in Africa. We must continue to search for the reasons why.

The Problem of Capacity

In chapter 4, we pointed to the importance of the fit between organizational form and function. It is a familiar issue in public administration and organizational analysis. It is also a problem that specialists in development administration have raised in the past, though it has received relatively little attention from senior officials responsible for managing aid agencies and for shaping systems and processes by which those agencies do their business. The new systems and processes that aid agencies are beginning to borrow from popular notions of "reinventing government" (including, above all, programming for measurable and immediate results) may, if not handled carefully, further complicate and reduce the flexibility of what are essentially experimental ventures in promoting development in Africa and elsewhere. And always, the goal of expanding or at least avoiding decreases in budgets remains a high priority, generating the familiar pressures to spend cited above.

What should the basic considerations of form and function be in managing aid for development? The most basic considerations are uncertainty and lack of control—uncertainty about how to accomplish risky tasks in unfamiliar environments that aid officials cannot control. Adding to their difficulties is the fact that their goals are often ambiguous and outcomes difficult to measure. These characteristics of the "task environment" of aid agencies suggest that such agencies, to be most effective, should have a number of key qualities: a maximum degree of decentralization of staff and authorities to the field where their work must be accomplished (but not so much as to lose broad program and policy coherence) and with the opportunity to spend time outside of field offices learning about the society in which they are posted, programming systems that permit and reward experimentation and learning, a technically qualified staff capable of managing all the various types of activities the aid agency undertakes, the involvement of local individuals and groups in the planning and implementation of aid-financed activities (consistent with the maintenance of programming standards and accountability), a system of evaluation that is reliable, comprehensive, accessible, and with incentives for staff to use its findings, and incentives for aid officials to decide not to plan and obligate monies where conditions are not supportive of the success of their programs or projects. The bottom line is that aid agencies, probably more than any other government agencies, need to be flexible, "learning" agencies with the ability to say no. However, these characteristics are present only to a limited degree in the agencies examined in this study, which are organized and function more like firms or public organizations where goals are relatively clear, measurable technologies for accomplishing them are known, and the environment in which those goals are achieved is easily controlled.

In reality, aid agencies tend to be highly centralized, with most decisions made at headquarters, to have elaborate, standardized, and at times rigid programming systems, to use the quantity of funds spent as a measure of the effectiveness of projects and programs while having weak and underused evaluation systems. As a result of these misfits, projects and programs are often poorly designed and implemented, pressures to spend drive programmatic decisions, the real impact of those programs and projects is often unknown, and what is known is seldom used to inform similar activities—with the result that mistakes in policy and programming are repeated many times before they are corrected. Aid agencies do learn, but slowly and expensively.

Why does this misfit exist and persist—despite the past critiques by a number of experts on aid administration? The main reasons are political: the size and often the use of the aid are driven by domestic political and bureaucratic imperatives, as the case studies in this book have shown. In contrast to many government agencies in Western countries, the intended beneficiaries of aid agencies—the poor in other countries—have very little say over how aid agencies are organized and run because those agencies are not accountable to those beneficiaries. One can imagine what kind of collective action European or American farmers would take if government programs intended to benefit them proved as ineffective as development aid programs in Africa. Pressures for more effective programs would likely force the adoption of more appropriate organizational and programmatic systems. Absent these pressures, aid agencies have tended to adopt programming systems similar to those that are known and used in other government agencies or preferred by legislators, bureaucrats, and policy-level officials keen to centralize power, to regularize processes, to spend available monies, to control programs, and to maximize political support for their activities and their budgets. We shall address the question undoubtedly in the reader's mind, what, if anything, is to be done about this problem, in the last part of this chapter.

The Autonomy of Aid Agencies

We posited at the beginning that the autonomy of an aid agency is influenced by the degree to which it has allies within governments and constituents outside it that support its development mission. Let us elaborate our findings in these two categories.

In terms of the relationships of aid agencies with other government agencies, there appear to be several findings from the case studies worth noting. One is that in the three-way contest for influence over aid funds within donor governments—between ministries of foreign affairs, economic ministries, and aid agencies themselves—ministries of foreign affairs have most often been the winners on issues of "high" diplomatic politics, that is, where important national or presidential priorities were involved. Where such issues were few or nonexistent in Africa (for example, for Sweden), these conflicts were far fewer and the priorities of aid agencies—promoting development—were more influential. However, where the ministry of foreign affairs had an interest in the aid program, it often limited the influence of economic ministries. This appears to have been the case in the United States, where the Department of State played an important—and the Department of Commerce and the Export-Import Bank a minor—role in the allocation of aid during the Cold War.

Despite the reliance of most aid agencies on ministries of foreign affairs (or their incorporation into those ministries), many have nevertheless managed to operate with a degree of autonomy. Thus, a second finding—contrary to what may have been expected—is that the institutional location of aid agencies does not necessarily determine their autonomy. The location of ODA within the British Foreign Office did not prevent it from exercising a considerable measure of autonomy over aid allocations in Africa, while the semi-independence of USAID from the Department of State has not prevented the latter from constraining the former's autonomy to a significant degree (at least during the Cold War). Other factors playing a role in autonomy include the organization and governance of the aid agency (or agencies), the respect accorded the development professionals and their mission by others in government, the leadership of the aid agency, and, very importantly, the size and influence of the constituency for development outside government.

Turning to the question of a constituency for development aid, this is the first study to examine and compare the role of NGOs—the primary development constituency for most aid agencies—in bolstering (or limiting) the autonomy of aid agencies. The materials and analysis generated by the case studies of aid donors point to a number of findings that are relevant not only to the practical interests of this book but to those parts of the fields of comparative government and international relations concerned with the role of transnational, nonstate actors in influencing policy choices of governments, and in the case of this study, of multilateral development banks as well.

1. NGOs interested in development and related issues (for example, humanitarian relief, the environment, or population problems) have been increasing in number, organization, political sophistication, and influence on policy. Their growth has been encouraged by the political space created by democratization in much of the world, by the prominence and encouragement given NGOs through the various UN summits of the 1990s, through the example of the influence of NGOs in developed countries—for instance, in the United States—and by NGOs themselves, which have established formal and informal networks of information, support, and advice. We have here in effect a rapidly expanding worldwide network of nonstate actors, acting at times separately, at times together, to influence government policy. They seek to influence not only governments but also multilateral institutions, including the two considered here—the World Bank and the European Commission. In the latter two cases, we have an instance of transnational nonstate actors seeking to influence other transnational, nonstate actors.

2. NGOs have become the most important constituency for the activities of development aid agencies. They have often supported the policies, programs, budgets, and, at times, survival of those agencies. But they have also at times been highly critical of those agencies and of their governments' policies. In either case, the tactics of influence pursued by

NGOs have varied according to the political systems in which they are functioning, much as institutionalists would predict. They typically seek important points of access to key policymakers and shape tactics according to the nature of that access. Where the legislature plays an important role in policy and individual legislators can be influential—as in the United States—NGOs focus on the legislature and adopt tactics intended to influence key legislators (for example, working through their constituents or using legislators supporting their positions to pressure other legislators for support). In governments where the legislature plays a limited role in influencing policy, NGOs have attempted to cultivate close relations with relevant policy officials, through personal contacts and through serving on government advisory boards. NGOs in Sweden appear to have relied primarily on this avenue of influence, assuming that it was adequate to promote and protect their interests. When it has proven possible, NGOs have turned to the courts (as in the United Kingdom), challenging government policies on the basis of existing legislation. In Japan, NGOs have resorted to *gaiatsu*—working through foreign NGOs to exert pressure on the Japanese aid bureaucracy (replicating the same tactic of influence used by Japanese government officials in alliance with foreign government officials). And in most places, NGOs have used the media—sometimes in a number of countries at the same time on the same issue—to prod or embarrass governments to adopt desired policies.

3. NGOs have also found ways to criticize, to support, and to influence multilateral development institutions. The World Bank and European Commission, as nonstate actors themselves, are accountable directly to their member states, but neither is directly accountable to a legislature. NGOs have sought to influence such institutions primarily through three channels: one has involved direct personal and institutional contacts, much as with bilateral aid agencies. The World Bank and the European Commission both have advisory bodies made up of NGOs. But NGOs have not relied solely on these channels for the good reason that they provide only limited influence. They have utilized the media to support or embarrass the multilaterals, much as they have with bilateral aid agencies. And where possible, they have worked through the legislatures of member states, again, much as NGOs have done with bilateral aid agencies, where that has proven possible. This has been most evident in the case of the United States. In the case of the World Bank, we also see the influence of institutions on tactics, where NGOs in major contributing countries have linked up with NGOs in borrowing countries to resist

certain Bank policies, especially in the area of the environment. Multilateral institutions, not surprisingly, produce multilateral tactics of influence.

4. We have noted the tendency of a number of aid agencies to expand the portfolio of activities they fund. This is most evident in the case of the World Bank, at least if the statements of its president are an indication of its intent. But it is also evident in most other aid donors—the United States, United Kingdom, Japan, the Europeans. In addition to the more traditional portfolios of infrastructure, health, education, and agriculture, aid is now provided for economic reforms, democratization, the environment, women in development, and other purposes. Most of these activities are not new. What appears to be novel is that most aid agencies want to do all of them. Despite declining budgets and calls for more coordination and specialization based on the comparative advantages of different agencies, portfolios of most aid agencies show every sign of expanding (or certainly not contracting). Why?

We can propose an answer based on the findings of this study. With the end of the Cold War, one of the main rationales of foreign aid for the United States and a significant or implicit rationale for a number of other governments for funding development in poor countries is gone. Additionally, with the real economic progress in much of Asia and Latin America, economic development is no longer the principal issue in the bilateral relations of rich and poor countries. Foreign ministries have a declining interest in aid as an instrument for achieving their diplomatic goals. Foreign-aid agencies are left to search for alternative rationales for what they do and a constituency that will support them in doing it. NGOs are the obvious constituency. But NGO interests run strongly in the direction of "people-oriented" development activities, and they are often organized to promote particular goals—such as improving the status of women or protecting the environment—rather than the broader goal of development. Aid agencies seeking their support are beginning to reflect their preferences but without dropping existing activities (in part because those activities have constituencies inside aid agencies in favor of their continuation). It appears that the political imperatives of finding relevance and garnering support are a key factor in the trend toward a broadening of aid agency portfolios.

5. Despite the recognition here of the growing influence of NGOs, it is also important to recognize that NGOs, although increasing in numbers and influence, still remain relatively weak in most political systems. Collective action is new for most of them; they are frequently based on

volunteers who feel strongly about a normative issue but whose fervor may wax and wane. And most of them are highly dependent on the financial support of their own governments, potentially limiting their abilities to take strongly critical positions of those same governments. But much of the future size and direction of development aid is likely to be dependent on them, as the foreign-policy uses of aid diminish.

Public Opinion and Foreign Aid

It is worth examining comparative findings vis-à-vis public opinion and development aid in the case studies included here. There are two interesting questions in this regard: what can we deduce about the role of public opinion in supporting and influencing foreign aid? And what influences public opinion on foreign aid? First, public opinion usually plays a relatively passive role in supporting foreign aid. A supportive public (as in the case of Sweden) provides aid agencies with a friendly political environment and so, greater autonomy and a broader scope for action and perhaps experimentation. A less supportive public—as in the United States—is likely to lead to greater scrutiny and criticism of aid funding, likely to tolerate or demand greater constraints on action and experimentation and to require greater public accountability. Second, while the public may be relatively passive on foreign aid, it can be aroused by shocks (humanitarian disasters or scandals in the aid program) and exert enormous pressure on its government to respond to those shocks. Third, where a high proportion of the public turns against foreign aid (as in Italy), it is difficult for governments to continue such programs.

What influences the degree of public support for foreign aid? It appears that public education and advocacy campaigns make a difference. Governments, like that of Sweden, which have spent relatively large amounts of money on such campaigns over a significant period of time have for the most part enjoyed a supportive public. Others, like the United States, have spent relatively little and have had considerably less public support for foreign aid. But public education is clearly only part of the answer. Another part is likely to be the basic values accepted by a country's public. In Sweden, for example, the public was long broadly supportive of the idea that the rich had an obligation to help the poor and government was an appropriate vehicle for organizing much of that support.[1] It was not difficult to make the case for development aid abroad to a public that already accepted these premises as bases for policies at home. However, in the United States, there has never been a strong consensus on the obligation of the rich to help the poor, and the role of government in U.S. society remains controversial. It appears that Americans often see foreign aid through a domestic welfare program optic and judge it accordingly. For this reason it may be much more difficult for a public education or advocacy program in the United States to gain significantly greater support for aid.

A third factor that clearly influences public opinion is economic conditions at home. Where countries suffer from recessions, their publics become less supportive of sending national resources abroad to help others. This is evident even in Sweden, with its high public support of foreign aid. Alternatively, where there are major disasters abroad, in which human suffering is made known to the publics of rich countries (as with the periodic droughts in Africa), support not only for relief but for overall development aid rises—at least for a time.

A Return to Hypotheses

Let us examine these findings in terms of the four hypotheses set out in chapter 4. Hypothesis number 1 was that the main impediment to aid effectiveness on the donor's side was the use of aid for nondevelopmental purposes, reflecting primarily the influence of ministries of foreign affairs over its allocation and use. The case studies here suggest that the allocation of aid for nondevelopmental purposes was at times an impediment, but greater impediments were the limitations on the capacity of aid agencies to undertake the types of aid interventions they chose to mount.

A second hypothesis was that field missions with delegated authorities led to more effective aid. The findings of this study suggest that while such field missions may be helpful, they are no guarantee of more effective aid, as the case of USAID demonstrates. What seems likely is that field missions can contribute to effectiveness—indeed, they may be essential—but only if those in the field have the technical and local knowledge and the time (along with appropriate programming processes) to gather and maintain that knowledge which will allow them to shape and manage aid programs and projects appropriate to local needs and capabilities.

A third hypothesis was that programming processes must fit the tasks demanded of aid officers. There is much in these studies that suggests this is correct. Finally, a fourth hypothesis was that there needed to be "ownership" locally of aid interventions if they were to be effective. This study suggests that a degree of local involvement is critical, but donors are unwise to turn over all authority over decisions on the uses of aid to recipients if they want to ensure their aid has the desired impact and proves sustainable.

Summing Up

Can we boil down the findings of this study to a few basic points? Yes, and they appear to be three. First, the challenges of development in Africa are especially difficult and complex and involve not only economic but political and social change. Second, because of the eagerness of Africans for aid and the willingness of donors to provide it in significant amounts during much of the period covered by this study, the weight of decision making on how that aid has been used has fallen largely to the donors along with the corresponding responsibility for making it work. Third, aid donors, often because of the domestic political and bureaucratic factors that influence their aid, have been limited in their capacity to use the aid to realize the economic, political, and social changes needed to further development in Africa. The first of these points will not be altered easily or quickly. But there are things to be done to change the second and third points to produce more effective aid in Africa, and these things involve the donors of that aid. It is to the reform of foreign aid that we now finally turn.

Whither Aid in Africa? Proposals for the Future

It is usually expected in public life that the person who raises problems also offers solutions. The solutions to the problems of effective aid in Africa need to include fundamental reforms in the way aid agencies do business in Africa, if that business is to be more effective in the future than it has been in the past in supporting development. As a general matter, aid programs need to be "depoliticized"—meaning that aid agencies need greater autonomy, within the requirements of public accountability, to manage those programs to realize their development goals. More importantly, the agencies themselves need to create organizational structures, staffing, and more flexible programming systems appropriate to their tasks. Most importantly, aid agencies and their staffs need to eliminate bureaucratic pressures to spend. Aid officials need to be able to decide not to commit funds without being penalized. Finally, aid agencies need to create mechanisms that will ensure greater coordination and coherence in their programs in particular African countries.

Changes such as these run against the grain of politics in most of the countries examined here. They would require an act of political will on the part of aid-giving governments in Africa to depart from traditional domestic political and bureaucratic practices. But the time is propitious for such an initiative on the part of aid donors. The Cold War (with its attendant influences over allocations) is over; aid to Africa is declining; and many donors are rethinking their overall aid programs and reorganizing their bureaucracies. Moreover, among both Africans and aid agencies, there is an increasing concern about ineffective aid and what can be done about it.

However, more than an act of political will is necessary to achieve more effective aid in Africa. A set of new mechanisms involving the management of that aid is required. The proposals below describe just such mechanisms. Some of them represent a radical departure from the way aid is organized and delivered in Africa at present. They will be criticized as impractical and politically naive. I believe they are neither. I would ask the reader to keep an open mind while reading them and to remember that in politics, what was believed to be impossible yesterday can seem inevitable today.

First, donors should shift much more responsibility for planning and programming their aid to their field staff in African countries receiving the aid, consistent with overall policy priorities of individual aid donors. That means a decentralization of staff to the field with delegated authorities to commit funds within agreed country budgetary levels, flexible programming systems to support field staff, and rigorous evaluation systems whose findings are widely disseminated and used. But decentralization is not enough, as the experience of USAID has demonstrated. Three other things are needed: field staff who have the time and incentives to work with potential recipients of their aid rather than spending time in their offices, much better coordination among donors in a country, and a much less intrusive approach to delivering the aid. These goals can be realized in a new organizational and programming mechanism shared by donors.

Joint Donor Missions

Donors should consider the establishment of joint missions in the field to which representatives of donor aid agencies would be accredited. Donor agencies would not surrender authority over decisions on the use of their aid to these missions,[2] but their representatives to them would have authority to commit aid funds to agreed activities provided those activities were in accord with the broad policies and regulatory requirements of their agencies. These missions would agree with a counterpart African agency (probably a government agency but with input from relevant elements of civil society) on an overall country strategy for assistance. (The aid donors would no longer draft such strategies themselves; this would have to be done by the Africans.) This strategy would provide a broad framework within which donors would plan their projects and programs. Different donors would then indicate which sectors or types of activities they would be willing to fund and the standards and conditions they would expect project and program proposals to meet.

The project and program proposals would be the responsibility of African governments and private-sector organizations to design and present to the joint donor mission for funding. This would be another departure from current practice. Aid donors could provide temporary technical assistance to African organizations if it were required for drafting fundable proposals. The proposals would be considered by the donors and approved for funding, rejected, or returned for revisions, much as philanthropic foundations do. Aid agencies would have to permit their representatives in the field to decline to spend available monies without negative consequences. Perhaps this would involve "no year" aid funding (that is, that aid monies appropriated for one year would remain available until spent). It would also mean that aid officials were evaluated not on how much money they committed but on the quality and, eventually, the outcome of the projects and programs they funded. They would have to remain in country or associated with country aid programs long enough for reasonable assessments of project or program outcomes to be made—more than the two or three years now common for aid assignments. This "demand-driven" approach would involve a far less intrusive posture on the part of aid donors and provide strong incentives for African institutions, public and private, to develop the capacity to design and manage aid-financed activities. It would also avoid the problems of "recipient-oriented" Swedish aid by requiring funding proposals to fit within overall strategies and individual donor priorities, and to meet agreed standards of quality and accountability.

I can almost hear the objections to these proposals. First, the Africans do not have the capacity to design and implement projects and programs. This may be true for many government agencies and NGOs at present. But it need not continue to be the case where there are incentives for capacity building. The problems of capacity in Africa today stem far less from the lack of trained manpower than ever in the past. Indeed, in many countries, there is an excess of educated Africans who could, where necessary, be further trained to manage development projects. What is needed are the incentives for governments and NGOs to utilize available capacity effectively. Where obtaining funding for development projects hinges on being able to design and implement such projects effectively, it is likely in all but the poorest countries that the capacity could quickly be developed or strengthened. This is unlikely to happen, however, if donors continue to do the work themselves.

A second objection is that donors would never be willing to cede a substantial amount of the responsibility for designing and managing their aid to Africans since donor aid agencies must be accountable to their publics for the use of monies appropriated to them; and a number of donor governments have, in any case, motives other than promoting effective development for providing their aid. There are several responses to these objections. First, the approach suggested here is less intrusive but not less accountable. Aid agencies would still adopt goals and seek the most effective and efficient means of achieving those goals. They would still audit and evaluate the use and impact of their expenditures. But rather than design the details of the projects they fund, they would hold the recipients responsible for designing the details and enable the recipients to alter those details as they learned from implementation or as the conditions affecting those projects shifted. It should also be recognized that mistakes and failures will occur in some aid projects designed and managed by Africans, at least in the early years of such an approach. But donors must be prepared to accept such mistakes as a price of improvements in the long-run effectiveness of their aid. It is difficult to believe that the publics in donor countries would not be willing to tolerate such failures as a price of learning and eventual success on the part of Africans.

Another possible objection to the approach proposed here is that it would limit the ability of NGOs, other private interests, legislatures, and other government agencies to influence the allocation and use of aid. This is true, and it is in fact part of the intent of this proposal. One of the advantages of enhanced donor coordination and joint donor missions working within agreed country development strategies is that they could bolster aid programs in African countries that are shaped more by local needs and opportunities than by domestic politics and bureaucratic imperatives in donor capitals. A joint mission with some stature in donor capitals could act in effect as a lobby with individual donor governments wanting to alter planned aid levels or spend aid funds for purposes inconsistent with those to which it has committed itself as part of the joint mission.

Finally, the reader may be asking what all these proposals imply for the level of aid to Africa. My response is that it is the wrong question. If there is one important finding in this book, it is that the level of aid to African countries is not as important as what the aid accomplishes. Aid levels for individual countries should be decided on the basis of conditions in that country and on what donors and Africans together can expect to accomplish. In countries where economic policies are supportive of development and additional capital would reduce the constraint on growth, it may make sense to focus on the size of aid flows—the "gap-filling" approach still evident in the thinking of a number of aid donors. In countries where economic policies are not supportive of development or where nonfinancial obstacles (social, political, institutional) impede that development, it is not the overall level of aid that is critical but what the aid can do to remove those obstacles and bring about beneficial changes.

But, a persistent reader may demand, won't the proposals outlined here result in lower levels of aid, at least in the short run, while African governments and NGOs gain the capacity to design and manage aid activities satisfactorily? This seems highly likely. But if less aid in the short run leads to more effective aid, a stronger local capacity, and a stronger sense of local responsibility (together with less dependent attitudes toward aid donors) in the long run, the decline would prove beneficial. Indeed, these results are essential to the effectiveness of aid and to the future of development in Africa.

Those familiar with the fashions in foreign-aid discussions will note that the catch phrases of today—in particular, "participation" and "selectivity"—have rarely been mentioned in this book. There is a reason for this. Their popularity combined with their ambiguity often obscures rather than furthers constructive discussions of the problems of aid effectiveness in Africa. Yet much of this book is about the core meanings of these words. The participation of the intended beneficiaries of aid—its "clients" in current-speak—need not only to be sought (often as far as "participation" goes on the part of aid donors) but needs to be part of the decision making on the use of foreign aid—in particular, its design and implementation. This does not mean, as some NGOs would have it, that beneficiaries ought to have complete say over how the aid is used. But to leave them out or involve them only perfunctorily as donors hasten to commit all their available monies is also a mistake and one not unfamiliar in donor practice.

Second, there is "selectivity." The meaning of this concept is clear—aid should be provided to those who can use it effectively. This is an easy policy for donors to support but a difficult one for them to implement, as suggested—nay, as demonstrated—by the history of aid in Africa. The absence of selectivity based on development considerations has been one of the greatest weaknesses of aid, a weakness attributable to the way aid donors have managed their resources. The decline in nondevelopmental interests of donors in Africa and the contraction in available aid monies may fortify donor commitment to greater selectivity. But the flexibility and capacity on the part of donors to say no to potential recipients and to terminate aid where it is not working or where recipients are not fulfilling their parts of aid agreements is central to the use of aid as an effective incentive.

This book has attempted to answer the question, why with so much aid has there been so little development in Africa? It is an important question, and the answers should affect policies as well as the lives of the many Africans foreign aid seeks to benefit. However, the answers and reforms proposed here are a beginning, not an end, to making foreign aid a more effective tool for promoting development. There is still much we do not know about African societies and polities as well as about the potential contribution of aid to the betterment of the lives of Africans. It is my hope that this work may contribute not only to a better understanding of aid and development in Africa, better policies and practices and more effective aid there, but also to continuing efforts on the part of the practitioners, scholars, and beneficiaries of that aid to push out the frontiers of our knowledge yet further. There is, indeed, so much still to be done.

Notes

Chapter One

1. *Africa* for the purposes of this study refers to the countries south of the Sahara, unless otherwise noted.

2. *The Autobiography of Kwame Nkrumah* (Edinburgh: Thomas Nelson and Sons, 1957), vii.

3. Development Assistance Committee, *Development Cooperation* (Paris: Organization for Economic Cooperation and Development, 1997), table 36, pp. A62–63. The only group of countries with a higher level of aid as a percentage of GNP (at nearly 20 percent) were the small island countries of the Pacific.

4. The heavy debt burden of many African countries, much of which is a result of large flows of aid credits, is widely viewed as a major impediment to future growth in the region. A number of initiatives have been undertaken to relieve this debt, but it remains at high levels for many countries. This study will not address African debt since that issue has been well studied elsewhere. See, for example, Carol Lancaster and John Williamson, eds., *African Debt and Financing* (Washington, D.C.: Institute for International Economics, 1986); Carol Lancaster, *African Economic Reform: The External Dimension* (Washington, D.C.: Institute for International Economics, 1991); and Matthew Martin, *The Crumbling Facade of African Debt Negotiations* (New York: St. Martin's, 1991). For data on African debt, see World Bank, *Global Development Finance* (Washington, D.C.: World Bank, 1997); and World Bank, *World Debt Tables* (Washington, D.C.: World Bank, various years).

5. Olusegun Obasanjo, "Africa: The Year 2000 and Beyond," United Nations, Third Economic Commission for Africa Silver Jubilee Lecture, Addis Ababa, 1987, p. 12. The major exceptions to this generalization tend to be among the most expensive aid projects in Africa, including the Tanzania-Zambian Railroad, constructed by the Peoples' Republic of China, the Ajoakuta steel mill, financed by the USSR, and the Volta River dam, financed by the United States, and the

Manantali Dam and barrage and irrigation works on the Senegal River, financed by Arab aid agencies and others.

6. Devesh Kapur, "The Weakness of Strength: The Challenge of Sub-Saharan Africa," in *The World Bank: Its First Half Century,* ed. Devesh Kapur, John P. Lewis, and Richard Webb (Washington, D.C.: Brookings Institution, 1997), 1:802.

7. See, for example, Andre Gunder Frank, *Capitalism and Underdevelopment in Latin America* (New York: Monthly Review Press, 1967); Samir Amin, *Neo-Colonialism in West Africa* (New York: Monthly Review Press, 1973); and Walter Rodney, *How Europe Underdeveloped Africa* (Washington, D.C.: Howard University Press, 1972).

8. See, for example, Teresa Hayter, *The Creation of World Poverty* (London: Pluto Press, 1981), and her *Aid as Imperialism* (Harmondsworth, Middlesex: Penguin, 1971).

9. Arturo Escobar, *Encountering Development: The Making and Unmaking of the Third World* (Princeton, N.J.: Princeton University Press, 1995), p. 9.

10. James Ferguson, *The Anti-Politics Machine: "Development," Depoliticization, and Bureaucratic Power in Lesotho* (New York: Cambridge University Press, 1990).

11. See Peter Bauer, *Dissent on Development* (Cambridge, Mass.: Harvard University Press, 1972).

12. See, for example, Robert Bates, *Markets and States in Tropical Africa* (Berkeley and Los Angeles: University of California Press, 1981); and Rudiger Dornbusch and Sebastian Edwards, eds., *The Macroeconomics of Populism in Latin America* (Chicago: University of Chicago Press, 1991).

13. See H. W. Arndt, *Economic Development: The History of an Idea* (Chicago: University of Chicago Press, 1987), for a detailed description of this era in thinking about development.

14. Graham Hancock, *Lords of Poverty: The Power, Prestige, and Corruption of the International Aid Business* (New York: Atlantic Monthly Press, 1989). Hancock asserts that aid provided by nongovernmental organizations avoids these problems. He overlooks the fact that much of the aid provided by NGOs comes from official aid agencies themselves.

15. See, for example, Howard White, "The Macroeconomic Impact of Development Aid: A Critical Survey," *Journal of Development Studies* 28, no. 2 (1992): 163–240. See also Paul Mosley, "Aid Effectiveness," final draft, 1995, photocopy; and Peter Boone, "The Impact of Foreign Aid on Savings and Growth," London School of Economics, 1994, mimeograph.

16. Craig Burnside and David Dollar, "Aid, Policies, and Growth," draft, Macroeconomics and Growth Division, Policy Research Department, World Bank, November 1996.

17. See Robert Cassen and Associates, *Does Aid Work? Report to an Intergovernmental Task Force,* 2d ed. (Oxford: Clarendon Press, 1994).

18. See Vernon Ruttan, Anne Krueger, and Constantine Michaelopolous, eds., *Aid and Development* (Baltimore: Johns Hopkins University Press, 1989).

19. Judith Tendler, *Inside Foreign Aid* (Baltimore: Johns Hopkins University Press, 1975); Dennis Rondinelli, *Development Projects as Policy Experiments* (New York: Methuen, 1983).

20. See Paul Mosley, Jane Harrigan, and John Toye, *Aid and Power: The World Bank and Policy-Based Lending,* 2 vols. (New York: Routledge, 1992).

21. Uma Lele, ed., *Aid to African Agriculture: Lessons from Two Decades of Donors' Experience* (Baltimore: Johns Hopkins University Press for the World Bank, 1991).

22. See Tony Killick, "The Developmental Effectiveness of Aid to Africa," Working Paper, Policy Research and External Affairs, International Economics Department, World Bank, 1991.

23. Nicolas van de Walle and Timothy Johnson, *Improving Aid to Africa,* Policy Essay No. 21 (Washington, D.C.: Overseas Development Council, 1996).

Chapter Two

1. Development is a value-laden concept, its definition often reflecting the values of the definer. For a discussion of various definitions, see Amartya Sen, "The Concept of Development," in *Handbook of Development Economics,* vol. 1, ed. Hollis Chenery and T. N. Srinivasan (New York: North Holland, 1988).

2. I have avoided the term *equity* here. Equity suggests a more equal division of national resources between the poor and rich—a worthy goal, but one that has lower priority than simply improving the standard of living of the poor. I have also avoided *poverty alleviation* since what is really needed in Africa and other poor regions is not the alleviation of poverty but its permanent reduction. And that, in turn, involves expanded access by the poor to assets or social services.

3. For an introduction to the evolution of thinking on economic development, see Arndt, *Economic Development.* For more detailed treatments of important topics in development economics, see the *Handbook of Development Economics,* vols. 1–2, 3b, ed. Hollis Chenery and T. N. Srinivasan (New York: North Holland, 1988–95), and vol. 3a, ed. Hollis Chenery, Jere Behrman, and T. N. Srinivasan (New York: North Holland, 1995).

4. For a discussion of the role of technology in development, see Robert Evenson, "Technological Change and Technology Strategy," in Behrman and Srinivasan, *Handbook of Development Economics,* vol. 3a. For an overview of recent and anticipated technologies relevant to development, see the National Research Council and World Bank, *Marshaling Technology for Development* (Washington, D.C.: National Academy Press, 1995).

5. Increases in the factors of production, technological advances, and changes in market conditions do not fully explain the rates of growth or their differences among countries. The "residual" is often significant, leading one economist to observe, "Right now, economists confronting the phenomenon of development are a bit like geologists confronting mountain ranges before the discovery of plate tectonics: we know a lot about the subject but can only speculate loosely about ultimate causes." Paul Krugman, "Cycles of Conventional Wisdom in Economic Development," *International Affairs* 72, no. 1 (1996): 717–32.

6. See, for example, Simon Kutzets, "Economic Growth and Income Inequality," *American Economic Review* 45 (1955): 1–29; and David Morawetz, *Twenty-*

five Years of Economic Development: 1950 to 1975 (Washington, D.C.: World Bank, 1977).

7. See, for example, Catherine Gwin and Joan Nelson, *Perspectives on Aid and Development,* Policy Essay No. 22 (Washington, D.C.: Overseas Development Council, 1997); Nancy Birdsall, David Ross, and Richard Sabot, "Inequality and Growth Reconsidered: Lessons from East Asia," *World Bank Economic Review* 9, no. 3 (1995): 477–508; Torsten Persson and Guido Tabellini, "Is Inequality Harmful to Growth?" *American Economic Review* 84, no. 3 (1994): 600–621.

8. See the World Bank, *The State in a Changing World* (Washington, D.C.: World Bank, 1997).

9. See Douglass North, *Institutions, Institutional Change, and Economic Performance* (New York: Cambridge University Press, 1990), p. 3. The idea that institutions (usually more narrowly defined as public agencies) play a key role in development is not new. It has been a theme in development work for decades. But what is new is the expansion in its definition and the increased appreciation on the part of economists and development practitioners of its importance.

10. For a lengthy analysis of Africa's development experience during the first three decades of independence, see World Bank, *Sub-Saharan Africa: From Crisis to Sustainable Growth* (Washington, D.C.: World Bank, 1989).

11. See World Bank, *Accelerated Development in Sub-Saharan Africa* (Washington, D.C.: World Bank, 1981), for a retrospective on the first two decades of development in Africa.

12. World Bank, *Sub-Saharan Africa* (1989), p. 269.

13. See Global Coalition for Africa, *African Social and Economic Trends,* Annual Report, 1996 (Washington, D.C.: n.p., 1997). The data are drawn from World Bank sources.

14. Some fourteen countries of sub-Saharan Africa share a common currency—the CFA franc—which is convertible to the French franc at a fixed rate. This rate was devalued in January 1994 and gave a boost to the exports of many CFA countries. For more detail, see chapter 6.

15. Global Coalition for Africa, *Social and Economic Trends,* p. 38. Investment includes public and private investment.

16. World Bank, *Sub-Saharan Africa* (1989), p. 163.

17. Global Coalition for Africa, *Social and Economic Trends,* p. 37.

18. Ibid., p. 37. Savings rates for Nigeria were not available in this data.

19. These figures were drawn from World Bank, *Accelerated Development* (1981); *Sub-Saharan Africa* (1989); and *Adjustment in Africa: Reforms, Results, and the Road Ahead* (Washington, D.C.: Oxford University Press for the World Bank, 1994), p. 38.

20. See, for example, Rodney, *How Europe Underdeveloped Africa;* Amin, *Neo-Colonialism in West Africa.*

21. World Bank, *Sub-Saharan Africa* (1989), p. 174, table 8.3.

22. I use the term *model* here loosely. It does not refer to a formal set of conditions, expressible mathematically. Rather it refers to a broad set of interrelated policies that African governments (and others elsewhere in the world) have pursued to manage their economies for growth. The term *sustainable development* is

used widely and with a number of different meanings. Many have used it since the UN Conference on Development and the Environment in 1992 to refer to development that is environmentally sustainable. Others use it more broadly to refer to development that continues over time. I am using it here in a narrow sense—to refer to the economic and financial aspects of sustainability only.

23. For more details, see Crawford Young, *Ideology and Development in Africa* (New Haven, Conn.: Yale University Press, 1982).

24. For a description of taxation systems in Africa, see International Monetary Fund, "Taxation in Sub-Saharan Africa," Occasional Paper No. 8, 1981; and Zmarak Shalizi and Lyn Squire, *Tax Policy in Sub-Saharan Africa* (Washington, D.C.: World Bank, 1988).

25. Shalizi and Squire, *Tax Policy,* p. 3.

26. Naomi Chazan et al., *Politics and Society in Contemporary Africa,* 2d ed. (Boulder, Colo.: Lynne Rienner, 1992), p. 55.

27. Tony Killick, *Development Economics in Action: A Study of Economic Policies in Ghana* (London: Heinemann Educational Books, 1978), pp. 1–2.

28. See, for example, Robert Bates's classic study of the role of these various interests in economic-policy choices in Africa, *Markets and States;* Jennifer Widener, "The Discovery of 'Politics': Smallholder Reactions to the Cocoa Crisis of 1988–90 in Côte d'Ivoire," in *Hemmed In,* ed. Thomas Callaghy and John Ravenhill (New York: Columbia University Press, 1993).

29. The term, coined by Professor Paul Collier, refers to those public agencies that are independent enough of the ruler's control to constrain the ruler in their particular area of responsibility. See Paul Collier, "Africa's External Economic Relations: 1960–1990," *African Affairs* 90 (1991): 339–57.

30. For a more detailed analysis of the fiscal impact of windfall increases in export revenues from commodity price fluctuations, see Jeffrey Davis, "The Economic Effects of Windfall Gains in Export Earnings," *World Development* 11, no. 2 (1983): 119–41.

31. See Jeffrey Herbst and Adebayo Olukoshi, "Nigeria: Economic and Political Reforms at Cross Purposes," in *Voting for Reform: Democracy, Political Liberalization, and Economic Adjustment,* ed. Stephan Haggard and Steven Webb (New York: Oxford University Press, 1994), p. 456.

32. For an assessment of the extent of policy and institutional reforms in Africa, see World Bank, *Adjustment in Africa.*

33. Richard Sandbrook, *The Politics of Africa's Economic Decline* (New York: Cambridge University Press, 1985), p. 94.

34. Professor Richard Sklar's observation that in Africa, "class relations, at bottom, are determined by relations of power, not production" helped crystallize the idea that those employed by or benefiting from the state were the predominant "class" in African societies. See his "Social Class and Political Action in Africa: The Bourgeoisie and the Proletariat," in *Political Development and the New Realism in Sub-Saharan Africa,* ed. David Apter and Carl Rosberg (Charlottesville: University of Virginia Press, 1994). See also Richard Sklar, "The Nature of Class Domination in Africa," *Journal of Modern African Studies* 17, no. 4 (1979): 531–52.

35. World Bank, *Sub-Saharan Africa* (1989), pp. 60–61.

36. See Freedom House, *Freedom in the World* (New York: Freedom House, 1997).

37. Freedom House, *Freedom in the World* (New York: Freedom House, 1995), p. 77.

38. For a brief analysis of private flows to sub-Saharan Africa, see Amar Bhatta-charya, Peter Montiel, and Sunil Sharma, "How Can Sub-Saharan Africa Attract More Private Capital Inflows?" in *Finance and Development* 34, no. 2 (1997): 3–7. A survey of potential investors found that civil strife, macroeconomic instabil-ity, slow growth and small markets, excessive regulations, high wages, poor infra-structure, and slow progress on privatization inhibited investors from risking their capital in Africa. And many feared that the economic-policy reforms already adopted might be reversed in the future.

39. See, for example, Goran Hyden, *No Shortcuts to Progress* (Berkeley and Los Angeles: University of California Press, 1983); David Leonard, "The Pol-itical Realities of African Management," *World Development* 15, no. 7 (1987): 899–910; Gelase Mutahaba, Rweikiza Baguma, and Mohamed Halfani, *Vit-alizing African Public Administration for Recovery and Development* (Hartford, Conn.: Kumarian Press in cooperation with the United Nations, 1993); and Jerker Carlsson, Gloria Somolekae, and Nicolas van de Walle, eds., *Foreign Aid in Africa: Learning from Country Experiences* (Uppsala: Nordiska Afrikainstitutet, 1997).

40. I want to thank Harris Mule, formerly Permanent Secretary in the Ministry of Finance of Kenya, for pointing this out to me.

41. One African government stands out as an exception to this pattern: that of Botswana. That government—one of the strongest in Africa by the 1990s—had a Ministry of Finance and Development that was competent enough and had enough authority to manage aid donors and its own spending ministries ef-fectively (see Gervase Maipose, Gloria Somolekae, and Timothy Johnson, "Ef-fective Aid Management: The Case of Botswana," in Carlsson, Somolekae, and van de Walle, *Foreign Aid in Africa,* pp. 16–35. Two factors distinguish Botswana from much of the rest of Africa: it has a well-run and relatively clean civil service, and it has been willing to reject aid programs and projects when they do not fit into Botswana's priorities. There are very few cases of African governments turn-ing away aid monies on these grounds.

42. Julius Nyerere, *Freedom and Socialism* (New York: Oxford University Press, 1968), p. 241.

43. The term is Ali Masrui's. See his "Socialism as a Mode of International Protest: The Case of Tanzania," in *Protest and Power in Black Africa,* ed. Robert Rotberg and Ali Mazrui (Oxford: Oxford University Press, 1970), p. 152.

44. Patrice Lumumba of the Congo attempted to switch when he appealed to the Soviets for help in the early years of independence. That appeal likely contrib-uted to his demise and death. Perhaps other leaders took a lesson on the dangers of switching Cold War partners.

45. For example, it is widely believed that several African leaders played a major role in the firing of the first minister of cooperation in French president Mitterrand's government—Jean Paul Cot. See, for example, Jean François Bay-art, *La Politique africaine de François Mitterrand* (Paris: Karthala, 1984).

46. Martin Staniland, "Francophone Africa: The Enduring French Connection," *Annals of the American Academy* 489 (1987): 61.

47. I have heard this story from several former U.S. ambassadors to Zaire. It is not, to my knowledge, documented anywhere.

Chapter Three

1. For an introduction to food aid and development, see Vernon Ruttan, *Why Food Aid?* (Baltimore: Johns Hopkins University Press, 1993). The data on food aid is drawn from the Development Assistance Committee, *Development Cooperation* (1997), pp. A3–4.

2. Ibid.

3. Ibid., pp. A21–22. Aid raised privately by NGOs amounted to $5.5 billion (pp. A3–4). Data on aid from NGOs is not as strong as one would hope. For example, the DAC shows ODA to NGOs at $1 billion in 1996 but grant aid from NGOs (raised privately and not counted as ODA) at $5.5 billion (Development Assistance Committee, *Development Cooperation*, pp. A3–4 and A21). However, we know that most NGOs working in development rely heavily on government grants to finance their work. Either much of this $5.5 billion in fact comes from bilateral and multilateral aid agency grants to NGOs, or the actual amount of aid funding managed by NGOs is far higher than the $5.5 billion estimate. Some DAC staff suspect the latter is in fact the case (personal communication, USAID representative to the DAC, December 1996).

4. See, for example, Roger Riddell et al., *Non-Governmental Organizations and Rural Poverty Alleviation* (London: Oxford University Press and the Overseas Development Institute, 1995). See also Overseas Development Institute, "The Impact of NGO Development Projects," *Briefing Paper* 2, London: ODI, 1996.

5. Data on aid henceforth is drawn from the DAC unless otherwise indicated. There are two annual DAC publications on the size of aid flows: the report *Development Cooperation*, by the chairman of the DAC, and the report *Geographical Distribution of Financial Flows to Developing Countries*.

6. The data in this figure and in tables in this book are in current dollars unless otherwise noted. (For aid flows to sub-Saharan Africa by donors in both current and constant dollars, see tables 4 and 5 in appendix A of this chapter.) While constant dollars are a better reflection of the real value of the resources transferred, current dollars provide a better indication of the political factors, such as the symbolism of rising and falling aid levels, that so often play an important role in decisions on aid and which are among our main concerns here.

7. Development Assistance Committee, *Development Cooperation* (1997), pp. A63–64. These figures are in 1995 prices and exchange rates.

8. Korea International Cooperation Agency, *Annual Report* (Seoul: Korea International Cooperation Agency, 1994), p. 93.

9. Vera Jerabkova, head of Africa Department, Ministry of Foreign Affairs, Czech Republic, interview by the author, Salzberg, Austria, June 1996.

10. On Korea, see Anne O. Krueger, *Economic Policies at Cross Purposes: The United States and Developing Countries* (Washington, D.C.: Brookings Institution, 1993), p. 52. Krueger also points out that aid to Taiwan ranged between 6 and

8 percent of GNP for just over a decade. U.S. aid to Turkey averaged 2 to 4 percent of GNP over roughly fifteen years. And aid to Jordan and Egypt reached 22 percent and 25 percent respectively of the GNPs of these countries during the 1980s. With the exception of the small island states of Oceania, these have been the main cases of continuously large aid flows in the postwar period. But they are still smaller in relative size and shorter in duration than aid to much of Africa. For the more recent percentages, see Development Assistance Committee, *Development Cooperation,* p. A62.

11. Development Assistance Committee, *Development Cooperation* (Paris: Organization for Economic Cooperation and Development, 1995), pp. A61–62.

12. Development Assistance Committee, *Development Cooperation* (1997), p. A61.

13. For a history of evolving ideas on aid and development, see (in addition to the works mentioned in chapter 1) Vernon Ruttan, *United States Development Assistance Policy* (Baltimore: Johns Hopkins University Press, 1996).

14. The classic statement of this proposition is Hollis Chenery and Alan Strout, "Foreign Assistance and Economic Development," *American Economic Review* 56, no. 4 (1966): 679–733.

15. Development Assistance Committee, *Development Cooperation* (Paris: Organization for Economic Cooperation and Development, 1996), pp. A3–4.

16. World Bank, *Sub-Saharan Africa* (1989).

17. The debate about aid and saving remains unresolved. For an overview of this and other broad issues of the impact of aid, see White, "Macroeconomic Impact of Aid."

18. The sources for the generalizations that follow are the evaluations and summaries of evaluation findings of all the aid agencies considered here, plus selected evaluations of aid agencies in Finland and the Netherlands. The documents and studies of the aid agencies are found in the footnotes to each case study. The challenges of data and methodology in assessing aid's effectiveness in Africa are considerable and are described briefly in appendix B to this chapter.

19. See, for example, Aehyung Kim and Bruce Benton, "Cost-Benefit Analysis of the Onchocerciasis Control Program," World Bank Technical Paper no. 282, 1995; John Dumm et al., *Evaluation of AID Family Planning Programs: Kenya Case Studies,* Technical Report 3 (Washington, D.C.: Center for Development Information and Evaluation, USAID, 1992).

20. See, for example, World Bank, *Effective Implementation: Key to Development Impact,* Portfolio Management Task Force, Washington, Annex C, 1992, p. 3; and World Bank, *Evaluation Results* (Washington, D.C.: Operations Evaluations Department, World Bank, 1994), p. 98.

21. There have been several significant exceptions to this generalization—cases of crop improvements in particular regions or countries being developed and disseminated by local research institutions in Africa. See, for example, Charles Johnson et al., *Kitale Maize: The Limits of Success* (Washington, D.C.: Center for Development Information and Evaluation, USAID, 1979).

22. Food production in Africa increased by 33 percent between 1980 and 1995, largely because the area cultivated expanded. (However, population in-

creased by just over 50 percent during the same period.) This increase was smaller than in most other parts of the developing world. See World Bank, *World Development Indicators* (Washington, D.C.: World Bank, 1997), pp. 34, 140, 144.

23. *Stabilization* is usually meant to refer to policy reforms intended to reduce inflation and imbalances in a country's external account. Stabilization policies typically include exchange rate adjustments, reductions in fiscal deficits, and credit controls. *Structural adjustment* may include these policies but usually refers to a broad array of reforms aimed at making an economy more efficient and stimulating investment and more rapid economic growth. Such policies might include trade liberalization; elimination of controls on wages, prices, and interest rates; and reforms in particular sectors or government institutions. While there may be considerable overlap between these two types of programs, stabilization programs are typically financed by the International Monetary Fund, and structural-adjustment programs are associated with the World Bank and other aid agencies.

24. The politics and tactics of reform on the part of aid donors and African governments is analyzed in detail in Mosley, Harrigan, and Toye, *Aid and Power*.

25. African Governors of the World Bank, "Partnership for Capacity Building in Africa: Strategy and Program of Action," Report for the President of the World Bank Group, mimeograph, September 28, 1996, p. 5.

26. World Bank, *Sub-Saharan Africa* (1989), p. 181. There are differences of opinion on this datum, with some believing that the numbers of technical assistants in Africa are only half this number. Personal communication, Professor Nicolas van de Walle, May 1997.

27. Jean Bossuyt, G. Laporte, and F. van Hoek, "New Avenues for Technical Cooperation in Africa," Occasional Paper (Maastricht: European Centre for Development Policy Management, 1992), p. 9.

28. Elliot Berg, *Rethinking Technical Cooperation: Reforms for Capacity Building in Africa* (New York: United Nations Development Program, 1993), p. 244.

29. Claude Ake, *Democracy and Development in Africa* (Washington, D.C.: Brookings Institution, 1996), p. 14.

30. See Bossuyt, Laporte and van Hoek, "New Avenues," p. 13; and Marc Wuyts, "Foreign Aid, Structural Adjustment, and Public Management: The Mozambican Experience," Institute of Strategic Studies, Working Paper General Series No. 206, November 1995.

31. See Paul Mosley and John Hudson, "Aid Effectiveness: A Study of the Effectiveness of Overseas Aid in the Main Countries Receiving ODA Assistance," November 1995, mimeograph. Mosley and Hudson found no significant relationship between aid and growth for six out of nine African countries examined (based on pooled, time series data over the period 1960–92). An ordinary least squares regression by this author of aid as a percentage of GNP on the rate of growth for thirty-nine African countries from 1970 to 1993, with a time lag of three years between aid and growth data, also failed to find a consistently significant relationship, either positive or negative. Only five of the countries showed a significance level of over 90 percent, but two of these showed a positive association, and three showed a negative association. One econometric effort did find a positive and significant correlation between investment and growth in sub-Saharan Africa (albeit the author found his conclusion "surprising"). See Victor

Levy, "Aid and Growth in Sub-Saharan Africa: The Recent Experience," *European Economic Review* 32 (1988): 1777–95.

32. Burnside and Dollar, "Aid, Policies, and Growth."

33. See Alex Duncan and Paul Mosley, "Aid Effectiveness: Kenya Case Study," commissioned by the Task Force on Concessional Flows of the World Bank/IMF Development Committee, August 1984, mimeograph, pp. 118ff.

34. Paul Collier, "Aid and Economic Performance in Tanzania," in *Transitions in Development,* ed. Uma Lele and Ijaz Nabi (San Francisco: International Center for Economic Growth, 1991).

35. See S. Van Wijnbergen, "Macroeconomic Aspects of the Effectiveness of Foreign Aid: The Two Gap Model, Home Goods Disequilibrium, and Real Exchange Rate Misalignment," *Journal of International Economics* 21 (1986): 123–37, for an overview of the Dutch disease and how it occurs.

36. See, for example, World Bank, *A Continent in Transition: Sub-Saharan Africa in the Mid-1990s* (Washington, D.C.: World Bank, Africa Region, 1995), p. 90.

37. S. D. Younger, "Aid and the Dutch Disease: Macroeconomic Management When Everybody Loves You," Working Paper 17, Cornell Food and Nutrition Policy Program, Ithaca, N.Y., 1991.

38. The argument developed here does not apply to aid provided by governments to nongovernmental organizations in recipient countries. Aid to NGOs remains, however, a small proportion of total aid flows.

39. I have personally been involved in a number of cases where foreign aid was initiated or increased intentionally as a symbol of approbation—for example, the doubling of U.S. aid to South Africa in the wake of the election of Nelson Mandela. The level of aid in this program was decided almost entirely on the basis of symbolism. I have also observed African leaders appeal for U.S. aid explicitly on the basis of its symbolism. I recall Jonas Savimbi, leader of the UNITA guerrillas challenging the Marxist government in Angola, saying a decade or so ago in a public meeting in Washington that he wanted U.S. aid (in this case, military aid) not because he needed the money but because he did not want to have to rely primarily on the South African government for help (which as a white-ruled, apartheid-based government undercut his claim to be a legitimate representative of black African aspirations). It is surely the case that President Mobutu of Zaire, who with access to the extensive government earnings from minerals exports, had no personal need for foreign aid but wanted U.S. assistance (and that of France and Belgium) as a sign of the approbation and implicit support of a great power. Finally, aid from the World Bank—particularly aid for structural adjustment—has come to symbolize that institution's approbation of the economic policies of governments receiving aid. African governments seek that aid because it helps them in their appeals to other donors for additional aid and to their creditors for debt relief. The Bank is well aware of this phenomenon and hesitates even to send appraisal missions for adjustment programs (which have a measure of symbolism themselves) to countries where it has serious doubts about the likelihood of that government's adopting a reform program.

40. See, for example, Robert Jackson and Carl Rosberg, "Sovereignty and Underdevelopment: Juridical Statehood in the African Crisis," *Journal of Modern African Studies* 24, no. 1 (1986): 1–31.

41. Nyerere, *Freedom and Socialism,* p. 238.

42. See for example Roger Riddell, *Aid Dependency,* project 2015 for the Swedish International Development Cooperation Agency (London: Overseas Development Institute, February 1996).

43. For a selection of studies on aid fungibility, see Howard Pack and Janet Rothenberg Pack, "Is Foreign Aid Fungible? The Case of Indonesia," *Economic Journal* 100, no. 399 (1990): 188–94, which found that aid was not highly fungible. However, another article by the same authors entitled "Foreign Aid and the Question of Fungibility," *Review of Economics and Statistics* 75, no. 2 (1993): 258–65, found aid to the Dominican Republic to be highly fungible. Others have found aid to be highly fungible when it is relatively small and not tied to the financing of particular projects. See, for example, N. M. Khilji and E. M. Zampelli, "The Fungibility of US Assistance to Developing Countries and the Impact on Recipient Expenditures: A Case Study of Pakistan," *World Development* 19, no. 8 (1991): 1095–1107. Peter Boone, in a 1994 econometric study, "Impact of Foreign Aid," found that when less than 15 percent of GNP, "virtually all aid goes to consumption" in the countries receiving it. Finally, a recent study by several economists at the World Bank found (with a better set of data than Peter Boone used) that aid was not associated with an increase in consumption but led rather to an equivalent increase in government expenditures. However, the increase in government expenditures was only equivalent to one-quarter of the amount of the aid. See Tarhan Feyzioglu, Vinaya Swaroop, and Min Zhu, "Foreign Aid's Impact on Public Spending," Policy Research Department, World Bank, 1996.

44. In his book *Foreign Aid Reconsidered* (Baltimore: Johns Hopkins University Press, 1987) Roger Riddell estimated that only around 10 percent of all aid since the late 1960s had been evaluated (p. 185). Most aid agencies only began to evaluate their projects and programs in a systematic fashion during the 1970s and have attempted to expand and upgrade the quality of their evaluations since then. It seems likely, therefore, that the percentage of activities evaluated may have increased somewhat since Riddell's book.

Chapter Four

1. This is a simplifying assumption—an unavoidable one in this study of eight different aid agencies. It is recognized here that a single public agency can encompass within it a variety of interests that may differ in their interpretation of agency goals and priorities and the best way to achieve them. These internal interests may also have close ties with external groups sharing the same interests, and these groups may work together to support or defeat agency policies. See, for example, a discussion of the natural and open-systems models of organizations in Richard Scott, *Organizations: Rational, Natural, and Open Systems* (Englewood Cliffs, N.J.: Prentice-Hall, 1987). Where different internal groupings have had an obvious impact on the functioning of an aid agency and the effectiveness of its assistance, these differences are noted in the case studies.

2. There is a significant literature that attempts to identify and assess the various motives of donors through econometric analysis of the distribution of aid.

It provides a useful overview of the broad motivations of donors, but because of the inability of quantitative data to disentangle a mix of motives, political nuances, and domestic influences, it is best used only as an introduction to understanding the broad motives of governments and international institutions providing aid. See, for example, Alfred Maizels and Machiko Nissanke, "Motivations for Aid to Developing Countries," *World Development* 12, no. 9 (1984): 879–900; Leonard Didley and Claude Montmarquette, "A Model of the Supply of Bilateral Foreign Aid," *American Economic Review* 66 (1976): 132–42; R. D. McKinlay, "The Aid Relationship: A Foreign Policy Model and Interpretation of the Distributions of Official Bilateral Economic Aid of the United States, the United Kingdom, France, and Germany, 1960–1970," *Comparative Political Studies* 11, no. 4 (1979): 411–63; William Cline and Nicholas Sargen, "Performance Criteria and Multilateral Aid Allocation," *World Development* 3, no. 6 (1975): 383–91; R. D. McKinlay and R. Little, "The French Aid Relationship: A Foreign Policy Model of the Distribution of French Bilateral Aid, 1964–70," *Development and Change* 9, no. 3 (1978): 459–78.

3. See David Newsom, *Diplomacy and the American Democracy* (Bloomington: Indiana University Press, 1988), p. 177.

4. These gifts are now termed *deliverables*. It was my task on occasion when I served in the U.S. Office of Management and Budget to try to block such deliverables (seldom successfully). Later, when I was serving in the Department of State, one of my tasks was to find aid monies for deliverables. Although I understood the reasons of political symbolism for this latter assignment, I confess that I often found the task distasteful. One of the pleasures of the end of the Cold War has been to discover, through the candid conversations now possible with former Soviet counterparts, that some of them had the same frustrating tasks and often found them equally distasteful.

5. Development Assistance Committee, *Development Cooperation* (1997), p. A52. "Partially tied" means that the aid can be spent only in the donor country or in another developing country.

6. For one example (involving the construction of the Turkwell Dam in Kenya), see Blain Harden, *Africa: Dispatches from a Fragile Continent* (New York: Houghton Mifflin, 1991).

7. The concept of autonomy is often used in political analyses to refer to the ability of the state to "formulate and pursue goals that are not simply reflective of the demands or interests of social groups, classes or society" (Peter Evans, Dietrich Rueschemeyer, and Theda Skocpol, *Bringing the State Back In* [New York: Cambridge University Press, 1985], p. 9). The concept of autonomy is applied here to an individual agency of the state—the aid agency—and that autonomy can be circumscribed not only by societal pressures but by the pressures of other agencies of the state and by the laws and regulations affecting the actions of the agency.

8. James Q. Wilson, *Bureaucracy* (New York: Basic Books, 1989), p. 28.

9. This point was convincingly demonstrated by Terry Moe in his study of the National Labor Relations Board ("Interests, Institutions, and Positive Theory: The Politics of the NLRB," in *Studies in American Political Development*, ed. Karen Orren and Stephen Skowronek [New Haven, Conn.: Yale University Press,

1987], 2:236–303), and we shall see evidence of the same in our case studies of aid agencies.

10. There are a few potential numerical indicators of autonomy. For example, the degree to which an agency's aid is tied to purchases in the donor country might indicate the influence of economic ministries on an aid agency's decision making. But this data can be misleading. First of all, the data that does exist is widely regarded by aid practitioners as being badly flawed. Second, a high proportion of tied aid might indicate greater autonomy of an aid agency rather than less if it "bought off" economic ministries by tying much of its aid. This is, in fact, the case in the United States, where a high proportion of aid is tied, but economic ministries nonetheless have relatively little influence over policy and allocative decisions. These kinds of data problems make measuring autonomy on the basis of available quantitative indicators a highly risky proposition.

11. The study of the implementation of policy choices and programs is a relatively recent one and has focused largely on domestic policies in the United States. An early work in this area was Jeffrey L. Pressman and Aaron B. Wildavsky, *Implementation* (Berkeley and Los Angeles: University of California Press, 1973). (For a review of the literature in part generated by this book, see the third edition, 1984.) Other important books in the evolving field of implementation include Daniel A. Mazmanian and Paul A. Sabatier, *Implementation and Public Policy* (Glenview, Ill.: Scott, Foresman, 1983); Eugene Bardach, *The Implementation Game: What Happens after a Bill Becomes a Law* (Cambridge, Mass.: MIT Press, 1977); Walter Williams et al., eds., *Studying Implementation: Methodological and Administrative Issues* (Chatham, N.M.: Chatham House, 1982); and Randall B. Ripley and Grace A. Franklin, *Policy Implementation and Bureaucracy* (Chicago: Dorsey Press, 1986). Pressman and Wildavsky and others in defining *implementation* understand that while it refers generally to the realization of policy ends with programmatic means, the lack of knowledge and control on the part of implementers, particularly in bringing about societal change, may require extensive adaptation and learning in the process of implementation (and even alterations in policy goals) if positive results are to be gained.

12. See, for example, Robert F. Zimmerman, *Dollars, Diplomacy, and Dependency* (Boulder, Colo.: Lynne Rienner for the Institute for the Study of Diplomacy, Georgetown University, 1993). Zimmerman begins his book with the statement that U.S. foreign aid "has largely failed to achieve its clearly stated economic and social development goals, primarily because this assistance has been first and foremost a diplomatic tool to promote U.S. political and security objectives" (p. 1).

13. See, for example, Tendler, *Inside Foreign Aid;* and Rondinelli, *Development Projects.* Rondinelli remarks, "The disjunction that exists between the nature of development problems and the methods of policy planning and implementation used by governments and international agencies has been a important factor accounting for the disappointing results of development programs in the past" (p. 13).

14. See, for example, World Bank, *Strengthening the Effectiveness of Aid* (Washington, D.C.: World Bank, 1995), p. ix.

15. This study takes into account many of the same elements of effective per-

formance that a study of European aid programs undertaken by the Overseas Development Institute identified. The ODI posited that "donor structures and organizations are considered more likely to be effective in aid delivery and potential development impact if: (a) they unify all aid instruments and aid recipients under single direction; (b) they have the maximum possible autonomy in relation to diplomatic and commercial pressures in the distribution of aid; (c) a high degree of operational freedom in the use and management of aid expenditures within countries; (d) adequate personnel in the field with substantial delegated responsibilities; and (e) a sufficient level and relevant range of specialist skills available to their organizations." Aidan Cox, John Healey, and Antonique Koning, *How European Aid Works* (London: Overseas Development Institute, 1996).

Chapter Five

1. Edward S. Mason, *Foreign Aid and Foreign Policy* (New York: Harper and Row for the Council on Foreign Relations, 1962).

2. U.S. Department of State, *The Scope and Distribution of U.S. Military and Economic Assistance Programs,* Report to the President of the United States from the Committee to Strengthen the Security of the Free World (Clay Committee), March 20, 1963, p. 4.

3. Raymond Copson, Theodor Galdi, and Larry Nowels, "U.S. Aid to Africa: The Record, the Rationales, and the Challenge," Congressional Research Service, Library of Congress, January 7, 1986, p. ix.

4. For historical data on U.S. aid to Africa, see USAID, *U.S. Overseas Loans and Grants,* vol. 4, *Sub-Saharan Africa, Obligations and Loan Authorizations Fiscal Year 1946–Fiscal Year 1994* (Washington, D.C.: USAID, 1994).

5. The Soviet offer of $100 million in aid to Haile Selassie was part of an effort to gain a strategic position in the Horn of Africa. Selassie accepted the offer as a signal of his unhappiness with Washington over the independence of Somalia. On this event, see, for example, Zaki Laidi, *The Super-powers and Africa: 1960–1990* (Chicago: University of Chicago Press, 1990), pp. 8–9.

6. For a history of this and other aspects of U.S. foreign assistance, see Vernon Ruttan, *United States Development Assistance Policy* (Baltimore: Johns Hopkins University Press, 1996), chap. 5.

7. Chester Crocker, *High Noon in Southern Africa* (New York: Norton, 1992), p. 409.

8. See, for example, Robert J. Berg and Jennifer Seymour Whitaker, eds., *Strategies for African Development,* a Study for the Committee on African Development Strategies sponsored by the Council on Foreign Relations and the Overseas Development Council, University of California, Berkeley, 1986.

9. See *Congressional Quarterly Almanac* 46 (1990): 832–33 and 47 (1991): 642–50.

10. See, for example, the press briefing by Senator Mitch McConnell, December 13, 1994, U.S. Information Agency Wireless File, December 14, 1994.

11. Copson, Galdi, and Nowels, "U.S. Aid to Africa," table 4.

12. There is a perhaps apocryphal story that circulates within USAID of a road project in Africa that was at various times presented as the "basic human needs"

road, the "policy reform" road and even the "democracy" road. I have never been able to verify this story, but I have heard it from several of USAID's most wily bureaucrats.

13. U.S. Agency for International Development, *Congressional Presentation, 1997* (Washington, D.C.: USAID, 1997).

14. Aid was seen by African leaders as a recognition of the recipient government as part of the world "club" of "legitimate countries with legitimate economic needs," according to Ambassador David Newsom, former U.S. assistant secretary of state for African affairs and undersecretary of state for political affairs, interview by the author, Washington, D.C., May 1996.

15. See U.S. Agency for International Development, *U.S. Overseas Loans and Grants* (Obligations and Authorizations), July 1, 1945, to September 30, 1995 (Cong-R-0105) (Washington, D.C.: USAID Bureau for Management, 1996).

16. USAID is one of the few aid agencies that undertakes and publishes "impact" evaluations—efforts to examine in depth the overall impact of particular projects or types of projects. These evaluations are often quite insightful, but their expense prohibits USAID from undertaking large numbers of them. USAID also produces completion reports of projects and programs. However, these are not well-enough developed to be useful for the purposes of this study. For example, one effort by USAID to derive patterns and lessons from such reports set out to analyze the performance of 277 projects of various types in Africa but found that the "data in AID's information system were often inconclusive as to what constitutes project success." Irving Rosenthau et al., *Signposts in Development Management: A Computer-Based Analysis of 277 Projects in Africa* (Washington, D.C.: Center for Development Information and Evaluation, USAID, May 1986).

17. On the effectiveness of projects in agriculture and livestock, see Bruce Johnston and Allan Hoben, *Assessment of AID Activities to Promote Agricultural and Rural Development in SubSaharan Africa* (Washington, D.C.: Center for Development Information and Evaluation, USAID, 1987); Johnson et al., *Kitale Maize;* John P. Lewis et al., *West Africa Rice Research and Development* (Washington, D.C.: Center for Development Information and Evaluation, USAID, 1983); C. Bryce Ratchford et al., *Tanzania Seed Multiplication* (Washington, D.C.: Center for Development Information and Evaluation, USAID, 1985); Peter Benedict et al., *Sudan: The Rahad Irrigation Project* (Washington, D.C.: Center for Development Information and Evaluation, USAID, 1982). All of these reports find that weak African institutions contributed to the limited success of aid projects. See also John Bennett, Steven Lawry, and James Riddell, *Land Tenure and Livestock Development in Sub-Saharan Africa* (Washington, D.C.: Center for Development Information and Evaluation, USAID, 1986); Krishna Kumar, *AID's Experience with Integrated Rural Development Projects* (Washington, D.C.: Center for Development Information and Evaluation, USAID, 1987); Dennis Rondinelli, *Development Management in Africa: Experience with Implementing Agricultural Development Projects* (Washington, D.C.: Center for Development Information and Evaluation, USAID, 1986); Louise While, *Managing Development Programs: Management Strategies and Project Interventions in Six African Agricultural Projects* (Washington, D.C.: Center for Development Information and Evaluation,

USAID, 1986). Other USAID activities that foundered because of institutional weaknesses of African governments or local NGOs include forestry projects in Mali, biological diversity projects in Madagascar, and agribusiness projects in Uganda.

18. Bruce Johnston, Allan Hoben, and William K. Jaeger, "United States Activities to Promote Agricultural and Rural Development in Sub-Saharan Africa," in *Aid to African Agriculture: Lessons from Two Decades of Donors' Experience,* ed. Uma Lele (Baltimore: Johns Hopkins University Press for the World Bank, 1991), p. 310.

19. Ibid., pp. 305–6.

20. On this latter point, see John Harbeson et al., *Area Development in Liberia: Toward Integration and Participation* (Washington, D.C.: Center for Development Information and Evaluation, USAID, 1984).

21. Siew Tuan Chew, *Natural Resources Management: Issues and Lessons from Rwanda* (Washington, D.C.: Center for Development Information and Evaluation, USAID, 1990).

22. Donald McClelland, *Forestry and the Environment: The Gambia Case Study* (Washington, D.C.: Center for Development Information and Evaluation, USAID, 1994).

23. The findings mentioned here are drawn from a variety of CDIE impact studies. See, for example, Jim Kelly et al., *Impact Review of the Onchocerciasis Control Program* (Washington, D.C.: Center for Development Information and Evaluation, USAID, May 1986); Robert Schmeding et al., *Evaluation of AID Child Survival Programs: Malawi Case Study* (Washington, D.C.: Center for Development Information and Evaluation, USAID, 1993); John Dumm et al., *AID Family Planning Programs;* David Dunlop et al., *Sustainability of US-Supported Health, Population, and Nutrition Programs in Tanzania: 1971–1988* (Washington, D.C.: Center for Development Information and Evaluation, USAID, 1990); Nancy Mock, Thomas Bossert, and Miatudila Milanga, *Sustainability of US-Supported Health, Population, and Nutrition Programs in Zaire: 1972–1988* (Washington, D.C.: Center for Development Information and Evaluation, USAID, 1990); Susan Adamchak et al., *Sustainability of US-Supported Health, Population, and Nutrition Programs in Senegal* (Washington, D.C.: Center for Development Information and Evaluation, USAID, 1990).

24. See Richard Martin, *AID's Child Survival Program: A Synthesis of Findings from Six Country Case Studies* (Washington, D.C.: Center for Development Information and Evaluation, USAID, October 1993), p. vi.

25. See Dumm et al., *AID Family Planning Programs.*

26. See ibid., for details.

27. See Donald McClelland et al., *Evaluation of AID Family Planning Programs: Ghana Case Study* (Washington, D.C.: Center for Development Information and Evaluation, 1993).

28. See Aurora Associates International and Creative Associates International, *Program Evaluation USAID/South Africa, Final Report,* sponsored by United States Agency for International Development, April 21, 1995.

29. Ibid., p. xv.

30. Joseph Lieberson, *AID Economic Policy Reforms Programs in Africa,* AID

Program and Operations Assessment Report No. 1 (Washington, D.C.: Center for Development Information and Evaluation, USAID, 1991), p. viii. This study examined USAID-financed reforms in Cameroon, Malawi, Mali, Uganda, Gambia, and Senegal. It was completed relatively soon after the reform programs were undertaken and, so, could not give an assessment of the sustainability of those reforms.

31. Ibid., pp. viii–ix.

32. Dumm et al., *AID Family Planning Programs,* p. 13.

33. See U.S. Agency for International Development, AFR/SD, "Results Review (R2)," April 17, 1996, mimeograph.

34. Johnston et al., "Assessment of A.I.D. Activities," p. 52.

35. A study of all U.S. aid programs, undertaken by the deputy secretary of state for the National Security Council in 1993 placed great weight on a recommendation: that promoting U.S. exports abroad should "remain separate" from development assistance programs. See the unpublished report by the Task Force to Reform A.I.D. and the International Affairs Budget, "Revitalizing A.I.D. and Foreign Assistance in the Post-Cold War Era" (the "Wharton Report"), September 1993, photocopy. The Departments of Commerce and Agriculture and the Export-Import Bank had relatively little influence over foreign-aid decisions during the first Clinton administration.

36. Members of Congress and their staffers threatened USAID officials that if directives were not followed, they would simply pass earmarks with the same requirements in the future.

37. Christopher Madison, "Foreign Aid Follies," *National Journal,* June 1, 1991, p. 1291.

38. See Sam Harris, *Reclaiming Our Democracy* (Philadelphia: Camino Books, 1994), for a fascinating description of how this very effective NGO operates within the U.S. political system.

39. There is also the Constituency for Africa, an umbrella organization made up of African American church groups, NGOs, citizen organizations, and others with an interest in Africa. This group, formed at the beginning of the 1990s, has remained relatively weak and thus far appears to have had little impact either on the size or distribution of foreign aid for Africa. Public-relations firms represent individual African governments in Washington, occasionally succeeding in getting aid legislation passed that benefits clients.

40. Some years ago, for example, environmental groups identified a "dirty dozen" congressmen who voted against important environmental issues and were able to embarrass them through the media (in opinion pieces, on radio and TV call-in programs, and other opportunities) in their home constituencies, with some effect.

41. The public is poorly informed about the amount of foreign aid, believing it to be around 18 percent of the federal budget when it is actually less than 1 percent. When informed of how small a proportion of the budget aid actually is, only a third still support cutting it. See Steven Kull, "Americans and Foreign Aid," Program on International Policy Attitudes, School of Public Affairs, University of Maryland, March 1, 1995.

42. See John E. Rielly, ed., *American Public Opinion and US Foreign Policy,*

1995 (Chicago: Chicago Council on Foreign Relations, 1995). This survey is taken every four years.

43. For a history of development thinking and policy in the United States, see Ruttan, *United States Development Assistance Policy.*

44. U.S. Agency for International Development, *Strategies for Sustainable Development* (Washington, D.C.: USAID, March 1994).

45. Rondinelli, *Development Projects,* pp. 70–71.

46. In an insightful report, *A Performance-Based Budgeting System for the Agency for International Development,* AID Program and Operations Assessment Report No. 4, commissioned by the Office of Evaluation of United States Agency for International Development (Washington, D.C.: USAID, 1993), Alan Schick remarks on the "uneven attention to evaluation in Missions and bureaus, weak headquarters leadership and accountability and a chronic failure to rely on evaluative findings in programming AID resources" (p. 15).

47. Cited in Center for Development Information and Evaluation, *Program Performance Measurement: Lessons Learned* (Washington, D.C., 1997), p. 2.

48. "Managing for results" is not USAID's first attempt to focus on measuring the impact of its activities abroad. Its "logical framework," which guided the presentation of project proposals to Washington for approval, also required objectively verifiable indicators. But identifying accurate indicators, establishing causality, and measuring meaningful results all proved exceedingly difficult, and the agency eventually moved away from trying. These problems challenge "managing for results" as well.

49. This only includes U.S. citizens who are full-time employees of USAID. The agency also hires foreign nationals and contractors. When all of these categories are totaled, USAID had a workforce of 9,642 in 1994. About three-quarters of all of these employees are located in USAID field missions. See Development Assistance Committee, *Development Cooperation* (1995), p. 33.

50. See Arthur Fell, "A Comparison of Management Systems for Development Assistance in OECD/DAC Member Countries," Development Assistance Committee, Organization for Economic Cooperation and Development, 1993, mimeograph. Fell's ratios do not include foreign nationals working for aid agencies. Even so, the U.S. ratio as of 1991 would have been one of the lower at $1.9 million per employee. Obviously, these are very approximate comparisons and do not reflect the quality of the staff.

51. John Koehring et al., *A.I.D.'s In-Country Presence,* AID Program and Operations Assessment Report No. 3 (Washington, D.C.: Center for Development Information and Evaluation, October 1992), p. viii.

52. Ibid.

53. Ibid.

54. Johnston et al., *Assessment of AID Activities,* p. 257.

Chapter Six

1. Cited in Teresa Hayter, *French Aid* (London: Overseas Development Institute, 1966), p. 29.

2. Jacques Adda and Marie-Claude Smouts, *La France face au Sud: Le miroir*

brisé (Paris: Karthala, 1989), p. 27. All translations are my own unless otherwise indicated.

3. John Chipman, *France in Africa* (London: Basil Blackwell, 1989), p. 1.

4. Georges Pompidou, *Discours sur la coopération, prononcé par M. Pompidou, Premier Ministre, devant L'Assemblée Nationale, Paris, 10 Juin, 1964* (Paris: La Documentation Française, 1964), p. 4. Concerns about the eroding use of French internationally may have contributed to the well-known resistance of French officials to the enlargement of World Bank influence in Africa. Pompidou remarked in the same speech, "It nevertheless remains true that multilateral aid, as it is handled by the large international organizations, leads to a strengthening of the position of the English language. But, I repeat, for us Frenchmen there is somehow a need to defend the French tongue. This is a fundamental reason to maintain bilateral aid."

5. Kaye Whiteman, "President Mitterrand and Africa," *African Affairs* 82, no. 328 (1983): 341.

6. For the 1963 Jenneneay Report, see *La Politique de coopération avec les pays en voie de développement* (Paris: La Documentation Française, 1963). For the Gorse Report, see Richard Robarts, *French Development Assistance: A Study in Policy and Administration,* Sage Professional Paper, Administrative and Policy Studies Series, vol. 2 (Beverly Hills, Calif.: Sage, 1974). (The Gorse Report was never published; this monograph summarizes its content.) And see also Stephane Hessel, "Les Relations de la France avec les pays en développpment," Report to the Prime Minister, Paris, 1990, mimeograph.

7. See Development Assistance Committee, *Development Cooperation* (1996), pp. A63–64, and Development Assistance Committee, *France,* Development Cooperation Review Series, no. 4 (Paris: Organization for Economic Cooperation and Development, 1994).

8. Development Assistance Committee, *Geographical Distribution of Financial Flows to Aid Recipients, 1989–93* (Paris: Organization for Economic Cooperation and Development, 1994), p. 103.

9. Ibid., p. 230.

10. Ibid., p. 78.

11. See Development Assistance Committee, *Development Cooperation* (1995), p. H20, and Development Assistance Committee, *Geographical Distribution of Financial Flows to Aid Recipients, 1990–94* (Paris: Organization for Economic Cooperation and Development, 1995), p. 92.

12. Hayter, *French Aid,* p. 166.

13. Mission Française de Coopération et d'Action Culturelle, "La Coopération franco-guinéenne: Bilan 1987," Conakry, Guinea, February 1987, mimeograph.

14. See, for example, Nicolas van de Walle, "The Decline of the Franc Zone: Monetary Politics in Francophone Africa," *African Affairs* 90, no. 360 (1991): 383–407.

15. The fears of French and African officials that a devaluation would destabilize African economies through provoking a cycle of inflation and further devaluation have proven groundless as balance of payments gaps have narrowed and growth in most franc zone countries has picked up significantly.

16. The material in this section was drawn from evaluations by the Ministry of Cooperation and summary reports of evaluations by the Caisse Française de Développement.

17. Unfortunately, most of the French government's evaluations of the impact of its aid in individual countries are not available to the public. The only one published is the one cited here.

18. Ministère de la Coopération et du Développement, *L'Aide française au Burkina Faso,* Evaluation No. 2 (Paris: Ministère de la Coopération et du Développement, June 1989), p. iv.

19. The March 3–10, 1994, edition of *La Lettre du continent,* a Paris-based newsletter with limited distribution, quotes from a confidential Ministry of Cooperation synthesis of six case studies and evaluations of aid activities during the period 1987–91. It is easy to understand why these evaluations are not available to the public.

20. See Claude Freud, *Quelle coopération? Un bilan de l'aide au développement* (Paris: Karthala, 1988), pp. 30–31.

21. It is not easy to obtain consistent statistics on the number of French cooperants in Africa. Claude Freud (a former employee of the Ministry of Cooperation) in his book *Quelle coopération* quotes a figure of twelve thousand *cooperants* at independence. A study of technical assistance commissioned by the Ministry of Cooperation entitled *L'Assistance technique française (1960–2000),* Study Report (Paris: La Documentation Française, 1994) shows a figure of 10,500 at that time and explains that complete data of all *cooperants,* consistent over time, does not exist.

22. See Philippe Hugon, "L'Education, la formation et l'emploi en Afrique," in *La France et l'Afrique: Vade-mecum pour un nouveau voyage,* ed. Serge Michailof (Paris: Karthala, 1993), p. 275.

23. For all these findings, see ibid., pp. 11–15.

24. See Caisse Française de Développement, "Deuxième Plan quinquennal des télécommunications de Côte d'Ivoire," *La Lettre de l'évaluation,* no. 7, Service Evaluations Retrospectives, October 1995, p. 3.

25. Caisse Française de Développement, "Réhabilitation, redressement et maintenance de la Société Tchadienne d'Eau et d'Electricite (STEE)," *Projets de Développement,* no. 4 (Paris: Caisse Française de Développement, March 1996).

26. *Les Echos* (Paris), December 6, 1995, p. 10.

27. *La Tribune* (Paris), July 2, 1997, p. 4.

28. French aid to Africa in 1994 amounted to $3.5 billion. In 1996, it was $2.5 billion. (Both figures are in 1995 prices.) See DAC, *Development Cooperation* (1997), pp. A63–64.

29. Jacques Foccart served in the French intelligence service before assuming the post of adviser to President de Gaulle on African affairs. Foccart's personal relationships with African leaders, his extensive networks of contacts in Africa and elsewhere, and his reputation as an intelligence operative made him both formidable and feared in the Franco-African community. For more on Foccard, see Philippe Gaillard, *Foccart parle* (Paris: Fayard, 1995), vols. 1 and 2.

30. Personal interview with a former senior official of the CFD, July 1996.

31. Freud, *Quelle coopération?* pp. 30–31.

32. See for example, Bayart, *Politique africaine de Mitterrand*.

33. Development Assistance Committee, *Development Cooperation* (1995), p. 21.

34. See for example, Benoit Cyrille, "La Politique française de coopération," *Projet* 241 (spring 1995). The author, writing under a pseudonym, is described as a French aid official. See also Stephen Smith and Antoine Glaser, *Ces Messieurs Afrique: Le Paris-Village du continent noir* (Paris: Calmann Levy, 1992), for an (undocumented) exposé.

35. See, for example, "France: Cot's Relance," *Africa Confidential* (London), June 1982, p. 7.

36. Stefan Brune, "Under Pressure to Reform: French Policies South of the Sahara," paper presented to the Conference on European-African Relations, Ebenhausen, May 1992, p. 7.

37. Because of the personal and political relationships between African and French elites, the influence wielded by the Africans in Paris was greater than any other recipient on a donor except perhaps Israel on the U.S.

38. EUROSTEP, ICUA, and InterAction, *The Reality of Aid, 1994* (London: Earthscan, 1995), p. 51.

39. Claude Freud, a former French aid official, has written: "The model of development advocated [by the French to Africans] is that which has succeeded in France after the Second World War, modernization thanks to advanced technologies within the structure of flexible planning in an environment of free trade. The objective: the welfare state (education and health services free), the reference point being European consumer societies" (*Quelle coopération?* p. 5).

40. Yves Berthelot, "French Aid Performance and Development Policy," *ODI Review* 6 (1973): 43.

41. The true antecedent to British aid in Africa was the 1940 Colonial Development and Welfare Act, which first authorized such aid. See, for example, Prosser Gifford and William Roger Louis, *The Transfer of Power in Africa* (New Haven, Conn.: Yale University Press, 1982).

42. United Kingdom Government, Command Paper 239 (London: Her Majesty's Stationery Office, 1957).

43. After further tensions with the Africans over the pension issue, the British finally took over full responsibility for paying the pensions and removed the financing of those pensions from their aid budgets.

44. See United Kingdom Government, *Annual Abstract of Statistics* (London: Central Statistical Office, various years).

45. United Kingdom Government, Foreign and Commonwealth Office, *The Government's Expenditure Plans, 1996–97 to 1998–99* (London: Her Majesty's Stationery Office, 1996), pp. 140–41.

46. United Kingdom Government, *Annual Abstract of Statistics,* various years.

47. United Kingdom Government, Command Paper 6270 (London: Her Majesty's Stationery Office, 1975).

48. Her Majesty's Treasury, *Aid to Developing Countries,* Command Paper 2174 (London: Her Majesty's Stationery Office, 1963), p. 5.

49. See, for example, United Kingdom Government, *Overseas Development: The Work of the New Ministry,* Command Paper 2736 (London: Her Majesty's

Stationery Office, 1965). This white paper, like one two years earlier, *Aid to Developing Countries* (Command Paper 2174), was largely descriptive of what the British government was already doing, with nothing in it that could be characterized as a "development doctrine."

50. Overseas Development Institute, "British Development Policies: Needs and Prospects," *ODI Review* 3 (1969): 9.

51. United Kingdom Government, Secretary of State for International Development, *Eliminating World Poverty: A Challenge for the 21st Century,* Command Paper 3739 (London: Her Majesty's Stationery Office, 1997).

52. The data on which this section on the effectiveness of British aid is based is drawn from several Evaluation Synthesis Studies of project completion reports undertaken by the Overseas Development Administration. These synthesis reports cover several hundred British aid projects in a variety of sectors worldwide, nearing completion or completed during the first half of 1990. They assess whether the objectives of the projects were achieved and project probable rates of sustainability. While they are useful for giving a sense of broad patterns of performance, the reports advise that the projects assessed are not a representative sample of all British aid projects worldwide; they are based on materials submitted by project managers and they are not impact focused. See Chris Athayde and Ann Bartholomew, *Project Completion Reports: Evaluation Synthesis Study,* Evaluation Report EV:571 (London: Overseas Development Administration, February 1994); and Nick Dyer and Ann Bartholomew, *Project Completion Reports: Evaluation Synthesis Study,* Evaluation Report EV:583 (London: Overseas Development Administration, June 1995). Other sources include John Howell, Kenneth Anthony, and Adrian Hewitt, "UK Agricultural Aid to Kenya, Tanzania and Malawi," draft report, Evaluation Department, Overseas Development Administration, May 1987. Also useful is John Healey, "The Management of British Bilateral Aid and Its Effectiveness," Working Paper no. 10 (Maastricht European Centre for Development Policy Management, 1996).

53. Foreign and Commonwealth Office, *Government's Expenditure Plans,* pp. 81–83.

54. Development Assistance Committee, *United Kingdom,* Development Cooperation Review Series, no. 1 (Paris: Organization for Economic Cooperation and Development, 1994), p. 7.

55. United Kingdom Government, Overseas Development Administration, "Fundamental Expenditure Review: Summary Report," <www.oneworld.oda>, July 1995.

56. Baroness Chalker, minister for development, interview by the author, Washington, D.C., May 1996.

57. See, for example, Independent Group on British Aid, *Missed Opportunities: Britain and the Third World* (London: Independent Group on British Aid, 1986); and, by the same group, *Real Aid: A Strategy for Britain* (London: Independent Group on British Aid, 1982).

58. See, for example, William Wallace, *The Foreign Policy Process in Britain* (London: Royal Institute of International Affairs, 1975), p. 191.

59. See, for example, Development Assistance Committee, *Development Cooperation* (1994), p. 8.

60. Paul Jendix, *The United Kingdom's Development Cooperation Policy* (Berlin: German Development Institute, 1986), p. 18.

61. The Commonwealth Development Corporation, which is formally independent of ODA but funded from loans out of its budget and CDC's own revenues from the sale of its equities and other sources, provides credits and equity investment to support private investment in developing countries. The National Resources Institute is the scientific arm of ODA.

62. In 1980, Neil Martin, then minister of ODA, announced that aid would take more account of British political and commercial interests abroad. However, this announcement seems to have had relatively little impact on British aid to Africa. And the government's emphasis on these goals diminished over recent years, especially with the 1997 white paper.

63. Development Assistance Committee, *Development Cooperation* (1994), p. 34; and Healey, "Management of British Aid," p. 14.

64. A DAC study on the management of aid agencies found that in 1991, ODA, CDC, and NRI employees handled $900,000 per year in aid, lower than the ratio of any other major aid agency. See Fell, "Comparison of Management Systems," p. 33.

65. Healey, "Management of British Aid," p. 5.

66. See, for example, John Howell, "British Aid to Agriculture in Kenya, Malawi, and Tanzania," in Lele, *Aid to African Agriculture.* Howell attributes the problems with project design in the agricultural area in part to the pressures to commit funds that prevented ODA from taking the time necessary to investigate thoroughly the technical aspects of these projects.

67. I am indebted to David Stanton, Alternative Executive Director at the World Bank for the United Kingdom for pointing this out to me. Personal correspondence, April 1997.

Chapter Seven

1. See Olav Stokke, *Western Middle Powers and Global Poverty* (Uppsala: Scandinavian Institute of African Studies and the Norwegian Institute of International Affairs, 1989), pp. 10–12.

2. "Nordic Voices," *Daedalus* 113, no. 2 (spring 1984): 28.

3. Marian Radetzki, "Swedish Aid to Kenya and Tanzania: Its Effect on Rural Development, 1970–84," in Lele, *Aid to African Agriculture,* pp. 242–43.

4. Christian Andersson, "Breaking Through," in *Swedish Development Aid in Perspective,* ed. Pierre Fruhling (Stockholm: Almqvist and Wiksell International, 1986), p. 42.

5. These countries, by size of Swedish aid, were Tanzania, Mozambique, South Africa, Angola, Ethiopia, Zambia, Zimbabwe, Uganda, Namibia, Kenya, Guinea Bissau, Botswana and Eritrea. See Development Assistance Committee, *Sweden,* Development Cooperation Review Series (Paris: Organization for Economic Cooperation and Development, 1996), p. 23. By 1990, about half of Swedish aid was provided these countries, a proportion that had been growing over the past decade.

6. Swedish International Development Authority, *Promoting Sustainable Livelihoods*, Report No. 5 (Stockholm: Secretariat for Analysis of Swedish Development Assistance, 1996), p. 24.

7. See ibid. for a brief history of Swedish aid.

8. See Development Assistance Committee, *Sweden*, p. 35.

9. Development Assistance Committee, *Development Cooperation* (1997), p. A64.

10. Gosta Edgren, "Changing Terms," in Fruhling, *Swedish Development Aid*, p. 49.

11. The discussion of the effectiveness of Swedish aid is drawn from several evaluation reports, including a review of a number of projects and programs in Zambia, and assessments of the impact of Swedish aid in particular African countries, including Botswana, Tanzania, and Namibia. These country-level reports provide useful insights into Swedish aid in particular countries but are quite diverse in methodology and quality and, so, permit only general comparisons among them or with other aid-financed programs in Africa. For the most part, they lack the rigor of evaluations by other donors, relying heavily on the judgments of evaluators rather than more objective measures, such as cost-benefit analysis or economic rates of return. This weakness is a reflection of the notion long held by Swedish aid officials that evaluation was the responsibility of the recipients. Efforts on the part of Sida to improve its evaluative services were undertaken in the mid-1980s.

12. Stefan Dahlgren et al., *SIDA Development Assistance to Botswana, 1966–1993* (Stockholm: Swedish International Development Authority, 1993), p. 108. This entire report was rather impressionistic and lacking in rigor.

13. Emma Ostaker, *Swedish Development Assistance to Zambia*, SASDA Report No. 5 (Stockholm: Swedish International Development Authority, January 1994), p. 10. The author criticizes Swedish aid projects for "a general trend of vague and unspecified goals" and a "lack of specification and quantification of objectives," forcing the evaluator to rely on interviews with those managing the projects for her judgments of project effectiveness rather than quantitative results of the projects themselves.

14. Development Assistance Committee, *Sweden*, p. 7.

15. Ibid., p. 162.

16. Ibid., p. 23.

17. One NGO commentator, predicting a greater commercial influence on Swedish aid in the future, has commented that "perhaps the main difference between the old and the new Sida is this: the old SIDA was a fairly politicized organization close to Social Democratic ideology and linking aid substantially to the Swedish Government's sometimes radical Third World policy. The new Sida very much likes to distance itself from that part of its predecessor's history. It therefore takes a much more technical approach. . . . this approach might give Sida a more pro-business and less radical position" (Svante Sandberg, "Sweden," in EUROSTEP et al., *The Reality of Aid, 1996* [London: Earthscan, 1997], p. 178). It is not at all clear, however, that the new Sida is so different from the "old" one. After all, the new Sida has the same staff as the old one and the same NGO constituency. And with the incorporation of BITS into Sida, the latter will

likely exert considerable influence on the programs of the former. What seems more likely is a Sida with more diplomatic influence on it.

18. Sixten Heppling, "The Very First Years: Memories of an Insider," in Fruhling, *Swedish Development Aid,* p. 16.

19. See, for example, Hans Lembke, *Sweden's Development Cooperation Policy* (Berlin: German Development Institute, 1986), p. 36; and Ruth Jacoby, "Idealism versus Economics," in Fruhling, *Swedish Development Aid,* for more details.

20. It is estimated that roughly one-fifth of Swedish bilateral aid is channeled through NGOs, one of the highest proportions among DAC members. See Development Assistance Committee, *Sweden,* pp. 64–65.

21. See EUROSTEP et al., *Reality of Aid* (1996), p. 218.

22. Development Assistance Committee, *Sweden,* p. 34.

23. Cited by Sandberg, "Sweden," p. 134.

24. Fell, "Comparison of Management Systems," p. 33.

25. In fact, Swedish aid officials in the field were well aware of the problems of a hands-off approach to aiding the Tanzanian government at this time, but their warnings had little impact in Stockholm. The belief in President Nyerere's commitment to social justice and his government's capacity to carry out effective aid programs was shared by both Social Democratic and Conservative governments (Professor Bertil Oden, Stockholm, personal correspondence, April 1997).

26. DAC, press release on Italian aid, 1993, cited in Development Assistance Committee, *Italy,* Development Cooperation Review Series (Paris: Organization for Economic Cooperation and Development, 1997).

27. While no polls on public attitudes toward foreign aid in recent years are available, Italian officials have stated, "Since 1992, there is less interest politically and on the part of the public for co-operation activities, following skepticism about the transparency of such activities" (Colm Foy and Henny Helmich, *Public Support for International Development* [Paris: Organization for Economic Cooperation and Development, 1996], p. 150). According to a DAC report on Italian aid, Italian political elites and the public "remain skeptical of aid activities." And aid officials see themselves working in a "climate of condemnation and ridicule" by the press and public for the failures of Italian aid. See Development Assistance Committee, *Italy,* p. 7.

28. Sergio Alessandrini, "Italian Aid: Policy and Performance," in *European Development Assistance,* ed. Olav Stokke (Oslo: Norwegian Institute of International Affairs, 1984), 1:262.

29. Richard Harlye, "Italians Cook Up Foreign Aid Plan to Help World's Hungry," *Christian Science Monitor,* January 29, 1982, p. 14.

30. M. C. Ercolessi, "Italia e Africa sub-sahariana negli anni Ottanta: Flussi d'aiuto e politica estera," *Note & Ricerche,* May 1989, cited in Jose Rhi-Sausi and M. Cristina Ercolessi, *Rapporto sulla cooperazione allo sviluppo 1990* (Rome: CeSPI, 1990), p. 7.

31. Wolfgang Achtner, "The Italian Connection: How Rome Helped Ruin Somalia," *Washington Post,* January 24, 1993, p. C3.

32. See ibid., which refers to allegations of aid-financed kickbacks and political-party financing.

33. Development Assistance Committee, Press Release A(85)37, Organization for Economic Cooperation and Development, Paris, May 31, 1985.

34. Rhi-Sausi and Ercolessi, *Rapporto sulla cooperazione,* pp. 18ff.

35. Achtner, "The Italian Connection," p. C3.

36. The Colombo Plan for Cooperative Economic Development in South and South East Asia, set up in 1951, was made up of sixteen Asian countries and six outside governments (including the United States, the United Kingdom, and, eventually, Japan). Its mission was to coordinate aid to the region. The stimulus for creating the plan was the Communist revolution in China

37. See Jide Owoeye, "Nigeria and Japan: A Study of Trade Relations," in *Nigeria's External Relations: The First Twenty-Five Years,* ed. G. O. Olusanya and R. A. Akindele (Ibadan: Nigerian Institute of International Affairs, University Press, 1986), for details on this story. The Japanese confirm this story in Economic Cooperation Bureau, *Annual Evaluation Report on Japan's Economic Cooperation* (Tokyo: Ministry of Foreign Affairs, 1990), p. 13.

38. Obafemi Awolowo, *Daily Sketch* (Lagos), December 16, 1983, cited in Owoeye, "Nigeria and Japan," p. 319.

39. Kweku Ampiah, "A One-Sided Partnership," *West Africa,* November 28– December 4, 1988, p. 2221.

40. Cited in Godfrey Morrison, "Japan's Year in Africa," in *Africa Contemporary Record, 1970–71,* ed. Colin Legum (London: Africa Publishing, 1971), p. 84.

41. For more on Japanese aid to Tanzania, see Kweku Ampiah, "Japanese Aid to Tanzania: A Study of the Political Marketing of Japan in Africa," *African Affairs* 95 (1996): 107–24.

42. David Newsom, interview.

43. Robert Orr Jr., *The Emergence of Japan's Foreign Aid Power* (New York: Columbia University Press, 1990), pp. 118–19.

44. Japanese officials acknowledge in private discussions the link between this and other international conferences and their government's goal of securing a seat on the Security Council (personal interview with U.S. official familiar with Japanese aid program and senior Japanese aid officials).

45. Alan Rix, *Japan's Foreign Aid Challenge: Policy Reform and Aid Leadership* (New York: Routledge, 1993), p. 242.

46. For more details on the role of the United States in pressuring the Japanese government on the size and worldwide distribution of its aid, see Orr, *Emergence of Japan's Aid,* chap. 5.

47. The Japanese prime minister announced at the 1987 G-7 Summit the creation of a $500 million fund for nonproject assistance mainly for African low-income countries, to be disbursed over the coming three years. In 1989, Japan made a further commitment to provide $600 million in nonproject aid to Africa over the coming three years. This type of aid was easy to disburse (compared to project aid), was consistent with mainstream development thinking at the time, and could be programmed through cofinancing with the World Bank.

48. An annual summary of evaluations undertaken in each year during the 1990s is available in English, and those surveys were used for this study. The English-language translation summarizes the outcomes of approximately 125 evaluations per year of Japan's aid worldwide conducted by various elements of

the Japanese government and outside experts. These evaluations typically examine whether the project or program has been implemented as planned, rather than its longer-term economic or social impact. These evaluations vary considerably in detail and methodology. For example, much of the analysis of the success of projects appears often to be based on impressions of the evaluators (and many of these are Japanese diplomats posted in the field) together with statements of appreciation by local officials. While they provide some insights into the effectiveness of Japanese aid in Africa, it is difficult to ascertain the extent to which programs and projects have been successful or unsuccessful and how their experience compares with similar projects or programs in other countries. See Economic Cooperation Bureau, *Annual Evaluation Report on Japan's Economic Cooperation* (Tokyo: Ministry of Foreign Affairs, 1990–96). I have also read a sample of the specific evaluation reports on which these summaries are based. These reports provide little more in the way of detail or useful comparative analysis.

49. See Economic Cooperation Bureau, *Annual Evaluation Report* (November 1991), pp. 11–23.

50. Ibid., p. 11.

51. Ibid., p. 12.

52. Ibid., p. 22.

53. See, for example, David Lindauer and Michael Roemer, *Asia and Africa* (San Francisco: Institute for Contemporary Studies Press, 1994).

54. When I was an official of USAID, a number of heads of other aid agencies warned me of exactly this consequence of the decrease in U.S. foreign aid.

55. Orr, *Emergence of Japan's Aid,* p. 49. See also Rix, *Japan's Foreign Aid Challenge,* p. 83.

56. One of the most articulate arguments to this effect is made by Rix, *Japan's Foreign Aid Challenge.*

57. Orr, *Emergence of Japan's Aid,* pp. 10–11.

58. The best description of the operation of these informal networks vis-à-vis Japanese aid is in David Arase, *Buying Power: The Political Economy of Japan's Foreign Aid* (Boulder, Colo.: Lynne Rienner, 1995).

59. Orr, *Emergence of Japan's Aid,* p. 63.

60. For details on the many interlocking relationships between government ministries and these private groups, see Arase, *Buying Power,* pp. 190ff.

61. The extent to which the Japanese government has, in fact, untied its aid is challenged by Margee Ensign in *Doing Good or Doing Well? Japan's Foreign Aid Program* (New York: Columbia University Press, 1992). While the extent to which the aid has been untied may be in dispute, there seems little doubt that more of it is now going to non-Japanese firms than in the past.

62. Interview with Keidanran official, June 1996, and with journalist from *Asahi Simbum,* July 1996.

63. Ministry of Foreign Affairs, *Japan's Official Development Assistance: Annual Report, 1995* (Tokyo: Ministry of Foreign Affairs, 1995), p. 228. These figures are double estimates by Japanese NGOs (see EUROSTEP et al., *The Reality of Aid* [1996], p. 238). The difference, according to officials from JANIC, an NGO umbrella organization, may be accounted for by the Japanese government's including funding for government and quasi-government foundations and other

organizations (which would be considered as parastatals in most countries), of which there are many in Japan. See Tatsuya Watanabe, "NGO Support Schemes of Japanese Government," JANIC, 1995, mimeograph.

64. Watanabe, "NGO Support Schemes," p. 94.

65. See EUROSTEP et al., *The Reality of Aid* (1996), pp. 144ff.

66. Orr, *Emergence of Japan's Aid*, p. 107.

67. Development Assistance Committee, *Japan*, Development Cooperation Review Series (Paris: Organization for Economic Cooperation and Development, 1996), p. 20.

68. Yasuo Uchida, "Japan: Public Knowledge and Attitudes towards ODA," in Foy and Helmich, *Public Support for Development*, p. 86.

69. Ministry of Foreign Affairs, *Japan's Official Development Assistance*, p. 253.

70. This is a shortcoming of which the Japanese government was well aware. A 1991 report by a government study group on aid to Africa warned that "Japanese assistance to Africa is expected to increase hereafter, although Japan has few special interest there, apart from the general concern for international solidarity. Japanese disinterestedness however, carries the weakness of the lack of knowledge and experience of Africa. Cooperation with other donor countries and institutions would be the expedient means to overcome this weakness and to enhance the effectiveness of Japanese aid to Africa." Masaya Hattori, chair, "Challenges of Japanese Development Assistance to Sub-Saharan Africa," Report of Study Group to Kensuke Yanagiya, president, Japanese International Cooperation Agency, February 1991, photocopy.

Chapter Eight

1. See, for example, Cheryl Payer, *The World Bank: A Critical Analysis* (New York: Monthly Review Press, 1982), who wrote that "the World Bank is perhaps the most important instrument of the developed capitalist countries for prying state control of its Third World member countries out of the hands of nationalists and socialists" (p. 20).

2. For a comprehensive look at the history and evolution of the World Bank, see Edward S. Mason and Robert E. Asher, *The World Bank since Bretton Woods* (Washington, D.C.: Brookings Institution, 1973); and Kapur, Lewis, and Webb, *The World Bank*.

3. For details on IDA, see World Bank, *IDA in Action, 1993–1996* (Washington, D.C.: World Bank, 1996).

4. World Bank, *Annual Report* (Washington, D.C.: World Bank, various years).

5. Executive directors from the United States, Belgium, and France all pressed Bank management to continue to lend there, according to Devesh Kapur, who had access to internal Bank documents and did extensive interviewing of staff on the issue of lending to Zaire. Some key staffers opposed continued lending, but senior officials decided otherwise (Kapur, interview by the author, May 1997).

6. For example, the concerns of, and pressures from, the French government to lend to the Ivory Coast were evident in World Bank internal memoranda and briefing notes made available to me as part of my research for "The World Bank in Africa since 1980," in Kapur, Lewis, and Webb, *The World Bank*.

7. World Bank, *Evaluation Results,* 1995, 2:62.

8. Ibid., p. 28.

9. Ibid., p. 33.

10. See World Bank, *Adjustment in Africa;* and Carl Jayarajah and William Branson, *Structural and Sectoral Adjustment: World Bank Experience, 1980–92,* Operations Evaluation Study (Washington, D.C.: World Bank, 1995).

11. Beatrice Buyck, "The Bank's Use of Technical Assistance for Institutional Development," World Bank, Policy Research and External Affairs, Working Papers, QPS 578, January 1991, p. v.

12. The study went on the explain these problems: "If any one factor can explain both the rather poor record of past Bank project assistance and the likely shortfalls in the growth objectives embedded in the current structural adjustment program, it is that the Bank has tended to overlook, downplay, or assume away major problems and issues. The Bank has also continued to provide advice and to make recommendations on the basis of very inadequate information and less than full understanding of the relationship between policy measures and policy objectives." World Bank, *The World Bank and Senegal, 1960–1987* (Washington, D.C.: Operations Evaluation Division, World Bank, 1989), p. iii.

13. For an analysis of the intellectual leadership of the World Bank, see Nicholas Stern with Francisco Ferreira, "The World Bank as an 'Intellectual Actor,'" in Kapur, Lewis, and Webb, *The World Bank.*

14. See the Economic Commission for Africa, *African Alternative Framework to Structural Adjustment Programmes for Socio-Economic Recovery and Transformation,* E/ECA/CM.15/6/Rev.3 (New York: United Nations, 1989).

15. Its cochairs as of 1996 were President Masire of Botswana, President Alpha O. Konare of Mali, Prime Minister Meles Zenawi of Ethiopia, Speaker of the House Frene Ginwala of the South African Parliament, Minister of Development Jan Pronk of the Netherlands, and Secretary of State for Africa Christine Stewart of Canada.

16. Some observers have characterized the GCA as a "cheerleader" for the Bank's economic-reform agenda. Creating more support for that agenda was certainly one of the motivations behind Bank support for its creation. For more details on the GCA, see Global Coalition for Africa, *African Social and Economic Trends.*

17. See for example, Bruce Rich, *Mortgaging the Earth* (Boston: Beacon Press, 1994); and Catherine Caufield, *Masters of Illusion* (New York: Henry Holt, 1996).

18. Moises Naim, "The World Bank: Its Role, Governance, and Organizational Culture," in Bretton Woods Commission, *Bretton Woods: Looking to the Future* (Washington, D.C.: Bretton Woods Commission, July 1994), p. 273.

19. Article 63, paragraph 2 of the United Nations Charter.

20. The World Bank is, in the words of Edward Mason and Robert Asher, a "special specialized agency" of the UN (*World Bank since Bretton Woods,* 58). This means that while the Bank is associated with the UN, its association is different from (and much more independent than) that of the Food and Agriculture Organization, the International Labor Organization, and other international agencies normally thought of as "specialized" UN agencies.

21. Article 4, paragraph 3 of the UN Agreement with the World Bank.

22. For details on this relationship, see Sidney Dell, "Relations between the United Nations and the Bretton Woods Institutions," *Development* 4 (1994): 27–38.

23. For a careful analysis of the influence of the United States on the World Bank, see Catherine Gwin, "U.S. Relations with the World Bank, 1945–92," Occasional Papers, Brookings Institution, 1994. Gwin argues that the United States has infrequently attempted to promote or block loans to particular countries or either opposed or encouraged specific activities. But when the United States does have a strong preference, issues are "often worked out between the United States and Bank management before they ever get to the board" (p. 56). Management and the board do on occasion decide against U.S. positions. But, Gwin points out, "Loans made despite strong opposition by the Bank's largest shareholder are the exceptions" (p. 76). For an earlier and also insightful study of U.S. influence in multilateral development banks, see Lars Schoultz, "Politics, Economics, and U.S. Participation in Multilateral Development Banks," *International Organization* 36, no. 3 (1982): 537–74.

24. Naim, "The World Bank," p. 281. See also Kapur, Lewis, and Webb, introduction to *The World Bank*, vol. 1. They argue that the autonomy of the Bank has diminished since the early 1980s with a succession of presidents lacking in the political skills and energy of Robert McNamara and, later, with the rise in influence of NGOs on the Bank.

25. Kapur, Lewis, and Webb, *The World Bank*, chap. 17 ("IDA: The Bank as a Dispenser of Concessional Aid"), 1:1148.

26. See, for example, Robert Wade, "Greening the Bank: The Struggle over the Environment, 1970–1995," in Kapur, Lewis and Webb, *The World Bank*. This essay is among the most insightful and balanced of any written on the Bank, the environment, and the role of NGOs in pressing the environmental agenda on the Bank; see also Rich, *Mortgaging the Earth*, chaps. 5 and 6.

27. U.S. House of Representatives, Committee on Appropriations, testimony of Bruce Rich, Director of the Environmental Defense Fund's International Program, March 1, 1993, cited in Elliot Berg and Donald Sherk, "The World Bank and Its Environmental Critics," in Bretton Woods Commission *Bretton Woods*, p. 308.

28. The more extreme criticisms of the Bank by U.S. NGOs, including suggestions that the funding for the organization be terminated, were not shared by the majority of U.S. NGOs and were even something of an embarrassment to them. But, as one senior official of a U.S. NGO umbrella organization said, the tactics of extremism proved useful to the others: "The more extreme criticisms of the Bank provide us with greater access and leverage with the organization," interview by the author, Washington, D.C., July 1996.

29. Mike Stevens and Shiro Gnanaselvam, "The World Bank and Governance," *Institute for Development Studies Bulletin* 25, no. 2 (1995): 103.

30. Wade, "Greening the Bank," pp. 675–78.

31. World Bank, *How the World Bank Works with Nongovernmental Organizations* (Washington, D.C.: World Bank, 1990), p. 8.

32. For a detailed description of this process, see Warren Baum and Stokes

Tolbert, *Investing in Development: Lessons of the World Bank Experience* (New York: Oxford University Press, 1985).

33. Ronald G. Ridker, *The World Bank's Role in Human Resource Development in Sub-Saharan Africa,* Operations Evaluation Study (Washington, D.C.: World Bank, 1994), p. 3.

34. Kapur, Lewis and Webb, *The World Bank,* 1:534.

35. One particular incident, widely recounted in Africa, between a vice president and President Nyerere has come to epitomize this problem. According to President Nyerere and his staff, the World Bank official used a meeting with the president to demand payment of debts overdue, offending Nyerere and causing him to terminate the meeting (Ambassador Charles Nyeribu, then minister of finance and present at the meeting, interview by the author, October 11, 1992; President Nyerere repeated this story to other Bank staff as well). The vice president denies that the meeting went as described (personal communication, 1996). Whatever the reality, the meeting fed the perception of an overbearing Bank.

36. Concerned about the adverse reaction on the part of many Africans to its 1981 report, *Accelerated Development in Sub-Saharan Africa,* and to the conditions it attached to its program lending in support of reforms, in 1983, the Bank asked an African consultant to undertake a study of African perceptions of the Bank. The report, which was never published and circulated only to a limited number of staff, came up with exactly these findings. Senior management of the Bank, while criticizing the report for being too limited in the numbers and types of Africans interviewed, nevertheless adopted policies intended to improve perceptions of the Bank, including the establishment of a Council of Economic Advisors. See Lancaster, "World Bank in Africa."

37. World Bank, "The Location of Bank Work: Background Materials," August 23, 1995, photocopy, p. 13.

38. See John Ravenhill, *Collective Clientism* (New York: Columbia University Press, 1985); and Enzo Grilli, *The European Community and the Developing Countries* (New York: Cambridge University Press, 1993).

39. For further details on phased programming in the EC, see Jean Bossuyt, "Phased Programming of Lome Funds: Lessons from Current EU and ACP Experiences," Policy Management Brief No. 2, European Centre for Development Policy Management, July 1994.

40. See M. K. Anyadike-Danes and M. N. Anyadike-Danes, "The Geographic Allocation of the European Development Fund under the Lome Conventions," *World Development* 20, no. 11 (1992): 1587–99.

41. Antonique Koning, "Strengths and Weaknesses in the Management of the European Development Fund," Working Paper No. 8 (Maastricht: European Centre for Development Policy Management, October 1995), p. 8.

42. John Healey and J. Rand, *The Effectiveness of EDF Development Aid to ACP Countries in the 1980s: A Final Report on EC Evaluations* (London: Overseas Development Institute, 1994).

43. Ibid., p. 20.

44. Ibid., p. 25.

45. Ibid., p. 45.

46. Koning, "Strengths and Weaknesses," p. 12.

47. European Commission, *Green Paper on Relations between the European Union and the ACP Countries on the Eve of the 21st Century* (Luxembourg: European Union, 1997), p. 6.

48. J. Deus de Pinhiero, quoted in *The Courier,* no. 150, March–April 1995, p. 25.

49. European Commission, "Communication from the Commission to the Council and the European Parliament: Guidelines for the Negotiation of New Cooperation Agreements with the African, Caribbean and Pacific (ACP) Countries," European Union, December 1997.

50. One European official interviewed for this study (Washington, D.C., June 1996) suggested that different donors tended to pursue different issues in the EDF committee. For example, Britain and France took a special interest in programs affecting their former colonies. Spain and Italy exhibited an interest in their nationals benefiting from EDF contracts (though the contract bidding process is open and apparently not easily influenced by national governments); and the Germans, Dutch, and Nordics showed a particular interest in new development themes, such as women in development.

51. House of Commons, Foreign Affairs Committee, *Monitoring of the European Community Aid Programme,* First Report, Session 1994–95, December 15, p. xii.

52. Overseas Development Institute, "Impact of NGO Projects, " pp. 29–30.

53. This may be in the process of changing. A senior official of the European Commission told me in 1996 that his goal was to encourage the formation of NGOs with which his directorate could deal directly as partners, both as advocates and implementers (personal conversation, Washington, D.C., September 1996).

54. This is drawn from an article by a staff member of EUROSTEP, "The Dreaming Dromedaries of the Desert Meet the Bothered Bureaucrats of Brussels," *The Courier,* no. 152, July–August 1995, pp. 81–82.

55. Jean Bossuyt, "The Future of EU-Africa Development Cooperation: With or without the Lome Convention?" Working Paper No. 95-2, European Centre for Development Policy Management, July 1995.

56. For more details, see Koning, "Strengths and Weaknesses," p. 20.

57. Ibid., p. 22.

58. These concerns were elaborated in the Development Assistance Committee, *Review of the Development Co-operation Policies and Programme of the European Community* (Paris: Organization for Economic Cooperation and Development, 1995).

Chapter Nine

1. International-relations specialists have long seen a relationship between the attitudes toward domestic welfare programs and toward foreign aid. See, for example, Alain Noel and Jean-Philippe Therien, "The Welfare State and Foreign Aid," *International Organization* 49, no. 3 (1995): 523–55.

2. This characteristic distinguishes this proposal from that of Professor Goran Hyden. Professor Hyden has proposed that national or sectoral funds be set up, financed at least in part with foreign aid, that would be legally independent enti-

ties responsible for allocating grants to qualified individuals or groups. See Goran Hyden, "From Bargaining to Marketing: How to Reform Foreign Aid in the 1990s," Michigan State University Working Papers on Political Reform in Africa, 1993. Hyden's proposal is an interesting one, but it does not address the problem of donor coordination at the country level, and by having donors transfer the authority to make allocative decisions to a foundation, it would likely encompass only a small proportion of the aid to individual countries. Donor governments are unlikely to relinquish authority over substantial proportions of their aid for reasons of accountability and politics.

Bibliography

Adamchak, Susan, et al. *Sustainability of US-Supported Health, Population, and Nutrition Programs in Senegal.* Washington, D.C.: Center for Development Information and Evaluation, USAID, 1990.

Adda, Jacques, and Marie-Claude Smouts. *La France face au Sud: Le miroir brisé.* Paris: Karthala, 1989.

African Governors of the World Bank. "Partnership for Capacity Building in Africa: Strategy and Program of Action." Report for the President of the World Bank Group, September 28, 1996.

Ake, Claude. *Democracy and Development in Africa.* Washington, D.C.: Brookings Institution, 1996.

Alessandrini, Sergio. "Italian Aid: Policy and Performance." In *European Development Assistance,* ed. Olav Stokke. Oslo: Norwegian Institute of International Affairs, 1984.

Amin, Samir. *Neo-Colonialism in West Africa.* New York: Monthly Review Press, 1973.

Ampiah, Kweku. "Japanese Aid to Tanzania: A Study of the Political Marketing of Japan in Africa." *African Affairs* 95 (1996): 107–24.

Andersson, Christian. "Breaking Through." In *Swedish Development Aid in Perspective,* ed. Pierre Fruhling. Stockholm: Almqvist and Wiksell International, 1986.

Anyadike-Danes, M. K., and M. N. Anyadike-Danes. "The Geographic Allocation of the European Development Fund under the Lome Conventions." *World Development* 20, no. 11 (1992): 1687–99.

Apter, David, and Carl Rosberg, eds. *Political Development and the New Realism in Sub-Saharan Africa.* Charlottesville: University of Virginia Press, 1994.

Arase, David. *Buying Power: The Political Economy of Japan's Foreign Aid.* Boulder, Colo.: Lynne Rienner, 1995.

Arndt, H. W. *Economic Development: The History of an Idea.* Chicago: University of Chicago Press, 1987.

Athayde, Chris, and Ann Bartholomew. *Project Completion Reports: Evaluation Synthesis Study.* Evaluation Report EV:571. London: Overseas Development Administration, February 1994.

Atwood, Brian. Remarks to the Center for National Policy, December 14, 1994. U.S. Information Agency Wireless File.

Aurora Associates International and Creative Associates International. *Program Evaluation USAID/South Africa, Final Report.* Sponsored by United States Agency for International Development. April 21, 1995.

Awolowo, Obafemi. *Daily Sketch* (Lagos), December 16, 1983. Cited in Jide Owoeye, "Nigeria and Japan: A Study of Trade Relations," in *Nigeria's External Relations: The First Twenty-Five Years,* ed. G. O. Olusanya and R. A. Akindele. Ibadan: Nigerian Institute of International Affairs, University Press, 1986.

Bardach, Eugene. *The Implementation Game: What Happens after a Bill Becomes a Law.* Cambridge, Mass.: MIT Press, 1977.

Bates, Robert. *Markets and States in Tropical Africa.* Berkeley and Los Angeles: University of California.Press, 1981.

Bauer, Peter. *Dissent on Development.* Cambridge, Mass.: Harvard University Press, 1972.

Baum, Warren, and Stokes Tolbert. *Investing in Development: Lessons of the World Bank Experience.* New York: Oxford University Press, 1985.

Bayart, Jean-François. *La Politique africaine de François Mitterrand.* Paris: Karthala, 1984.

Behrman, Jere, and T. N. Srinivasan, eds. *Handbook of Development Economics.* Vol. 3a. New York: North Holland, 1995.

Benedict, Peter, et al. *Sudan: The Rahad Irrigation Project.* Washington, D.C.: Center for Development Information and Evaluation, USAID, 1982.

Bennett, John, Steven Lawry, and James Riddell. *Land Tenure and Livestock Development in Sub-Saharan Africa.* Washington, D.C.: Center for Development Information and Evaluation, USAID, 1986.

Berg, Elliot. *Rethinking Technical Cooperation: Reforms for Capacity Building in Africa.* New York: United Nations Development Program, 1993.

Berg, Elliot, and Donald Sherk. "The World Bank and Its Environmental Critics." In Bretton Woods Commission, *Bretton Woods: Looking to the Future.* Washington, D.C.: Bretton Woods Commission, July 1994.

Berg, Robert J., and Jennifer Seymour Whitaker. *Strategies for African Development.* Study for the Committee on African Development Strategies sponsored by the Council on Foreign Relations and the Overseas Development Council, University of California, Berkeley, 1986.

Boone, Peter. "The Impact of Foreign Aid on Savings and Growth." London School of Economics, 1994. Mimeograph.

Bossuyt, Jean. "The Future of EU-Africa Development Cooperation: With or without the Lome Convention?" Working Paper No. 95-2, Maastricht, European Centre for Development Policy Management, July 1995.

———. "Phased Programming of Lome Funds: Lessons from Current EU and ACP Experiences." Policy Management Brief No. 2, Maastricht, European Centre for Development Policy Management, July 1994.

Bossuyt, Jean, G. Laporte, and F. van Hoek. "New Avenues for Technical Cooperation in Africa." Maastricht, European Centre for Development Policy Management Occasional Paper, 1992.

Brune, Stefan. "Under Pressure to Reform: French Policies South of the Sahara." Paper presented to the Conference on European-African Relations, Ebenhausen, May 1992.

Bruno, Michael, Martin Ravallion, and Lyn Squire. "Equity and Growth in Developing Countries." World Bank Policy Research Working Paper 1563, January 1996.

Burnside, Craig, and David Dollar. "Aid, Policies, and Growth." Macroeconomics and Growth Division, Policy Research Department, World Bank, November 1996. Draft.

Buyck, Beatrice. "The Bank's Use of Technical Assistance for Institutional Development." Policy Research and External Affairs, Working Papers, QPS 578, World Bank, January 1991.

Caisse Française de Développement. "Deuxième Plan quinquennal des télécommunications de Côte d'Ivoire." La Lettre de l'évaluation, no. 7. Service Evaluations Retrospectives, Paris, October 1995.

———. "Réhabilitation, redressement et maintenance de la Société Tchadienne d'Eau et d'Electricite (STEE)." Projets de Développement, no. 4. Paris: Caisse Française de Développement, March 1996.

Callaghy, Thomas, and John Ravenhill, eds. Hemmed In. New York: Columbia University Press, 1993.

Carlsson, Jerker, Gloria Somolekae, and Nicolas van de Walle, eds. Foreign Aid in Africa: Learning from Country Experiences. Uppsala: Nordiska Afrikainstitutet, 1997.

Cassen, Robert, and Associates. Does Aid Work? Report to an Intergovernmental Task Force. 2d ed. Oxford: Clarendon Press, 1994.

Caufield, Catherine. Masters of Illusion. New York: Henry Holt, 1996.

Center for Development Information and Evaluation. Program Performance Measurement: Lessons Learned. Washington, D.C.: U.S. Agency for International Development, May 1994.

———. Program Performance Measurement: Lessons Learned. Washington, D.C.: U.S. Agency for International Development, 1997.

Chazan, Naomi, et al. Politics and Society in Contemporary Africa. 2d ed. Boulder, Colo.: Lynne Rienner, 1992.

Chenery, Hollis, and Alan Strout. "Foreign Assistance and Economic Development." American Economic Review 56, no. 4 (1966): 679–733.

Chenery, Hollis, and T. N. Srinivasan, eds. Handbook of Development Economics, vols. 1–2, 3b. New York: North Holland, 1988–95.

Chenery, Hollis, Jere Behrman, and T. N. Srinivasan, eds. Handbook of Development Economics, vol. 3a. New York: North Holland, 1995.

Chew, Siew Tuan. Natural Resources Management: Issues and Lessons from Rwanda. Washington, D.C.: Center for Development Information and Evaluation, USAID, 1990.

Chipman, John. France in Africa. London: Basil Blackwell, 1989.

Collier, Paul. "Africa's External Economic Relations: 1960–1990." African Affairs 90 (1991):339–57.

———. "Aid and Economic Performance in Tanzania." In *Transitions in Development*, ed. Uma Lele and Ijaz Nabi. San Francisco: International Center for Economic Growth, 1991.

Copson, Raymond, Theodore Galdi, and Larry Nowels. "U.S. Aid to Africa: The Record, the Rationales, and the Challenge." Congressional Research Service, Library of Congress, January 7, 1986.

Cox, Aidan, John Healey, and Antonique Koning. *How European Aid Works*. London: Overseas Development Institute, 1996.

Cox, Aidan, and Antonique Koning. *Understanding European Community Aid*. London: Overseas Development Institute, 1997.

Crocker, Chester. *High Noon in Southern Africa*. New York: Norton, 1992.

Dahlgren, Stephan, et al. *SIDA Development Assistance to Botswana, 1966–1993*. Stockholm: Swedish International Development Authority, 1993.

Davis, Jeffrey. "The Economic Effects of Windfall Gains in Export Earnings." *World Development* 11, no. 2 (1983): 119–41.

Dell, Sidney. "Relations between the United Nations and the Bretton Woods Institutions." *Development* 4 (1994): 27–38.

Development Assistance Committee. *Development Cooperation*. Paris: Organization for Economic Cooperation and Development, various years.

———. *France*. Development Cooperation Review Series, no. 4. Paris: Organization for Economic Cooperation and Development, 1994.

———. *Geographical Distribution of Financial Flows to Aid Recipients*. Paris: Organization for Economic Cooperation and Development, various years.

———. *Italy*. Development Cooperation Review Series. Paris: Organization for Economic Cooperation and Development, 1997.

———. *Japan*. Development Cooperation Review Series. Paris: Organization for Economic Cooperation and Development, 1996.

———. Press Release A(85)37. Paris: Organization for Economic Cooperation and Development, May 31, 1985.

———. *Review of the Development Co-operation Policies and Programme of the European Community*. Paris: Organization for Economic Cooperation and Development, 1995.

———. *Sweden*. Development Cooperation Review Series. Paris: Organization for Economic Cooperation and Development. 1996.

———. *United Kingdom*. Development Cooperation Review Series, no. 1. Paris: Organization for Economic Cooperation and Development, 1994.

Dornbusch, Rudiger, and Sebastian Edwards, eds. *The Macroeconomics of Populism in Latin America*. Chicago: University of Chicago Press, 1991.

Dudley, Leonard, and Claude Montmarquette. "A Model of the Supply of Bilateral Foreign Aid." *American Economic Review* 66 (1976): 132–42.

Dumm, John, et al. *Evaluation of AID Family Planning Programs: Kenya Case Studies*. Technical Report 3. Washington, D.C.: Center for Development Information and Evaluation, USAID, 1992.

Duncan, Alex, and Paul Mosley. "Aid Effectiveness: Kenya Case Study." Commissioned by the Task Force on Concessional Flows of the World Bank/IMF Development Committee. August 1984. Mimeograph.

Dunlop, David, et al. *Sustainability of US-Supported Health, Population, and Nutrition Programs in Tanzania: 1971–1988.* Washington, D.C.: Center for Development Information and Evaluation, USAID, 1990.

Dyer, Nick, and Ann Bartholomew. *Project Completion Reports: Evaluation Synthesis Study.* Evaluation Report EV:583. London: Overseas Development Administration, June 1995.

Economic Commission for Africa. *African Alternative Framework to Structural Adjustment Programmes for Socio-Economic Recovery and Transformation.* E/ECA/CM.15/6/Rev.3. New York: United Nations, 1989.

Economic Cooperation Bureau. *Annual Evaluation Report on Japan's Economic Cooperation.* Tokyo: Ministry of Foreign Affairs, various years.

Edgren, Gosta. "Changing Terms." In *Swedish Development Aid in Perspective,* ed. Pierre Fruhling. Stockholm: Almqvist and Wiksell International, 1986.

Ensign, Margee. *Doing Good or Doing Well? Japan's Foreign Aid Program.* New York: Columbia University Press, 1992.

Escobar, Arturo. *Encountering Development: The Making and Unmaking of the Third World.* Princeton, N.J.: Princeton University Press, 1995.

European Commission. "Communication from the Commission to the Council and the European Parliament: Guidelines for the Negotiation of New Cooperation Agreements with the African, Caribbean and Pacific (ACP) Countries." European Union, December 1997.

———. *Green Paper on Relations between the European Union and the ACP Countries on the Eve of the 21st Century.* Luxembourg: European Union, 1997.

EUROSTEP. "The Dreaming Dromedaries of the Desert Meet the Bothered Bureaucrats of Brussels." *The Courier,* no. 152, July–August 1995.

EUROSTEP, ICUA, and InterAction. *The Reality of Aid.* London: Earthscan, various years.

Evans, Peter. *Embedded Autonomy: States and Industrial Transformation.* Princeton, N.J.: Princeton University Press, 1995.

Evans, Peter, Dietrich Rueschemeyer, and Theda Skocpol. *Bringing the State Back In.* New York: Cambridge University Press, 1985.

Evenson, Robert. "Technological Change and Technology Strategy." In *Handbook of Development Economics,* ed. Jere Behrman and T. N. Srinivasan, vol. 3a. New York: North Holland, 1995.

Fell, Arthur. "A Comparison of Management Systems for Development Assistance in OECD/DAC Member Countries." Development Assistance Committee, Organization for Economic Cooperation and Development. June 7, 1993. Mimeograph.

Ferguson, James. *The Anti-Politics Machine: "Development," Depoliticization, and Bureaucratic Power in Lesotho.* New York: Cambridge University Press, 1990.

Feyzioglu, Tarhan, Vinaya Swaroop, and Min Zhu. "Foreign Aid's Impact on Public Spending." Policy Research Department, World Bank, 1996.

Foy, Colm, and Henny Helmich. *Public Support for International Development.* Paris: Organization for Economic Cooperation and Development, 1996.

"France: Cot's Relance." *Africa Confidential* (London), June 8, 1982.

Frank, Andre Gunder. *Capitalism and Underdevelopment in Latin America.* New York: Monthly Review Press, 1967.

Freedom House. *Freedom in the World.* New York: Freedom House, various years.

Freud, Claude. *Quelle coopération? Un bilan de l'aide au développement.* Paris: Karthala, 1988.

Fruhling, Pierre, ed. *Swedish Development Aid in Perspective.* Stockholm: Almqvist and Wiksell International, 1986.

Gifford, Prosser, and William Roger Louis. *The Transfer of Power in Africa.* New Haven, Conn.: Yale University Press, 1982.

Global Coalition for Africa. *African Social and Economic Trends.* Annual Report, 1996. Washington, D.C.: n.p., 1997.

Grilli, Enzo. *The European Community and the Developing Countries.* New York: Cambridge University Press, 1993.

Guess, George M. *The Politics of United States Foreign Aid.* New York: St. Martin's, 1987.

Gwin, Catherine. "U.S. Relations with the World Bank, 1945–92. " Occasional Papers, Brookings Institution, 1994.

Gwin, Catherine, and Joan Nelson. *Perspectives on Aid and Development.* Policy Essay No. 22. Washington, D.C.: Overseas Development Council, 1997.

Haggard, Stephan, and Steven Webb. *Voting for Reform: Democracy, Political Liberalization, and Economic Adjustment.* New York: Oxford University Press for the World Bank, 1994.

Hancock, Graham. *Lords of Poverty: The Power, Prestige, and Corruption of the International Aid Business.* New York: Atlantic Monthly Press, 1989.

Harbeson, John, et al. *Area Development in Liberia: Toward Integration and Participation.* Washington, D.C.: Center for Development Information and Evaluation, USAID, 1984.

Harden, Blain. *Africa: Dispatches from a Fragile Continent.* New York: Houghton Mifflin, 1991.

Harlye, Richard. "Italians Cook Up Foreign Aid Plan to Help World's Hungry." *Christian Science Monitor,* January 29, 1982.

Harris, Sam. *Reclaiming Our Democracy.* Philadelphia: Camino Books, 1994.

Hattori, Masaya, chair. "Challenges of Japanese Development Assistance to Sub-Saharan Africa." Report of Study Group to Kensuke Yanagiya, president, Japanese International Cooperation Agency, February 1991. Photocopy.

Hayter, Theresa. *Aid as Imperialism.* Harmondsworth, Middlesex: Penguin, 1971.

———. *The Creation of World Poverty.* London: Pluto Press, 1981.

———. *French Aid.* London: Overseas Development Institute, 1966.

Healey, John. "The Management of British Bilateral Aid and Its Effectiveness." Working Paper no. 10, Maastricht, European Centre for Development Policy Management, 1996.

Healey, John, and J. Rand. *The Effectiveness of EDF Development Aid to ACP Countries in the 1980s: A Final Report on EC Evaluations.* London: Overseas Development Institute, 1994.

Heppling, Sixten. "The Very First Years: Memories of an Insider." In *Swedish*

Development Aid in Perspective, ed. Pierre Fruhling. Stockholm: Almqvist and Wiksell International, 1986.

Her Majesty's Treasury. *Aid to Developing Countries.* Command Paper 2174. London: Her Majesty's Stationery Office, 1963.

Herbst, Jeffrey, and Adebayo Olukoshi. "Nigeria: Economic and Political Reforms at Cross Purposes." In *Voting for Reform: Democracy, Political Liberalization, and Economic Adjustment,* ed. Stephan Haggard and Steven Webb. New York: Oxford University Press, 1994.

Hessel, Stephane. "Les Relations de la France avec les pays en développment." Report to the Prime Minister. Paris, 1990. Mimeograph.

Hook, Steven. *Foreign Aid Toward the Millennium,* Boulder, Colo., Lynne Rienner, 1996.

———. *National Interest and Foreign Aid,* Boulder, Colo., Lynne Rienner, 1995.

House of Commons. Foreign Affairs Committee. *Monitoring of the European Community Aid Programme.* First Report, Session 1994–95, December 15.

Howell, John, Kenneth Anthony, and Adrian Hewitt. "UK Agricultural Aid to Kenya, Tanzania, and Malawi." Draft report, Evaluation Department, Overseas Development Administration, May 1987.

Hugon, Philippe. "L'Education, la formation et l'emploi en Afrique." In *La France et l'Afrique: Vade-mecum pour un nouveau voyage,* ed. Serge Michailof. Paris: Karthala, 1993.

Hyden, Goran. "From Bargaining to Marketing: How to Reform Foreign Aid in the 1990s." Michigan State University Working Papers on Political Reform in Africa, 1993.

———. *No Shortcuts to Progress.* Berkeley and Los Angeles: University of California Press, 1983.

Independent Group on British Aid. *Missed Opportunities: Britain and the Third World.* London: Independent Group on British Aid, 1986.

———. *Real Aid: A Strategy for Britain.* London: Independent Group on British Aid, 1982.

International Monetary Fund. "Taxation in Sub-Saharan Africa." Occasional Paper no. 8, 1981.

Jacoby, Neil. "An Evaluation of United States Economic Aid to Free China, 1951-1965." USAID Discussion Paper No. 11, 1966.

Jacoby, Ruth. "Idealism versus Economics." In *Swedish Development Aid in Perspective,* ed. Pierre Fruhling. Stockholm: Almqvist and Wiksell International, 1986.

Jayarajah, Carl, and William Branson. *Structural and Sectoral Adjustment: World Bank Experience, 1980–92.* Operations Evaluation Study. Washington, D.C.: World Bank, 1995.

Jeanneneay Commission. *The Jeanneneay Report.* Abridged translation of *La Politique de Coopération avec les Pays en Voie de Développement.* London: Overseas Development Institute, 1964.

Jendix, Paul. *The United Kingdom's Development Cooperation Policy.* Berlin: German Development Institute, 1986.

Johnson, Charles, et al. *Kitale Maize: The Limits of Success.* Washington, D.C.: Center for Development Information and Evaluation, USAID, 1979.

Johnston, Bruce, and Allan Hoben. *Assessment of AID Activities to Promote Agricultural and Rural Development in Sub-Saharan Africa.* Washington, D.C.: Center for Development Information and Evaluation, USAID, 1987.

Johnston, Bruce, Allan Hoben, and William K. Jaeger. "United States Activities to Promote Agricultural and Rural Development in Sub-Saharan Africa." In *Aid to African Agriculture: Lessons from Two Decades of Donors' Experience,* ed. Uma Lele. Baltimore: Johns Hopkins University Press for the World Bank, 1991.

Kapur, Devesh. "The Weakness of Strength: The Challenge of Sub-Saharan Africa." In *The World Bank: Its First Half Century,* ed. Devesh Kapur, John P. Lewis, and Richard Webb. Washington, D.C.: Brookings Institution, 1997.

Kapur, Devesh, John P. Lewis, and Richard Webb. *The World Bank: Its First Half Century.* 2 vols. Washington, D.C.: Brookings Institution, 1997.

Katzenstein, Peter, ed. *Between Power and Plenty: Foreign Economic Policies of Advanced Industrial States,* Madison, University of Wisconsin, 1978.

Kelly, Jim, et al. *Impact Review of the Onchocerciasis Control Program.* Washington, D.C.: Center for Development Information and Evaluation, USAID, May 1986.

Khilji, N. M., and E. M. Zampelli. "The Fungibility of US Assistance to Developing Countries and the Impact on Recipient Expenditures: A Case Study of Pakistan." *World Development* 19, no. 8 (1991): 1095–1107.

Killick, Tony. *Development Economics in Action: A Study of Economic Policies in Ghana.* London: Heinemann Educational Books, 1978.

———. "The Developmental Effectiveness of Aid to Africa." Working Paper, Policy Research and External Affairs, International Economics Department, World Bank, 1991.

Kim, Aehyung, and Bruce Benton. "Cost-Benefit Analysis of the Onchocerciasis Control Program." World Bank Technical Paper no. 282, 1995.

Koehring, John, et al. *AID's In-Country Presence.* AID Program and Operations Assessment Report No. 3. Washington, D.C.: Center for Development Information and Evaluation, October 1992.

Koning, Antonique. "Strengths and Weaknesses in the Management of the European Development Fund." Working Paper No. 8, Maastricht, European Centre for Development Policy Management, October 1995.

Korea International Cooperation Agency. *Annual Report.* Seoul: Korea International Cooperation Agency, 1994.

Krueger, Anne O. *Economic Policies at Cross Purposes: The United States and Developing Countries.* Washington, D.C.: Brookings Institution, 1993.

Krugman, Paul. "Cycles of Conventional Wisdom in Economic Development." *International Affairs* 72, no. 1 (1996), pp. 717–32.

Kull, Steven. "Americans and Foreign Aid." Program on International Policy Attitudes, School of Public Affairs, University of Maryland, March 1, 1995.

Kumar, Krishna. *AID's Experience with Integrated Rural Development Projects.* Washington, D.C.: Center for Development Information and Evaluation, USAID, 1987.

Kuznets, Simon. "Economic Growth and Income Inequality." *American Economic Review* 45, no. 1 (1955): 1–29.

Laidi, Zaki. *The Super-powers and Africa: 1960–1990.* Chicago: University of Chicago Press, 1990.

Lancaster, Carol. *African Economic Reform: The External Dimension.* Washington, D.C.: Institute for International Economics, 1991.

———. "The World Bank in Africa since 1980: The Politics of Structural Adjustment Lending." In *The World Bank: Its First Half Century,* ed. Devesh Kapur, John P. Lewis, and Richard Webb. Washington, D.C.: Brookings Institution, 1997.

Lancaster, Carol, and John Williamson. *African Debt and Financing.* Washington, D.C.: Institute for International Economics, 1989.

Legum, Colin, ed. *Africa Contemporary Record, 1970–71.* London: Africa Publishing, 1971.

Lele, Uma, ed. *Aid to African Agriculture: Lessons from Two Decades of Donors' Experience.* Baltimore: Johns Hopkins University Press for the World Bank, 1991.

Lele, Uma, and Manmohan Agarwal, "Four Decades of Economic Development in India and the Role of External Assistance." In *Transitions in Development: The Role of Aid and Commercial Flows,* ed. Uma Lele and Ijaz Nabi. San Francisco: International Center for Economic Growth, 1991.

Lele, Uma, and Ijaz Nabi, eds. *Transitions in Development: The Role of Aid and Commercial Flows.* San Francisco: International Center for Economic Growth, 1991.

Lembke, Hans. *Sweden's Development Cooperation Policy.* Berlin: German Development Institute, 1986.

Leonard, David. "The Political Realities of African Management." *World Development* 15, no. 7 (1987): 899–910.

La Lettre du Continent (Paris), March 3–10, 1994.

Levinson, Jerome, and Juan de Onis. *The Alliance That Lost Its Way: A Twentieth Century Fund Study.* Chicago: Quadrangle Books, 1970.

Levy, Victor. "Aid and Growth in Sub-Saharan Africa: The Recent Experience." *European Economic Review* 32 (1988): 1777–95.

Lewis, John P., and Richard Webb. "The Bank as a Dispenser of Concessional Aid." In *The World Bank: Its First Half Century,* ed. Devesh Kapur, John P. Lewis, and Richard Webb. Washington, D.C.: Brookings Institution, 1997.

Lewis, John P., et al. *West Africa Rice Research and Development.* Washington, D.C.: Center for Development Information and Evaluation, USAID, 1983.

Lieberson, Joseph. *AID Economic Policy Reform Programs in Africa.* AID Program and Operations Assessment Report No. 1. Washington, D.C.: Center for Development Information and Evaluation, USAID, 1991.

Lindauer, David, and Michael Roemer. *Asia and Africa.* San Francisco: Institute for Contemporary Studies Press, 1994.

Madison, Christopher. "Foreign Aid Follies." *National Journal,* June 1, 1991.

Maizels, Alfred, and Machiko Nissanke. "Motivations for Aid to Developing Countries." *World Development* 12, no. 9 (1984): 879–900.

Marshall, Rick. "McConnell Proposes Cuts, Reorientation of U.S. Foreign Aid." U.S. Information Agency Wireless File, December 14, 1994.

Martin, Matthew. *The Crumbling Facade of African Debt Negotiations.* New York: St. Martin's, 1991.

Martin, Richard. *AID's Child Survival Program: A Synthesis of Findings from Six Country Case Studies.* Washington, D.C.: Center for Development Information and Evaluation, USAID, October 1993.

Mason, Edward S. *Foreign Aid and Foreign Policy.* New York: Harper and Row for the Council on Foreign Relations, 1962.

Mason, Edward S., and Robert E. Asher. *The World Bank since Bretton Woods.* Washington, D.C.: Brookings Institution, 1973.

Mason, Edward S., et. al. *The Economic and Social Modernization of the Republic of Korea: Studies in the Modernization of the Republic of Korea; 1945–1975.* Cambridge, Mass.: Council on East Asian Studies, Harvard Institute for International Development and the Korean Development Institute, 1979.

Masrui, Ali. "Socialism as a Mode of International Protest: The Case of Tanzania." In *Protest and Power in Black Africa,* ed. Robert Rotberg and Ali Masrui. Oxford: Oxford University Press, 1970.

Mazmanian, Daniel A., and Paul A Sabatier. *Implementation and Public Policy.* Glenview, Ill.: Scott, Foresman, 1983.

McClelland, Donald. *Forestry and the Environment: The Gambia Case Study.* Washington, D.C.: Center for Development Information and Evaluation, USAID, 1994.

McClelland, Donald, et al. *Evaluation of AID Family Planning Programs: Ghana Case Study.* Washington, D.C.: Center for Development Information and Evaluation, USAID, 1993.

McConnell, Mitch. Press briefing by Senator Mitch McConnell, December 13, 1994. U.S. Information Agency Wireless File, December 14, 1994.

McKinlay, R. D. "The Aid Relationship: A Foreign Policy Model and Interpretation of the Distributions of Official Bilateral Economic Aid of the United States, the United Kingdom, France, and Germany, 1960–1970." *Comparative Political Studies* 11, no. 4 (1979): 411–63.

McKinlay, R. D., and R. Little. "The French Aid Relationship: A Foreign Policy Model of the Distribution of French Bilateral Aid, 1964–70." *Development and Change* 9, no. 3 (1978): 459–78.

Michailof, Serge, ed. *La France et l'Afrique: Vade-mecum pour un nouveau voyage.* Paris: Karthala, 1993.

Ministère de la Coopération et du Développement. *L'Aide française au Burkina Faso.* Evaluation no. 2. Paris: Ministère de la Coopération et du Développement, June 1989.

———. *L'Assistance technique française (1960–2000).* Study Report. Paris: La Documentation Française, 1994.

Ministry of Foreign Affairs. *Japan's Official Development Assistance: Annual Report, 1995.* Tokyo: Ministry of Foreign Affairs, 1995.

Mission Française de Coopération et d'Action Culturelle. La Coopération franco-guinéenne: Bilan 1987. Conakry, Guinea, February 1987. Mimeograph.

Mock, Nancy, Thomas Bossert, and Miatudila Milanga. *Sustainability of US-*

Supported Health, Population, and Nutrition Programs in Zaire: 1972–1988. Washington, D.C.: Center for Development Information and Evaluation, USAID, 1990.

Moe, Terry. "Interests, Institutions, and Positive Theory: The Politics of the NLRB." In *Studies in American Political Development,* ed. Karen Orren and Stephen Skowronek, 2:236–303. New Haven, Conn.: Yale University Press, 1987.

Morawetz, David. *Twenty-five Years of Economic Development: 1950 to 1975.* Washington, D.C.: World Bank, 1977.

Morrison, Godfrey. "Japan's Year in Africa." In *Africa Contemporary Record, 1970–71,* ed. Colin Legum. London: Africa Publishing, 1971.

Mosley, Paul, and John Hudson. "Aid Effectiveness: A Study of the Effectiveness of Overseas Aid in the Main Countries Receiving ODA Assistance." November 1995. Mimeograph.

Mosley, Paul, Jane Harrigan, and John Toye. *Aid and Power: The World Bank and Policy-Based Lending.* 2 vols. New York: Routledge, 1991.

Muscat, Robert. *Thailand and the United States: Development, Security, and Foreign Aid.* New York: Columbia University Press, 1990.

Mutahaba, Gelase, Rweikiza Baguma, and Mohamed Halfani. *Vitalizing African Public Administration for Recovery and Development.* Hartford: Kumarian Press in cooperation with the United Nations, 1993.

Naim, Moises. "The World Bank: Its Role, Governance, and Organizational Culture." In Bretton Woods Commission, *Bretton Woods: Looking to the Future.* Washington, D.C.: Bretton Woods Commission, July 1994.

National Research Council and World Bank. *Marshaling Technology for Development.* Washington, D.C.: National Academy Press, 1995.

Newsom, David. *Diplomacy and the American Democracy.* Bloomington: Indiana University Press, 1988.

Noel, Alain, and Jean-Philippe Therien. "The Welfare State and Foreign Aid." *International Organization* 49, no. 3 (1995): 523–55.

"Nordic Voices." *Daedalus* 113, no. 2 (spring 1984): 28.

North, Douglass. *Institutions, Institutional Change, and Economic Performance.* New York: Cambridge University Press, 1990.

Nowels, Larry Q. "Foreign Aid Reform Legislation: Background, Contents, and Issues." Congressional Research Service Report for Congress, Library of Congress, January 10, 1994.

———. "Foreign Operations Appropriations for FY 1997: Funding and Policy Issues." Congressional Research Service Report for Congress, Library of Congress, October 1, 1996.

Nurske, Ragnar. *Problems of Capital Formation in Underdeveloped Countries.* New York: Oxford University Press, 1953.

Nyerere, Julius. *Freedom and Socialism.* New York: Oxford University Press, 1968.

Obasanjo, Olesegun. "Africa: The Year 2000 and Beyond." United Nations, Third Economic Commission for Africa Silver Jubilee Lecture, Addis Ababa, 1987.

Olusanya, G. O., and R. A. Akindele, eds. *Nigeria's External Relations: The First Twenty-Five Years.* Ibadan: Nigerian Institute of International Affairs, University Press, 1986.

Oman, Charles, and G. Wignaraja. *The Post-War Evolution of Development Thinking.* New York: St. Martin's, 1991.

Orr, Robert, Jr. *The Emergence of Japan's Foreign Aid Power.* New York: Columbia University Press, 1990.

Ostaker, Emma. *Swedish Development Assistance to Zambia.* SASDA Report No. 5. Stockholm: Swedish International Development Authority, January 1994.

Overseas Development Institute. "The Impact of NGO Development Projects." *Briefing Paper* 2, London: Overseas Development Institute, May 1996.

Owoeye, Jide. "Nigeria and Japan: A Study of Trade Relations." In *Nigeria's External Relations: The First Twenty-Five Years,* ed. G. O. Olusanya and R. A. Akindele. Ibadan: Nigerian Institute of International Affairs, University Press, 1986.

Pack, Howard, and Janet Rothenberg Pack. "Foreign Aid and the Question of Fungibility." *Review of Economics and Statistics* 75, no. 2 (1993): 258–65.

———. "Is Foreign Aid Fungible? The Case of Indonesia." *Economic Journal* 100, no. 399 (1990): 188–94.

Payaslian, Simon. *U.S. Foreign Economic and Military Aid.* Lanham, Md.: University Press of America, 1996.

Payer, Cheryl. *The World Bank: A Critical Analysis.* New York: Monthly Review Press, 1982.

Persson, Torsten, and Guido Tabellini. "Is Inequality Harmful to Growth?" *American Economic Review* 84, no. 3 (1994): 600–622.

Pompidou, Georges. *Discours sur la coopération, prononcé par M. Pompidou, Premier Ministre, devant L'Assemblée Nationale, Paris, 10 Juin, 1964.* Paris: La Documentation Française, 1964.

Portfolio Management Task Force. *Effective Implementation: Key to Development Impact.* Washington, D.C.: World Bank, 1992.

Pressman, Jeffrey L., and Aaron B. Wildavsky. *Implementation.* Berkeley and Los Angeles: University of California Press, 1973.

Radetzki, Marian. "Swedish Aid to Kenya and Tanzania: Its Effect on Rural Development, 1970–84." In *Aid to African Agriculture: Lessons from Two Decades of Donors' Experience,* ed. Uma Lele. Baltimore: Johns Hopkins University Press for the World Bank, 1991.

Ratchford, C. Bryce, et al. *Tanzania Seed Multiplication.* Washington, D.C.: Center for Development Information and Evaluation, USAID, 1985.

Ravenhill, John. *Collective Clientism.* New York: Columbia University Press, 1985.

Rhi-Sausi, Jose, and M. Cristina Ercolessi. *Rapporto sulla cooperazione allo sviluppo 1990.* Rome, CeSPI, 1990.

Rice, Andrew E., and Donald Gordon. "A Constituency for Foreign Assistance." In *U.S. Foreign Assistance: Investment or Folly?* ed. John Wilhelm and Gerry Feinstein. New York: Praeger, 1984.

Rich, Bruce. *Mortgaging the Earth.* Boston: Beacon Press, 1994.

Riddell, Roger. *Aid Dependency.* Project 2015 for the Swedish International Development Cooperation Agency. London: Overseas Development Institute, February 1996.

———. *Foreign Aid Reconsidered.* Baltimore: Johns Hopkins University Press, 1987.

Riddell, Roger, et al. *Non-Governmental Organizations and Rural Poverty Alleviation.* London: Oxford University Press and the Overseas Development Institute, 1995.

Ridker, Ronald G. *The World Bank's Role in Human Resource Development in Sub-Saharan Africa.* Operations Evaluation Study. Washington, D.C.: World Bank, 1994.

Rielly, John E., ed. *American Public Opinion and US Foreign Policy, 1995.* Chicago: Chicago Council on Foreign Relations, 1995.

Ripley, Randall B., and Grace A. Franklin. *Policy Implementation and Bureaucracy.* Chicago: Dorsey Press, 1986.

Rix, Alan. *Japan's Foreign Aid Challenge: Policy Reform and Aid Leadership.* New York: Routledge, 1993.

Robarts, Richard. *French Development Assistance: A Study in Policy and Administration.* Sage Professional Paper, Administrative and Policy Studies Series, vol. 2. Beverly Hills, Calif.: Sage, 1974.

Rodney, Walter. *How Europe Underdeveloped Africa.* Washington, D.C.: Howard University Press, 1981.

Rondinelli, Dennis. *Development Management in Africa: Experience with Implementing Agricultural Development Projects.* Washington, D.C.: Center for Development Information and Evaluation, USAID, 1986.

———. *Development Projects as Policy Experiments.* London: Methuen, 1983.

Rosenthau, Irving, et al. *Signposts in Development Management: A Computer-Based Analysis of 277 Projects in Africa.* Washington, D.C.: Center for Development Information and Evaluation, USAID, May 1986.

Rostow, W. W. *Eisenhower, Kennedy, and Foreign Aid.* Austin: University of Texas Press, 1985.

Ruttan, Vernon W. *United States Development Assistance Policy.* Baltimore: Johns Hopkins University Press, 1996.

———. *Why Food Aid?* Baltimore: Johns Hopkins University Press, 1993.

Ruttan, Vernon W., Anne O. Krueger, and Constantine Michaelopolous, eds. *Aid and Development.* Baltimore: Johns Hopkins University Press, 1989.

Sandberg, Svante. "Sweden." In EUROSTEP, *The Reality of Aid 1996.* London: Earthscan, 1997.

Sandbrook, Richard. *The Politics of Africa's Economic Decline.* New York: Cambridge University Press, 1985.

Schick, Alan. *A Performance-Based Budgeting System for the Agency for International Development.* AID Program and Operations Assessment Report No. 4. Commissioned by the Office of Evaluation of United States Agency for International Development. Washington, D.C.: USAID, 1993.

Schmeding, Robert, et al. *Evaluation of AID Child Survival Programs: Malawi Case Study.* Washington, D.C.: Center for Development Information and Evaluation, USAID, 1993.

Schoultz, Lars. "Politics, Economics, and U.S. Participation in Multilateral Development Banks." *International Organization* 36, no. 3 (1982): 537–74.

Schultz, Theodore. *Transforming Traditional Agriculture.* New Haven, Conn.: Yale University Press, 1964.

Scott, Richard. *Organizations: Rational, Natural, and Open Systems.* Englewood Cliffs, N.J.: Prentice-Hall, 1987.

Sen, Amartya. "The Concept of Development." In *Handbook of Development Economics,* vol. 1, ed. Hollis Chenery and T. N. Srinivasan. New York: North Holland, 1988.

Sewell, John W., and Christine E. Contee. "U.S. Foreign Aid in the 1980s: Reordering Priorities." In *U.S. Foreign Policy and the Third World: Agenda 1985,* ed. John W. Sewell et al. New Brunswick, N.J.: Transaction, 1985.

Sewell, John W., et al., eds. *U.S. Foreign Policy and the Third World: Agenda 1985.* New Brunswick, N.J.: Transaction, 1985.

Shalizi, Zmarak, and Lyn Squire. *Tax Policy in Sub-Saharan Africa.* Washington, D.C.: World Bank, 1988.

Sklar, Richard. "The Nature of Class Domination in Africa." *Journal of Modern African Studies* 17, no. 4 (1979): 531–52.

———. "Social Class and Political Action in Africa: The Bourgeoisie and the Proletariat." In *Political Development and the New Realism in Sub-Saharan Africa,* ed. David Apter and Carl Rosberg. Charlottesville: University of Virginia Press, 1994.

Smith, Stephen, and Antoine Glaser. *Ces Messieurs Afrique: Le Paris-Village du continent noir.* Paris: Calmann Levy, 1992.

Southworth, Herman, and Bruce Johnston, eds. *Agricultural Development and Economic Growth.* Ithaca, N.Y.: Cornell University Press, 1967.

Stern, Nicholas, with Francisco Ferreira. "The World Bank as an 'Intellectual Actor.'" In *The World Bank: Its First Half Century,* ed. Devesh Kapur, John P. Lewis, and Richard Webb. Washington, D.C.: Brookings Institution, 1997.

Stokke, Olav. *Western Middle Powers and Global Poverty.* Uppsala: Scandinavian Institute of African Studies and the Norwegian Institute of International Affairs, 1989.

———, ed. *European Development Assistance.* Vol. 1. Oslo: Norwegian Institute of International Affairs, 1984.

Swedish International Development Authority. *Promoting Sustainable Livelihoods.* Report No. 5. Stockholm: Secretariat for Analysis of Swedish Development Assistance, 1996.

Task Force to Reform A.I.D. and the International Affairs Budget. "Revitalizing A.I.D. and Foreign Assistance in the Post-Cold War Era" ("Wharton Report"). September 1993. Photocopy.

Tendler, Judith. *Inside Foreign Aid.* Baltimore: Johns Hopkins University Press, 1975.

Uchida, Yasuo. "Japan: Public Knowledge and Attitudes towards ODA." In *Public Support for International Development,* ed. Colm Foy and Henny Helmich. Paris: Organization for Economic Cooperation and Development, 1996.

United Kingdom Government. *Annual Abstract of Statistics.* London: Central Statistical Office, various years.

———. Command Paper 239. London: Her Majesty's Stationery Office, 1957.

———. Command Paper 6270. London: Her Majesty's Stationery Office, 1975.

———. *Overseas Development: The Work of the New Ministry.* Command Paper 2736. London: Her Majesty's Stationery Office, 1965.

———. Foreign and Commonwealth Office. *The Government's Expenditure Plans, 1996–97 to 1998–99.* London: Her Majesty's Stationery Office, 1996.

———. Overseas Development Administration. "Fundamental Expenditure Review: Summary Report." <www.oneworld.oda>. July 1995.

———. Secretary of State for International Development. *Eliminating World Poverty: A Challenge for the 21st Century.* Command Paper 3739. London: Her Majesty's Stationery Office, 1997.

U.S. Agency for International Development. *Congressional Presentation, 1997.* Washington, D.C.: USAID, 1997.

———. *Results Review, 1995.* Washington, D.C.: USAID, 1996.

———. *Strategies for Sustainable Development.* Washington, D.C.: USAID, March 1994.

———. *U.S. Overseas Loans and Grants* (Obligations and Authorizations), July 1, 1945, to September 30, 1995 (Cong-R-0105). Washington, D.C.: USAID Bureau for Management, 1996.

———. *U.S. Overseas Loans and Grants.* Vol. 4, *Sub-Saharan Africa, Obligations and Loan Authorizations Fiscal Year 1946–Fiscal Year 1994.* Washington, D.C.: USAID, 1994.

U.S. Department of State. *The Scope and Distribution of U.S. Military and Economic Assistance Programs.* Report to the President of the United States from the Committee to Strengthen the Security of the Free World (Clay Committee). Washington, D.C.: U.S. Department of State, March 20, 1963.

U.S. House Committee on Foreign Affairs. *Assistance to Greece and Turkey.* Hearings, March 20, 1947.

U.S. Senate. Senator Jesse Helms. "The U.S. Foreign Aid Program: Congress Has Broken the Bank and the Backs of the American Taxpayer." *Congressional Record,* May 18, 1982.

———. Senator Patrick Leahy. "The Mission of Foreign Aid in the Post-Cold-War Era." *Congressional Record,* March 19, 1993.

———. Senator Patrick Leahy. "A Strategy for Foreign Aid Reform." *Congressional Record,* January 28, 1993.

Van Wijnbergen, S. "Macroeconomic Aspects of the Effectiveness of Foreign Aid: The Two Gap Model, Home Goods Disequilibrium, and Real Exchange Rate Misalignment." *Journal of International Economics* 21, nos. 1–2 (1986): 123–37.

van de Walle, Nicolas. "The Decline of the Franc Zone: Monetary Politics in Francophone Africa." *African Affairs* 90, no. 360 (1991): 383–407.

van de Walle, Nicolas, and Timothy Johnson. *Improving Aid: The Challenge to Donors and African Governments,* New Brunswick, N.J.: Transaction, 1996.

———. *Improving Aid to Africa.* Policy Essay No. 21. Washington, D.C.: Overseas Development Council, 1996.

Wade, Robert. "Greening the Bank: The Struggle over the Environment, 1970–1995." In *The World Bank: Its First Half Century,* ed. Devesh Kapur, John

P. Lewis, and Richard Webb. Washington, D.C.: Brookings Institution, 1997.

Wallace, William. *The Foreign Policy Process in Britain.* London: Royal Institute of International Affairs, 1975.

Watanabe, Tatsuya. "NGO Support Schemes of Japanese Government." JANIC, 1995. Mimeograph.

While, Louise. *Managing Development Programs: Management Strategies and Project Interventions in Six African Agricultural Projects.* Washington, D.C.: Center for Development Information and Evaluation, USAID, 1986.

White, Howard. "The Macroeconomic Impact of Development Aid: A Critical Survey." *Journal of Development Studies* 28, no. 2 (1992): 163–240.

White, John A. *The Politics of Foreign Aid.* New York: St. Martin's, 1974.

Whiteman, Kaye. "President Mitterrand and Africa." *African Affairs* 82, no. 328 (1983): 329–45.

Widener, Jennifer. "The Discovery of 'Politics': Smallholder Reactions to the Cocoa Crisis of 1988–90 in Cote d'Ivoire." In *Hemmed In,* ed. Thomas Callaghy and John Ravenhill. New York: Columbia University Press, 1993.

Wilhelm, John, and Gerry Feinstein, eds. *U.S. Foreign Assistance: Investment or Folly?* New York: Praeger, 1984.

Williams, Walter, et. al., eds. *Studying Implementation: Methodological and Administrative Issues.* Chatham, N.M.: Chatham House, 1982.

Wilson, James Q. *Bureaucracy.* New York: Basic Books, 1989.

World Bank. *Accelerated Development in Sub-Saharan Africa.* Washington, D.C.: World Bank, 1981.

———. *Adjustment in Africa: Reforms, Results, and the Road Ahead.* New York: Oxford University Press for the World Bank, 1994.

———. *Annual Report.* Washington, D.C.: World Bank, various years.

———. *A Continent in Transition: Sub-Saharan Africa in the Mid-1990s.* Washington, D.C.: World Bank, Africa Region, 1995.

———. *The East Asian Miracle.* New York: Oxford University Press, 1993.

———. *Effective Implementation: Key to Development Impact.* Portfolio Management Task Force, Annex C. Washington, D.C.: World Bank, 1992.

———. *Evaluation Results.* Washington, D.C.: Operations Evaluations Department, World Bank, various years.

———. *Global Development Finance.* Washington, D.C.: World Bank, 1997.

———. *How the World Bank Works with Nongovernmental Organizations.* Washington, D.C.: World Bank, 1990.

———. *IDA in Action, 1993–1996.* Washington, D.C.: World Bank, 1996.

———. "The Location of Bank Work: Background Materials." August 23, 1995. Photocopy.

———. *The State in a Changing World.* Washington, D.C.: World Bank, 1997.

———. *Strengthening the Effectiveness of Aid.* Washington, D.C.: World Bank, 1995.

———. *Sub-Saharan Africa: From Crisis to Sustainable Growth.* Washington, D.C.: World Bank, 1989.

———. *The Twelfth Annual Review of Project Performance Results.* Washington, D.C.: Operations Evaluation Department, World Bank, 1987.

———. *Toward Sustained Development in Sub-Saharan Africa.* Washington, D.C.: World Bank, 1984.

———. *The World Bank and Senegal, 1960–1987.* Washington, D.C.: Operations Evaluation Department, World Bank, 1989.

———. *World Bank Atlas.* Washington, D.C.: World Bank, 1997.

———. *World Debt Tables.* Washington, D.C.: World Bank, 1995.

———. *World Development Indicators.* Washington, D.C.: World Bank, 1995.

———. *World Development Indicators.* Washington, D.C.: World Bank, 1997.

———. *World Tables.* Washington, D.C.: World Bank, 1995.

Wuyts, Marc. "Foreign Aid, Structural Adjustment, and Public Management: The Mozambican Experience." Institute of Strategic Studies Working Paper General Series No. 206, November 1995.

Young, Crawford. *Ideology and Development in Africa.* New Haven, Conn.: Yale University Press, 1982.

Younger, S. D. "Aid and the Dutch Disease: Macroeconomic Management When Everybody Loves You." Working Paper 17, Cornell Food and Nutrition Policy Program, Ithaca, N.Y., 1991.

Zimmerman, Robert F. *Dollars, Diplomacy, and Dependency.* Boulder, Colo.: Lynne Rienner for the Institute for the Study of Diplomacy, Georgetown University, 1993.

Index

The letters *t* and *f* attached to locators refer to tables and figures.

Index